The
Manager's
Guide to HR

The Manager's Guide to HR

Hiring, Firing, Performance
Evaluations, Documentation,
Benefits, and Everything Else
You Need to Know

Max Muller

AMACOM

SOCIETY FOR HUMAN
RESOURCE MANAGEMENT

American Management Association

New York • Atlanta • Brussels • Chicago • Mexico City
• San Francisco • Shanghai • Tokyo • Toronto • Washington, D.C.

This publication is designed to provide accurate and authoritative information in regard to the subject matter covered. It is sold with the understanding that the publisher is not engaged in rendering legal, accounting, or other professional service. If legal advice or other expert assistance is required, the services of a competent professional person should be sought.

Various names used by companies to distinguish their software and other products can be claimed as trademarks. The following trademarks are used in this book: O★NET, O★NET OnLine, FlexiLedger, Intuit QuickBooks, Intuit Quicken, Quicken Elite, CRSTL Compliance Positioning System, FLS eDP.Payrolltax, Intrax ProcedureNet, Paisley Cardmap, Accutrac, OmniRM, AcornSystems Corporate Performance Management, AMS Services AMS Sagitta, Cartesis ES Magnitude, AuditWare, MethodWare ProAudit Advisor, RSM McGladrey Auditor Assistant, and E-Verify. AMACOM uses such names throughout this book for editorial purposes only, with no intention of trademark violation. All such software or product names are in initial capital letters or ALL CAPITAL letters. Individual companies should be contacted for complete information regarding trademarks and registration.

Library of Congress Cataloging-in-Publication Data

Muller, Max, 1947-
    The manager's guide to HR : hiring, firing, performance evaluations, documentation, benefits, and everything else you need to know / Max Muller.
        p. cm.
    Includes index.
    ISBN-13: 978-0-8144-1076-9 (hbk.)
    ISBN-10: 0-8144-1076-6 (hbk.)
    1. Personnel management. 2. Supervision of employees. 3. Labor laws and legislation—United States. I. Title.
    HF5549.M786   2009
    658.3—dc22

                                                                    2008042204

The Society for Human Resource Management (SHRM) is the world's largest professional association devoted to human resource management. Our mission is to serve the needs of HR professionals by providing the most current and comprehensive resources, and to advance the profession by promoting HR's essential, strategic role. Founded in 1948, SHRM represents more than 225,000 individual members in over 125 countries, and has a network of more than 575 affiliated chapters in the United States, as well as offices in China and India. Visit SHRM at www.shrm.org.

Printing number

10 9 8 7 6 5 4 3 2 1

Contents

CHAPTER 1

Hiring

Introduction

Hiring dumb is easy. Hiring smart is hard.

All it takes to hire dumb is to select a job description written by someone once upon a time, a long time ago—one that is hopelessly out of date when compared with the job as it currently exists—and then use that job definition to recruit a candidate who fits the job description, not the actual job.

Hiring dumb also involves advertising job openings in ways that discriminate against potential candidates based on their race, religion, age, sex, national origin, physical disabilities, or other legally protected characteristics.

Hiring smart involves defining the job properly, and then developing a job description that is more than a bullet list of generalized descriptors of technical skills.

A well-researched and well-developed job description is the foundation stone of smart recruiting, interviewing, and hiring, as well as staff retention.

Defining the Job

The first order of business in hiring smart is to analyze the job in terms of:

- Skills and knowledge required
- How the work is performed
- Typical work settings

Analytic Steps

Identify and determine in detail the particular job duties, requirements, and the relative importance of these duties and requirements for a given job by undertaking the following steps:

1. Review existing job description, if any.
2. Review public source information and job classification systems.
3. Conduct incumbent surveys and interviews.
4. Conduct supervisor surveys and interviews.

Review Existing Job Description

Although your existing job description could well be out of date, it does represent a starting point from which to derive basic technical skills, reporting relationships, and other information.

The existing description also provides you with a baseline against which to measure the current job—in other words, how the job has evolved or materially changed.

Review Public Source Information and Job Classification Systems

Looking at how other companies describe jobs will help you write a good job description. Here are some examples of public sources of that information:

The Occupational Information Network (O★NET®) System
(www.onetcenter.org)

- Database of occupational requirements and worker attributes

- Comprehensive source of descriptors, with ratings of importance, level, relevance, or extent, for more than nine hundred occupations
- Common language and terminology describing occupational requirements

The *Occupational Outlook Handbook* (OOH) (http://www.bls.gov/oco/home.htm)

- Publication of the U.S. Department of Labor Bureau of Labor Statistics
- Includes information about the nature of the work, working conditions, training and education, earnings, and job outlook for hundreds of different occupations
- Released biennially with its companion publication the *Career Guide to Industries*

These sources will give you a good idea of how to classify a job.

Conduct Incumbent Surveys and Interviews

Find out what the people who have actually been doing the job think. What technical skills do they think are required, to whom do they believe they report (irrespective of what an organization chart says), whom do they believe reports to them, whom do they interact with on an ongoing basis, how do they believe the job is actually performed, what percentage of their time is being spent on various tasks or undertakings, and so forth?

Help them help you. Most staff members do not think of their jobs in an organized fashion or spend any time trying to measure how many minutes or hours per day they engage in any particular task versus any other. However, that is precisely the information you need to successfully analyze the job and develop a meaningful job description. Consequently, provide incumbents with box checklists, surveys, and questionnaires to fill out.

Box Checklists Here is an example of a portion of a box checklist related to bookkeeping, accounting, or auditing clerks.

Check if you perform the task listed ☑

Task	Frequency		
	Daily	Weekly	Monthly
Check figures, postings, and documents for correct entry, mathematical accuracy, and proper codes.	☐	☐	☐
Operate computers programmed with accounting software to record, store, and analyze information.	☐	☐	☐
Comply with federal, state, and company policies, procedures, and regulations.	☐	☐	☐
Debit, credit, and total accounts on computer spreadsheets and databases, using specialized accounting software.	☐	☐	☐
Classify, record, and summarize numerical and financial data to compile and keep financial records, using journals and ledgers or computers.	☐	☐	☐
Calculate, prepare, and issue bills, invoices, account statements, and other financial statements according to established procedures.	☐	☐	☐
Compile statistical, financial, accounting, or auditing reports and tables pertaining to such matters as cash receipts, expenditures, accounts payable and receivable, and profits and losses.	☐	☐	☐
Code documents according to company procedures. Access computerized financial information to answer general questions as well as those related to specific accounts.	☐	☐	☐
Operate ten-key calculators, typewriters, and copy machines to perform calculations and produce documents.	☐	☐	☐
OTHER: Please identify	☐	☐	☐
OTHER: Please identify	☐	☐	☐

Surveys and Questionnaires Here is an example of a portion of a survey related to bookkeeping, accounting, or auditing clerks.

Please specify the tools and equipment you use in your job:

____ Desktop computers
____ Scanners
____ Other: _____
____ Other: _____

Please specify the technology you use in your job:

Accounting software

____ FlexiLedger software
____ Intuit QuickBooks
____ Intuit Quicken software
____ Quicken Elite software
____ Other: _____
____ Other: _____

Compliance software

____ CRSTL Compliance Positioning System
____ FLS eDP.Payrolltax
____ Intrax ProcedureNet
____ Paisley Cardmap
____ Other: _____
____ Other: _____

Document management software

____ Accutrac software
____ OmniRIM software
____ Records management software
____ Other: _____
____ Other: _____

Enterprise resource planning ERP software

____ AcornSystems Corporate Performance Management

___ AMS Services AMS Sagitta
___ Business performance management BPM software
___ Cartesis ES Magnitude
___ Other: _____
___ Other: _____

Financial analysis software

___ Auditing software
___ AuditWare software
___ MethodWare ProAudit Advisor
___ RSM McGladrey Auditor Assistant
___ Other: _____
___ Other: _____

Please explain the following relationships as they are related to your job:

• Supervision given and received.
• Relationships with internal people.
• Relationships with external people.

People who have had the job before are probably your best source of information about the day-to-day responsibilities, so make sure you ask them. You also, however, need to check with their managers, because the job may be changing or the manager may not have liked the way the employee handled the position.

Conduct Supervisor Surveys and Interviews

Surveying and interviewing supervisors will provide you with the information you need to determine the core competencies required for the specific job in question. For example, you should discuss the following:

KNOWLEDGE	
Clerical	Knowledge of administrative and clerical procedures and systems such as word processing, managing files and records, stenography and transcription, designing forms, and other office procedures and terminology.

Mathematics	Knowledge of arithmetic, algebra, geometry, calculus, statistics, and their applications.
English Language	Knowledge of the structure and content of the English language including the meaning and spelling of words, rules of composition, and grammar.
Economics and Accounting	Knowledge of economic and accounting principles and practices, financial markets, banking, and analysis and reporting of financial data.
Customer and Personal Service	Knowledge of principles and processes for providing customer and personal services. This includes customer needs assessment, meeting quality standards for services, and evaluation of customer satisfaction.
Computers and Electronics	Knowledge of circuit boards, processors, chips, electronic equipment, and computer hardware and software, including applications and programming.
SKILLS	
Mathematics	Using mathematics to solve problems.
Reading Comprehension	Understanding written sentences and paragraphs in work-related documents.
Time Management	Managing one's own time and the time of others.
Active Listening	Giving full attention to what other people are saying, taking time to understand the points being made, asking questions as appropriate, and not interrupting at inappropriate times.
Critical Thinking	Using logic and reasoning to identify the strengths and weaknesses of alternative solutions, conclusions, or approaches to problems.
Active Learning	Understanding the implications of new information for both current and future problem solving and decision making.
Learning Strategies	Selecting and using training and instructional methods and procedures appropriate for the situation when learning or teaching new things.
Social Perceptiveness	Being aware of others' reactions and understanding why they react as they do.
Writing	Communicating effectively in writing as appropriate for the needs of the audience.

Speaking	Talking to others to convey information effectively.
ABILITIES	
Near Vision	The ability to see details at close range (within a few feet of the observer).
Mathematical Reasoning	The ability to choose the right mathematical methods or formulas to solve a problem.
Problem Sensitivity	The ability to tell when something is wrong or is likely to go wrong. It does not involve solving the problem, only recognizing there is a problem.
Deductive Reasoning	The ability to apply general rules to specific problems to produce answers that make sense.
Information Ordering	The ability to arrange things or actions in a certain order or pattern according to a specific rule or set of rules (e.g., patterns of numbers, letters, words, pictures, or mathematical operations).
Oral Comprehension	The ability to listen to and understand information and ideas presented through spoken words and sentences.
Written Comprehension	The ability to read and understand information and ideas presented in writing.
Written Expression	The ability to communicate information and ideas in writing so others will understand.
Oral Expression	The ability to communicate information and ideas in speaking so others will understand.
Speech Clarity	The ability to speak clearly so others can understand you.

Information related to bookkeeping, accounting, or auditing clerks was from the O★NET OnLine system.

Development Steps

After completing information gathering through the analytic steps discussed in the table, distill the information into a useable form through the creation of a Job Audit Form and an Essential/Nonessential Duties and Responsibilities Chart.

Job Audit Form

A Job Audit Form is not a job description; however, it forms a basis on which to draft the job description, such as in the following example:

Job Audit Form

Audit conducted by: _____   Date: _____

Job title: _____   Department: _____

Major duties: Minor duties:

Reporting relationships:

    Supervised by: Supervises:

Training required: Education required:

Certificates/licenses required:

Experience required:

Physical requirements:

On-the-job hazards/working conditions:

Source(s) of job-audit information:

Essential/Nonessential Duties and Responsibilities Chart

(E) = Essential functions   (N) = Nonessential functions

Percentage of Time Devoted	Essential/ Nonessential	Task
35	E	Check figures, postings, and documents for correct entry, mathematical accuracy, and proper codes.
55	E	Operate computers programmed with accounting software to record, store, and analyze information.
5	N	Compile statistical, financial, accounting, or auditing reports and tables pertaining to such matters as cash receipts, expenditures, accounts payable and receivable, and profits and losses.
2	N	Work with the public.

Writing the Job Description

Minimum Requirements

Start with developing the minimum job requirements including:

- *Summary Statement*—provides a synopsis of the major purpose of a position and its role in the department.
- *Duties*—major subdivisions of work performed by one individual.
- *Tasks*—work operations that are logical, essential steps in the performance of a duty. The "tasks" section of the description defines the methods, procedures, and techniques by which duties are carried out. It should show:
  - What is done (action)
  - How it is done (procedures, materials, tools, or equipment)
  - Why it is done (purpose)

  Begin each task statement with an action verb in the first-person present tense (e.g., *write, calibrate, analyze, coordinate, approve, accept, devise,* or *develop*).
- *Degree of Supervision*—supervision either given or received.

Once you have the essential minimum requirements, put them into your job template.

Job Description Template

Job Title:
Department:
Reports to:
FLSA Status:

SUMMARY

ESSENTIAL DUTIES AND RESPONSIBILITIES [Other duties may be assigned]

SUPERVISORY RESPONSIBILITIES

QUALIFICATIONS

EDUCATION AND/OR EXPERIENCE

LANGUAGE SKILLS

MATHEMATICAL SKILLS

REASONING ABILITY

CERTIFICATES, LICENSES, REGISTRATIONS

PHYSICAL DEMANDS

WORK ENVIRONMENT

Recruiting

Recruiting Generally

Successful recruiting is centered on techniques to attract a large pool of qualified applicants.

Internal Job Postings

Because they already possess working knowledge of your organization's policies, procedures, and so on, current employees are an immediately available and important applicant pool for job vacancies. Job vacancies may represent desirable promotions (upward moves) or transfers (lateral moves).

In general, all vacancies should be publicized through internal physical postings on bulletin boards, at meetings, or through the organization's website or Web blog. These postings will help you discover qualified employees within your organization and could help in meeting equal employment opportunity (EEO) commitments.

Many organizations limit how soon or how often a current employee can apply for any opening. For example, an employee must be with the company for at least a year and in his or her current job for six months to become eligible to apply for a vacancy.

It is neither legally necessary nor operationally desirable to give present employees first refusal on all vacancies; however, a promotion-and-transfer system can build employee trust and enhance morale.

Note: A common problem with internal recruiting is that managers will deliberately sabotage the promotion chances of their best employees in order to retain them.

Employee Referrals

Current employee referrals, especially from good performers, are an effective job applicant source. People generally make friends with people similar to themselves.

Good people want to work with good people. Hard workers gravitate to other hard workers. Therefore, referrals from your best performers are likely to be highly desirable applicants. And, word of mouth is a strong method of advertising open positions. Also, referred applicants tend to have a more realistic picture of an organization and can be reached at practically no cost.

Note: A major disadvantage of employee referrals can be the current worker's expectation that all referred applicants should receive job offers.

Also Note: Employee referral programs may be perceived as discriminatory in practice.

> **EXAMPLE:** If an existing work group is fairly homogeneous—that is, 98 percent of all workers are white women—you will likely end up hiring more people within the same limited group and having a disparate impact on all others. So employee referrals should not be your only recruitment method, especially if you have a primarily homogeneous group.

External Sources

The Internet, certainly including the company's own website, is becoming a primary source of attracting talent. External to the organization and to the Internet are an array of recruiting sources including, but not limited to, newspaper and trade publication advertisements, educational institutions, labor and community organizations, job fairs, state agencies, professional search firms, online recruiting sites, employee leasing, temporary agencies, billboards, and past employees.

Recruiting and Discrimination

Discriminatory Recruitment

Section 703, Civil Rights Act of 1964 (CRA); other federal laws; and the fair employment practice acts (FEPAs) of almost every state make it an unlawful employment practice for any employer, employment agency, or labor organization to deprive any individual of employment opportunities because of the applicant's race, color, religion, sex, national origin, physical disability, or other characteristic protected by law. (See Chapter 6, Employment Laws.")

Because of these laws, employers cannot fail or refuse to hire an individual because he or she is a member of a protected class or print or publish, or cause to be printed or published, a job advertisement that may adversely affect a member of a protected class. Since you are trying to recruit applicants whose skills and abilities match the job(s) in question, advertisements should contain words and phrases that focus on the job. Job-related language is your best defense against printing or publishing discriminatory advertisements.

Job-Related Advertising Language

A discriminatory job advertisement is one that indicates, or that might reasonably be understood as indicating, that an employer intends to commit an act of unlawful discrimination when determining who should be offered employment or promotion. Intent to discriminate is determined from what an employer says or does—not from what it *actually* meant. For example, an employer seeking applicants for an entry-level position may say in its job advertisement, "Perfect for those just starting their careers." This seems to indicate people over age 40 are not being sought. More appropriate wording would simply state that the job is an entry-level position.

An advertisement must be read as a whole and you must be careful of not only the words you use but also the pictures.

> **EXAMPLE:** A job advertisement for a mechanic that features a male mechanic or an advertisement for a nurse that presents a picture of a female nurse could indicate a preference based on sex (gender).

A central issue is whether the advertisement's language has a *disparate impact* on one or another protected group. Disparate impact is where an employment practice appears to be neutral; however, in practice, it disproportionately and adversely impacts members of a protected group. It doesn't have to eliminate everyone in the protected group, merely a statistically significant number of that group.

> **EXAMPLE:** A job advertisement that states a height requirement may have a disparate impact on women or Asians (national origin discrimination).

A narrow exception exists regarding discriminatory job requirements if there is a characteristic that a candidate must possess to actually do the job in question. This is called a *bona fide occupational qualification* (BFOQ). The BFOQ must be significantly necessary for operation of the employer's business. For example, being female is not a BFOQ for working in a women's health club in such positions as a manager or trainer; however, it could be for being an attendant in the women's locker room.

Other areas where issues related to disparate impact might arise include the following:

- Educational standards
- No facial hair standards for men where there is no operational or safety-related reason for the policy
- Preemployment testing
- Referrals from current workforce (if current workforce is predominantly of one race, gender, etc.)

Retention of Applications and Résumés

Applications in Response to Job Advertisements

You must retain for one year any résumés or applications you receive in response to job advertisements you have placed in any media.

Title 29 Code of Federal Regulations Section 1602.14 Preservation of Records Made or Kept, says, among other things:

> Any personnel or employment record made or kept by an employer (including but not necessarily limited to requests for reasonable accommodation, application forms submitted by applicants and other records having to do with hiring, promotion, demotion, transfer, lay-off or termination, rates of pay or other terms of compensation, and selection for training or apprenticeship) shall be preserved by the employer for a period of one year from the date of the making of the record or the personnel action involved, whichever occurs later.

Although you must retain applications for one year, unless you are going to actively review applications when a new job opening occurs, it is recommended you advise applicants that applications and résumés will be kept active only for sixty days after they are received and that they must reapply if they have an interest in any job with your company after that time. This will eliminate any argument a potential plaintiff may have that your retention of an application was an implied promise that you would consider him or her in the future.

Unsolicited Applications and Résumés

Hard-Copy Applications and Résumés Individuals who physically send you unsolicited applications and résumés are not automatically applicants for employment. You may dispose of unsolicited applications and résumés you receive unless it is your organizational practice to keep and use an open file of such unsolicited applications and résumés.

A walk-in applicant whom you allow to fill out and hand you an application form probably is considered to be an applicant for employment and you should retain his or her application for one year.

Electronic Applications and Résumés In order for an individual to be an applicant in the context of the Internet and related electronic data-processing technologies, the following must have occurred:

- The employer has acted to fill a particular position.
- The individual has followed the employer's standard procedures for submitting applications.
- The individual has indicated an interest in the particular position.

If someone is an electronic applicant in that he or she has properly responded to an advertisement you posted on the Internet, you must retain his or her application or résumé for one year.

Preemployment Screening

Companies will sometimes receive dozens of applications for an open position and will seek to narrow the field of applicants it actually wishes to interview. Two common methods used in preemployment screening are preemployment testing and using a screening tool to quickly select the most-qualified candidates.

Preemployment Testing

It *is* legal to test job applicants to see if they possess relevant skills. Title VII, CRA (the portion of the federal law that establishes protected classes of people) permits the use of professionally developed ability tests as long as they are not designed or administered in a discriminatory manner. Specifically, an employer is prohibited from using preemployment tests that have an adverse statistical impact on minority groups unless it has taken measures to demonstrate the business relevance of the test results. *Validation* is the term that describes a study of this kind.

The Equal Employment Opportunity Commission's (EEOC's) "Uniform Guidelines on Employee Selection Procedures" ("Uniform Guidelines") allows three basic methods of test validation: content, construct, and criterion.

1. *Content validation* involves analyzing the content of the tests and demonstrating that it corresponds to the job tasks as set out in a complete job analysis.
2. *Construct validation* involves showing that the test measures specific personal characteristics that are shown to be necessary for performance of the job.
3. *Criterion validation* involves showing a statistical correlation between performance on the test and actual job performance as measured by specific criteria.

Screening Tools

An efficient method of quickly screening a large pool of applicants is to use your Job Audit Form and Essential/Nonessential Duties and Responsibilities Chart to create an analytic spreadsheet using the following steps:

1. Select skill sets or background characteristics you feel are truly important for the position in question.
2. Utilize symbols that represent whether the applicant does or does not possesses the requisite skill or background or has a related skill or background. (See "Example—Screening Tool" on the facing page.)
3. Quickly screen all applications using the screening tool.
4. Interview only those applicants who most closely match your significant requirements.

Example—Screening Tool

Legend:
+ = possesses skill set or background
− = related skill set or background
0 = does not possess skill set or characteristic

Skill Set or Background	Applicant A	Applicant B	Applicant C	Applicant D
Check figures, postings, and documents for correct entry, mathematical accuracy, and proper codes.	0	+	+	−
Operate computers programmed with accounting software to record, store, and analyze information.	−	+	+	0
Work with the public.	+	+	+	+
Lift heavy objects.	0	+	+	+
Work alone.	−	+	+	+

Screening Applications and Résumés

A careful review of applicants' applications and résumés will assist you in deciding which applicants to actually interview and provide you with areas to pursue (e.g., relevance of experience stated) and to get clarification on (e.g., "What were your actual duties when you . . . ?").

The Application Form

Have applicants fill out your application form even if they have a professionally produced résumé. A professionally produced résumé will often hide as much as it reveals, such as reasons for leaving a prior job. Your application form forces the employee to not only personally fill in the information you reasonably require but also to attest to the truthfulness of the data through his or her signature.

Your application should have important disclaimers and representations from your organization to applicants as well as representations you want them to make to you through their signatures—for example, "I represent that all of the information stated is true and correct. . . ."

What to Look For

The following is a list of areas to focus on when reviewing an application or résumé. It is not meant to be exhaustive nor is it presented in any order of importance.

Overall Appearance When reviewing an application or résumé, always keep in mind the job you are hiring for. Improper grammar on the application for a common laborer is irrelevant; however, on an application for an executive position it could be highly significant.

Blanks or Omissions of Information Note and ask about missing dates, job titles, addresses, and other contact information related to former employers and similar fact-based information.

Gaps in Employment Resist being judgmental about why someone has gaps in his or her employment history. Gaps in employment are merely one consideration among many in the hiring decision.

Overlaps in Employment Ask if it is inherently plausible that someone could have been doing whatever the applicant has indicated on a concurrent basis. Going to school during the same time frame someone was working is plausible, but working two full-time direct manual labor jobs may not be.

Frequency of Job Changes In the past, if someone changed jobs every few years, they were deemed to be unreliable. That concept is somewhat dated. People are far more mobile today than ever before, and the old notion that if you were loyal to an organization it would be loyal to you is simply gone. Also, many companies now hire people on an almost "project" basis, and when the effort is completed, the worker "changes" jobs.

It is far more important that you analyze why applicants have changed jobs than the mere fact that they did or that they did it within a short time frame.

Logical Inconsistencies A more subtle item to look for is a mismatch between someone's educational or work background and jobs they have been recently doing. For example, it would seem illogical for someone with an advanced degree in engineering to be working as a server in a fast-food restaurant. Seek clarification whenever these types of logical inconsistencies appear.

Nondescriptive Job Titles or Statement of Job Duties Take note and seek clarification of job titles that do not actually explain what the applicant did for a past employer, such as "accounting clerk" or "handled receiving."

Reasons for Leaving Past Employment Seek clarification of nonexplanatory reasons for leaving past employment such as, "personal reasons" or "no room for growth."

Compensation Ask yourself if there is a valid relationship between what the applicant is seeking and your ability to satisfy his or her needs. For example, if an applicant has been making $62,500 per year for several years and you are trying to fill a job with a top end compensation of $65,000 per year, will that applicant stay with you for more than a short time if hired? Probably not.

Interviewing

Structured Interviews

Treating an interview in a casual manner is a surefire way to find yourself being charged with discrimination. (See Chapter 6, "Employment Laws," for a full discussion of federal and state laws dealing with discrimination.) Under Title VII and the EEOC Uniform Guidelines interviews are considered to be selection procedures on a par with preemployment tests because they are one means by which an employer disqualifies an applicant from consideration for a job.

Employers that use unstructured interviews tend to use subjective, rather than objective, criteria. Questions or comments that do not focus on job-related issues can open the employer to charges of discrimination. Your safest legal course is to center interview questions and comments on job-related issues and, to the greatest extent possible, ask all applicants the same core questions. (See "Competency-Based Questions" in this chapter.)

In preparing to interview you should:

- Define, as objectively as possible, the qualifications of the job in question.
- Devise questions that are job related.
- Ask questions in a consistent, objective manner.

EXAMPLE: Do not ask a female applicant what she will do with her young children when she travels, but rather simply ask if she will be able to travel on business. And, ask male applicants the same core question in the same way.

Note: If an applicant volunteers information related to protected class status—for example, "I'm over age 40," "I have a special needs child," or "I'm a Muslim"—be sure to openly state that your organization is an equal opportunity employer and makes hiring decisions based on job-related qualifications without regard to race, religion, age, sex, national origin, physical disability, or other legally protected characteristics.

Interviews and the Americans with Disabilities Act

Pre-Offer Stage

What You Can and Cannot Ask Under the Americans with Disabilities Act (ADA), an employer may ask disability-related questions and require medical examinations of an applicant only after the applicant has been given a conditional job offer.

At the pre-offer stage, an employer cannot ask questions that are likely to elicit information about a disability, including directly asking whether an applicant has a particular disability. You also cannot ask questions that are closely related to disability.

Focus application and interview questions on nonmedical job qualifications. An employer may ask a wide range of questions designed to determine an applicant's qualifications for a job.

What you can ask:

- Whether the applicant can perform the essential functions of a job (describe them to the applicant) with or without a reasonable accommodation

- Whether the applicant has the right education, training, and skills for the position
- How much time off the applicant took in a previous job (but not why), the reason he or she left a previous job, and any past discipline

What you cannot ask:

- Whether the applicant needs an accommodation to do the job
- Questions about the applicant's physical or mental impairment or how he or she became disabled (e.g., questions about why the applicant uses a wheelchair)
- Questions about the applicant's use of medication
- Questions about the applicant's prior workers compensation history

When an employer could reasonably believe that an applicant will not be able to perform a job function because of a known disability, the employer may ask that particular applicant to describe or demonstrate how he or she would perform the function. An applicant's disability would be a *known disability* either because it is obvious—for example, the applicant uses a wheelchair—or because the applicant has voluntarily disclosed that he or she has a hidden disability.

> **EXAMPLE:** During a job interview, you may ask a blind applicant interviewing for a position that requires working with a computer whether he or she will need a reasonable accommodation, such as special software that will read information on the screen.

Documentation of a Disability If the need for accommodation is not obvious, an employer may ask an applicant for reasonable documentation about his or her disability if the applicant requests reasonable accommodation for the hiring process—for example, a request for the employer to reformat an examination or a request for an accommodation in connection with a job demonstration.

Since the employer is entitled to know that the applicant has a covered disability and that he or she needs an accommodation, the applicant may be required to provide documentation from an appropriate professional, such as a doctor or a rehabilitation counselor, concerning the applicant's disability and functional limitations.

Confidentiality and the ADA An employer must keep any medical information on applicants or employees confidential, with the following limited exceptions:

- Supervisors and managers may be told about necessary restrictions on the work or duties of the employee and about necessary accommodations.

- First aid and safety personnel may be told if the disability might require emergency treatment.

- Government officials investigating compliance with the ADA must be given relevant information on request.

- Employers may give information to state workers compensation offices, state second injury funds, or workers compensation insurance carriers in accordance with state workers compensation laws.

- Employers may use the information for insurance purposes.

Medical information may be given to—and used by—appropriate decision makers involved in the hiring process so they can make employment decisions consistent with the ADA. As mandated by the Americans with Disabilities Act, keep medical information in a medical records file separate from an applicant's or employee's regular personnel file.

Post-Offer Stage

After making a job offer, you may ask disability-related questions and conduct medical examinations as long as you do this for everybody in the same job category.

The job offer may be conditioned on the results of post-offer disability-related questions or medical examinations. You may withdraw an offer from an applicant with a disability only if it becomes clear that he or she cannot do the essential functions of the job or would pose a direct threat—for example, a significant risk of substantial harm to the health or safety of himself or herself or others.

Examples of What You Can Do

- If you want to give a medical examination to someone who has been offered a job that involves heavy labor, you must give the same exam to anyone who is offered the same kind of job.

- You may withdraw an offer of a manufacturing job involving the use of dangerous machinery if you learn during a post-offer medical exam that the applicant has frequent and unpredictable seizures.

Examples of What You Cannot Do

- You can't withdraw an offer to an HIV-positive applicant because you are concerned about customer and client reactions or because you assume that anyone with HIV infection will be unable to work long and stressful hours.

Interview Questions

Acceptable vs. Unacceptable Questions

Subject	Acceptable	Unacceptable
Name	Can ask if applicant has ever worked for the company under another name.	Have you ever had any other names?
Birthplace	No acceptable questions.	Where were you born? Where were your parents born? Requiring a birth certificate.
Age	Can ask if the applicant meets any age-required conditions of the job.	How old are you? Any questions attempting to determine the age of the applicant are unacceptable unless BFOQ related (e.g., being at least age 21 to serve hard liquor in a lounge).
Religion	No acceptable questions unless religion is a bona fide occupational qualification (e.g., teaching at a parochial school).	Questions about religion generally or about what days the applicant may need off for religious observance.
Work Schedule	Can ask if the applicant meets the attendance requirements of the position.	Any questions about health conditions that would lead to absences from work.
Race	No acceptable questions.	Any questions seeking to elicit what race the applicant is or other questions indicating race or color.

Subject	Acceptable	Unacceptable
Photographs	Unacceptable unless BFOQ (e.g., some sort of acting role).	Please attach a photograph.
Citizenship	The only acceptable question is whether the applicant will be able to prove that he or she is employable in the event he or she is offered the job. Employment authorization and identity must be verified and Form I-9 completed within three days of when the individual begins employment.	Any questions asking or seeking to elicit what nationality the applicant is.
National Origin	Languages that the applicant can read, write, or speak and his or her level of fluency.	Any questions about the applicant's national lineage or his or her date of entry into the United States. Any questions concerning the national origin of the applicant's spouse or mother. Any questions such as, "What is your mother tongue?"
Education	Applicant's educational background.	When did you graduate from high school? When did you receive your college degree?
Experience	Can ask questions like: What is your work experience? Why did you leave your last job?	What type of discharge did you receive from the military?
Arrests	In most states, no acceptable questions.	Have you ever been arrested?
Felony Convictions	Can ask about felony convictions in all states. In many states, may only disqualify applicant for a job-related reason and not just because of the conviction itself.	Have you ever been indicted for a crime?
Relatives	Names of any relatives employed by the company.	Are you married? What relatives live with you? With whom do you reside?
Physical Condition	Can you perform the essential functions of the position for which you are interviewing with or without a reasonable accommodation?	Are you disabled? Are you healthy? Any pre-job offer questions concerning workers compensation.

Subject	Acceptable	Unacceptable
Miscellaneous	A statement that any material misstatements made by the applicant may result in immediate dismissal.	Any questions that are not related to the position or necessary to evaluate the applicant's capability to perform the job.

Competency-Based Questions

Modern human resource management practices suggest that the core of an interview be made up of competency-based questions. This type of question focuses on relating past job performance to probable on-the-job behavior. Answers to competency-based questions are indicators, not predictors, of future performance.

Competency-based questions are derived from your having done a job analysis that identifies the specific job-related skills, abilities, and traits required for successful performance of the job in question.

This type of question seeks specific examples from the applicant's past that will allow you to project how this person will perform in similar circumstances or conditions at your organization.

Competency-based interviews do not, of course, consist solely of competency-based questions. Although the core of the interview will be made up of these types of questions, there will also be closed-end "yes/no" questions to confirm information given, confirming questions to address answers the applicant gives, and open-ended follow-up questions to other answers provided.

Common competency-based question lead-ins are:

- "Describe a time when you . . ."
- "Describe the circumstances under which you most recently . . ."
- "Tell me about a time when you . . ."
- "Give an example of a time in which you . . ."
- "Tell me about a specific job experience in which you . . ."
- "Give me an example of a specific occasion when you . . ."
- "Describe a situation in which you were called upon to . . ."
- "Describe the most significant . . ."
- "What did you do in your last job in order to . . ."
- "How often in the past year were you called upon to . . ."

- "Tell me about a time when you didn't want to _____;
  what happened?"
- "Describe a situation in which you felt _____; what was
  the result?"
- "Identify [number] of your [greatest] [best] [weakest] [worst]
  _____ . . ."
- "Which of your _____ do you apply when faced with
  _____?"

Verifying Employment Eligibility

Form I-9

The Immigration Reform and Control Act made all U.S. employers responsible for verifying the employment eligibility and identity of all employees hired to work in the United States after November 6, 1986. To
implement the law, employers are required to complete Employment Eligibility Verification forms (Form I-9) for all employees, including U.S.
citizens.

Completing Form I-9

Every U.S. employer with four or more workers must have a Form I-9 in
its files for each current employee unless the employee was hired before
November 7, 1986, and has been continuously employed by the same
employer.

Form I-9 need not be completed for those individuals who provide:

- Domestic services in a private household that are sporadic, irregular, or intermittent.
- Services for the employer as an independent contractor.
- Services for the employer under a contract, subcontract, or exchange entered into after November 6, 1986. (In such cases, the
  contractor is the employer for I-9 purposes; for example, a temporary employment agency.)

Missing or Materially Incorrect I-9s

Because significant penalties can be levied by the Department of Home-
land Security's Immigration Customs Enforcement (ICE) department if

you do not have an I-9 for current employees or if I-9s contain material omissions, such as missing signatures or dates, you should show good faith and reduce your liability by taking the following steps:

- Audit your I-9 files.
- Identify missing or materially incorrect I-9s regarding current employees.
- Immediately work with appropriate employees to complete new I-9s.
  - Complete new forms; do not merely change existing forms.
  - Retain old, incorrect form with new form.
- Draft an explanatory memo to the file. Example:

  On [DATE] the [Company Name] undertook a voluntary self-audit of its I-9 Forms and discovered that there were no forms for certain of its current employees and that some forms contained material errors or omissions. Consequently, all employees in question completed new Form I-9s no later than [DATE]. The employees in question are: [List alphabetically]

Employee's Responsibility Regarding Form I-9

Completion Date Have the employee complete Section 1 at the time of the hire (when he or she begins to work) by filling in the correct information and signing and dating the form. Ensure that the employee prints the information clearly.

If the employee cannot complete Section 1 without assistance or if he or she needs the Form I-9 translated, someone may assist him or her.

- The preparer or translator must read the form to the employee, assist him or her in completing Section 1, and have the employee sign or mark the form in the appropriate place.
- The preparer or translator must complete the Preparer/Translator Certification block on the Form I-9.

The employee's signature holds him or her responsible for the accuracy of the information provided and no documentation from the employee is required to substantiate Section 1 information provided by the employee. However, the employer is responsible for reviewing and ensuring that the employee fully and properly completes Section 1.

Social Security Number and E-Verify The United States Citizenship and Immigration Service (USCIS) operates an electronic employment eligibility verification system called E-Verify. E-Verify provides an automated link to federal databases to help employers determine the employment eligibility of new hires.

Employees must provide their Social Security number (although not necessarily a Social Security card) if you are a participant of the E-Verify Program.

E-Verify is free to employers and is available in all fifty states, as well as U.S. territories except for American Samoa and the Commonwealth of the Northern Mariana Islands.

Employers who participate in the E-Verify Program complete a Form I-9 for each newly hired employee, as is required of all employers in the United States. E-Verify employers may accept any document or combination of documents acceptable on the Form I-9, but if the employee chooses to present a List B and C combination, the List B (identity only) document must have a photograph.

After completing Form I-9 for a new employee, E-Verify employers must submit an electronic query that includes information from Sections 1 and 2 of Form I-9 (see Exhibits 1-1 and 1-2). After submitting the query, the employer will receive an automated response from the E-Verify system regarding the employment eligibility of the individual.

You must reverify an employee's status on or before the expiration date of the employee's authorization.

Exhibit 1-1. Attestation of alien work authorization.

I attest, under penalty of perjury, that I am (check one of the following):

☐ A citizen or national of the United States

☐ A lawful permanent resident (Alien #) A _____

☐ An alien authorized to work until _____

(Alien # or Admission #) _____

Employers can register online for E-Verify at https://www.vis-dhs. com/EmployerRegistration

Employer's Responsibility Regarding Form I-9 Section 2

Acceptance of Documents The employer must fully complete Section 2 no later than the end of the third day that employment services begin (see Exhibit 1-2). You must examine one document from List A (List of Acceptable Documents) or one from List B and one from List C. Record the title, issuing authority, number, and expiration date (if any) of the document(s); fill in the date of hire and correct information in the certification block; and sign and date Form I-9.

The employee must present you with an *original* document or documents that establish identity and employment eligibility within three business days of the date employment begins. A receipt indicating that an individual has applied for initial work authorization or for extension of an expiring work authorization, although *not* acceptable proof of employment eligibility on the Form I-9, may be accepted as proof of temporary employment eligibility during the initial three days of employment. An original document must be presented within ninety days. Receipts are never acceptable if employment lasts for less than three business days.

When the employee provides an acceptable receipt, you should record the document title in Section 2 of the Form I-9 and write the word *receipt*

Exhibit 1-2. List of acceptable documents in I-9 Section 2.

List A	OR	List B	AND	List C

Section 2. Employer Review and Verification. To be completed and signed by employer. Examine one document from List A OR examine one document from List B and one from List C, as listed on the reverse of this form, and record the title, number and expiration date, if any, of the document(s).

Document title:

Issuing authority:

Document #:

   Expiration Date *(if any)*:

Document #:

   Expiration Date *(if any)*:

CERTIFICATION - I attest, under penalty of perjury, that I have examined the document(s) presented by the above-named employee, that the above-listed document(s) appear to be genuine and to relate to the employee named, that the employee began employment on *(month/day/year)* **and that to the best of my knowledge the employee is eligible to work in the United States.** (State employment agencies may omit the date the employee began employment.)

Signature of Employer or Authorized Representative	Print Name	Title
Business or Organization Name and Address *(Street Name and Number, City, State, Zip Code)*		Date *(month/day/year)*

and any document number in the "Document #" space. When the employee presents the actual document, you should cross out the word *receipt* and any accompanying document number, insert the number from the actual document presented, and initial and date the change.

You must accept any documents from the List of Acceptable Documents presented by the individual that reasonably appear on their face to be genuine and to relate to the person presenting them. The employer is under no legal obligation to research the validity of a document that reasonably appears to be genuine.

Remote Hires—Agents

If you hire a new employee who doesn't physically come to your office to complete paperwork, you may designate agents to carry out your I-9 responsibilities. Agents may include notaries public, accountants, attorneys, personnel officers, foremen, and the like. Choose an agent cautiously, since your organization will be held responsible for the actions of that agent.

Remote Hires—Nonoriginal Documents

Employers should not carry out I-9 responsibilities by means of documents faxed by a new employee or through identifying numbers appearing on acceptable documents. The employer *must* review original documents. Also, the employer must complete Section 2. Therefore, Form I-9 should not be mailed to a new employee to complete Section 2 himself or herself.

Acceptable Documents Some documents establish the following:

- Both identity and employment eligibility (List A)
- Identity only (List B)
- Employment authorization only (List C)

The employee can choose which document(s) he or she wants to present from the List of Acceptable Documents. You (the employer) may not specify which document(s) an employee must present.

Photocopying Verification Documents You *may* but *are not required* to photocopy the documents presented. It is strongly recommended that you *do not* photocopy the documents presented as part of the verification process! If you do photocopy the documents, you must keep them with the I-9 and cannot use them for any purpose other than verification. Even if you photocopy the documents you must still completely fill out Section 2. (You cannot photocopy, staple the copies to the I-9, and write, "See attached.") Therefore, *by photocopying you are putting into your files documents that ICE can later challenge.*

After Form I-9 Is Completed—Dos and Don'ts

Do not file the I-9 forms with the U.S. Government.

Do maintain I-9 records in your own files for three years after the date of hire or one year after the date the employee's employment is terminated, whichever is later. Examples include the following:

- A worker is hired today and works for only three weeks. Retain his or her I-9 for three years from the date of hire.

- A worker works for you for ten years and then separates from the company. Retain this employee's I-9 for one year after the date of separation.

Note: You may retain the I-9 in the employee's personnel file; however, it is a best practice to keep these forms in a separate, stand-alone file. If ICE requests to see your I-9s you must provide them within three business days. Having your I-9s in a separate file will greatly assist you with your compliance efforts.

No-Match Letters

A Social Security no-match letter is a notice sent by the Social Security Administration (SSA) to employers and employees to inform them that the employee's name or Social Security number listed on an employee's W-2 does not match the SSA records.

A Social Security no-match letter is *not* a notice of wrongdoing. There are many ordinary reasons why a no-match discrepancy may occur, such as misspelled names, transposed numbers, unreported name changes, or clerical errors. The no-match letter is not a notice that the employer should threaten or take any adverse action against an employee listed in the no-match letter.

Suggestions if You Receive a No-Match Letter

- Take reasonable steps to resolve the no-match (check for spelling errors, transposed numbers, etc.).

- Apply these steps uniformly to all employees listed in the SSA letter. For example, investigating only workers with Hispanic surnames would be national origin discrimination. (See Chapter 6, "Employment Laws.")

- Promptly (no later than thirty days) check to make sure the error was not the result of an error on the part of the employer.

- If this does not resolve the problem, ask the employee to confirm the accuracy of the employer's records.

- If necessary, ask the employee to resolve the issue with SSA. Inform the employee he or she has ninety days from the date the employer received the no-match letter to resolve the matter with SSA.

- If none of the foregoing measures resolves the matter within ninety days of receipt of the no-match letter, the employer should:

  - Complete within three days a new Form I-9 as if the employee in question were newly hired, except that no document may be used to verify the employee's authorization for work that uses the questionable Social Security number.

  - Additionally, have the employee present a document that contains a photograph in order to establish identity or both identity and employment authorization.

No-Match Risk

If the employer cannot confirm that the employee is authorized to work (by following the previous procedures), the employer risks liability for violating the law by knowingly continuing to hire unauthorized workers.

Reverifying Employment Authorization for Current Employees

When an employee's work authorization expires, you must reverify his or her employment eligibility.

You may use Section 3 of Form I-9, or, if Section 3 has already been used for a previous reverification or update, use a new Form I-9. If you use a new form, write the employee's name in Section 1, complete Section 3, and retain the new form with the original.

The employee must present a document that shows either an extension of the employee's initial employment authorization or new work authorization. If the employee cannot provide you with proof of current work authorization—for example, any document from List A or List C, including an unrestricted Social Security card—you cannot continue to employ that person.

Reverifying or Updating Employment Authorization for Rehired Employees

When you rehire an employee, you must ensure that he or she is still authorized to work by completing a new Form I-9 or you may reverify or update the original form by completing Section 3.

If you rehire an employee who has previously completed a Form I-9, you may reverify on the employee's original Form I-9 (or on a new Form I-9 if Section 3 of the original has already been used) if:

- You rehire the employee within three years of the initial date of hire.
- The employee's previous grant of work authorization has expired, but he or she is currently eligible to work on a different basis or under a new grant of work authorization than when the original Form I-9 was completed.

To reverify, you must:

- Record the date of rehire.
- Record the document title, number, and expiration date (if any) of any document(s) presented.
- Sign and date Section 3.
- If you are reverifying on a new Form I-9, write the employee's name in Section 1.

2

Performance Evaluations

Introduction

One of the most uncomfortable moments in any manager's working year is when he or she must conduct a performance evaluation. Whether an uncomfortable moment or not, performance evaluations are an important management tool with which to assess any given employee's performance and to motivate him or her to either improve or continue to perform to company standards.

Proper preparation and structuring of a performance evaluation can transform it from a confrontation into a worthwhile collaboration between you, the employer, and your employee.

The Job Description

The natural starting point for preparing to undertake a performance review is to begin with the employee's job description. By its nature, the job description should define the nature of the worker's job, the tasks involved, the reporting relationships, and so forth.

As stated in Chapter 1, "Hiring," a well-researched and well-developed job description is the foundation stone of smart recruiting, interviewing, and hiring, as well as staff retention.

However, although the job description is the final manifestation of an organization's statement of its expectations of a position and the reporting relationships surrounding it, by itself, it is not detailed enough to serve as a proper metric by which to measure performance. The detailed information with which to measure performance lies within the analysis that led up to the job description—the breakdown of the core competencies, knowledge, skills, attitudes, and so on that are required for the job.

Core Competencies

An enumeration of core competencies sets up a review structure. For example, assume that we were seeking an accounting clerk with knowledge of spreadsheet software. For the job in question, what level of knowledge did we require? Was it someone who could perform the following:

- Display an existing spreadsheet and merely repopulate the cells with new information he or she was provided.
- Create a spreadsheet from scratch using simple formulae.
- Create multiple spreadsheets that automatically imported or exported information to and from other spreadsheets or files within a larger database.

Once we understand the level of knowledge required, we can assess how well the employee actually performed. It is this author's opinion that most people want to do a good job—if management would just tell them what a good job is. Being able to tell an employee what we believe a good job is begins with our understanding the job in question and determining what metrics will be used to measure satisfactory performance.

The more competencies we examine and compare the employee's performance against, the better chance we have of truly entering into a collaborative dialogue with the worker where specifics rather than purely subjective criteria are used.

As an example, consider one portion of the knowledge requirement for an accounting clerk, namely clerical skills. The requirement might read: "Knowledge of administrative and clerical procedures and systems such as word processing, managing files and records, stenography and transcription, designing forms, and other office procedures and terminology."

Each of the requirements should be considered individually. For example, you should define what "managing files and records" means within the context of your organization. Does it involve hard-copy paper records, electronic records, document retention, document destruction, and so forth? Once you have a clear understanding of the requirements, you will be able to discuss the worker's specific actions and performance in carrying out the company's expectations.

It has become a well-known truism that a manager cannot motivate someone unless he or she can bring the employee's own desires and needs into alignment with the organization's objectives, goals, and expectations. An individual's desires and views are independent of those of the organization. By focusing a review on individual competencies, skills, and attitudes, the reviewer has more opportunities to understand not only what the employee has done during the review period but also why. Understanding the employee's motivations is a major step toward either motivating the employee to continue performing at an acceptable level or changing and modifying undesirable actions or attitudes.

The Paradox of Measurement

We've all received simple letter or number grades from grade school on. These types of measurements make it easy to rate individuals and to aggregate, compare, and contrast information on groups of individuals. The problem is that the simpler the measurements are and the lower the number of criteria used the less chance you have of successfully rating the individual on a qualitative basis.

Based on the previous paradox, you should set up a rating system that uses a broad range of competencies and metrics—for example, number or letter ratings, coupled with detailed definitions of what the numbers or letters mean.

Performance Rating Descriptions

EXAMPLE 1:

1	Consistently failed to meet performance standards. A remedial action plan is being developed to include specific training, coaching, or other support, with a timetable to achieve specific results.
2	Occasionally failed to meet performance standards. An appropriate development plan has been established and is stated in the "Development Plans" section.

3	Consistently met performance standards.
4	Frequently exceeded performance standards.
5	Consistently exceeded performance standards. This is the highest level of performance that can be attained by the employee and should be reserved for those few employees achieving results of the highest attainable level.

EXAMPLE 2:

E—Exceeded Expectations: A preponderance of the employee's work exceeded expectations. The employee consistently did outstanding work, regularly going far beyond what is expected of employees doing this type of work. Performance that exceeded expectations was due to the effort and skills of the employee.

M—Met Expectations: Performance fully met the established job expectations and may on occasion have exceeded expectations. The employee generally performs very well and requires little additional guidance.

I—Improvement Needed: Performance met some of the job expectations but did not fully meet the remainder. The employee generally performs at a minimal level and improvement is needed to fully meet expectations. Performance deficiencies were due to the employee's lack of effort or skills.

F—Failed to Meet Expectations: Performance generally failed to meet the established expectations or required frequent, close supervision and/ or the redoing of work. The employee did not perform at the level expected for employees doing this type of work. Unacceptable job performance was due to the employee's lack of effort or skills.

Evaluation of Performance for Each Principal Function

Functions/Competencies

| 1 | Provide active feedback and encouragement. |
| 2 | Allow subordinates the opportunity to assume greater responsibilities. |

Use the next part to record information about actual performance discussed with the employee during the performance review.

Principal Function #	Actual Performance	Performance Rating
1	Contributes to subordinates' annual development plans. Allows subordinates to take training courses. Promotes diversity.	4
2	Does not delegate time-sensitive tasks. Tends to delegate only mundane and repetitive tasks.	2

Employee Self-Review

In order to ensure a full dialogue between the reviewer and the employee, employees should rate themselves using the same published criteria the reviewer will use.

This self-assessment should take place in advance of the supervisor-employee review session. Often self-realization of deficiencies makes it easier for the manager to guide the worker in correcting and improving performance.

Performance Factors	Employee Rating	Supervisor Rating
Knowledge of Work: Understands assigned duties and responsibilities; establishes priorities and plans work; uses appropriate procedures, tools, equipment, and materials for assigned work.		
Quality of Work: Work is complete, neat, accurate, timely, and thoughtful.		
Quantity of Work: Completes all assignments within specified time limits; adjusts to unexpected changes in work demands to meet timetables.		
Initiative: Self-starter requires minimal supervision, requests additional assignments or responsibilities; suggests and implements improved work methods.		

40   THE MANAGER'S GUIDE TO HR

Performance Factors	Employee Rating	Supervisor Rating
Cooperation: Projects a positive work attitude; relates effectively with coworkers, supervisors, and others; uses tact and diplomacy, acts professionally at all times.		

Structured Performance Reviews and Discrimination

As discussed in Chapter 6, "Employment Laws," an employer cannot deprive an individual of employment opportunities because he or she is a member of a protected class. Employment opportunities include not only hiring and firing issues but also working hours, working conditions, rates of pay, training and advancement opportunities, and performance reviews.

By following a structured performance review process that focuses on the employee's actual performance measured against the specific requirements of the job in question, you can avoid charges of discrimination.

Unstructured reviews that are based on a supervisor's subjective beliefs without regard to any objective criteria or metrics are an invitation to litigation.

CHAPTER 3

Training

Introduction

An old joke goes like this:

> **"Why should I train my employees? As soon as I get them trained they'll leave."**
>
> **"Yes, but what if you don't and they stay?"**

A workforce untrained in safety, discrimination, and harassment will lead to physical and emotional harm, litigation, manager/employee and employee/employee oppression, internal miscommunication, and so on.

Purpose

Training will lead to increased employee:

- Job satisfaction and morale among employees
- Motivation
- Work throughput rates

- Capacity to adopt new technologies and methods
- Innovation

Training will reduce employee turnover and enhance the organization's image.

Training is an integral part of risk management, including training about safety, sexual harassment, and diversity.

Safety

Basically, every private enterprise in the United States and its territories is subject to the Occupational Safety and Health Act (OSHA), as are federal facilities. Twenty-six states and territories have their own approved safety and health programs covering public sector employees, such as state, county, and city workers. (States and their political subdivisions are not governed by federal OSHA.)

Many OSHA regulations (standards) expressly mandate that workers must be trained in various safety matters. Some standards that apply to a majority of businesses include those related to hazardous chemicals, personal protective equipment, fire safety, and emergency action plans.

Sexual Harassment

As several Supreme Court cases have made clear, employee awareness of the organization's harassment policy is a prerequisite for an entity to defend itself from claims of sexual and other forms of harassment. See Chapter 7, "Hot-Button Issues."

Diversity

Since the intent to discriminate can be proven circumstantially (see Chapter 7, "Hot-Button Issues," and Chapter 6, "Employment Laws"), supervisors must understand what they can and cannot say and do in the workplace.

Strategy

Opening Issues

You should begin any employee HR training effort by asking yourself three questions:

1. What are the goals of the training? In other words, where are we going?

2. What is the instructional method and medium going to be? In other words, how are we going to get there?

3. How will we measure success? In other words, how will we know we've arrived?

Identify Training Goals

To best identify training goals, you should focus on what the employee is expected to do and how he or she is expected to do it.

An obvious starting point for identifying training needs and goals is to review your employees' job descriptions. This job analysis pinpoints what employees need to know in order to perform a job; with whom they will interact both above and below their own status levels, as well as laterally within their own working environment; and their educational level (which, in turn, will help determine the type of training that will be most effective for them).

Clearly stated instructional goals will help you identify what you, the employer, want employees to do, to do better, or to stop doing. Learning objectives should:

- Be written.
- Be clear and measurable.
- Identify how employees will demonstrate (1) that they understand the subjects presented or (2) that they have acquired the desired skills or knowledge.
- Define what constitutes acceptable performance or behavior.

Develop Learning Activities

People have widely disparate language skills; for example, some read and write English fluently, whereas others are functionally illiterate. Also, people learn in a variety of ways.

Auditory Learners This type of individual learns primarily through listening. They learn best through verbal lectures, discussions, talking things through, and listening to what others have to say. They focus their attention on your words, listening carefully to everything you say.

Effective training for these individuals allows them to talk rather than write. They relish the opportunity to discuss what they've heard.

Visual Learners This type of individual learns primarily through seeing and visualizing. They generally think in pictures and learn best from visual displays, such as diagrams, illustrated textbooks, overhead transparencies, videos, flipcharts, and handouts. So that they can "see" the information, they will often take detailed notes.

Kinesthetic or Tactile Learners This type of individual learns best through a hands-on approach. They like to move, touch, and explore. They don't do well in settings where they must sit for long periods of time.

Because of the diverse styles in which people learn, training should employ a wide range of techniques, including group sessions, one on one, lecture, video, interactive CD, hands-on, observation of others actually performing the task, testing, charts, job aids, overhead transparencies, role playing, and demonstrations.

Presenting It

There are two basic approaches to presenting information:

1. Straight presentation based on the idea that the learner knows little, if anything, about the topic
2. Questioning students about concepts and ideas and allowing them to come to their own conclusions

Both approaches are necessary. Which you use should reflect what you are trying to achieve—for example, presentation of facts, analysis of concepts, or presentation of a process.

Evaluate

It is imperative to test how effectively the information was received, learned, and assimilated. That determination can be made through written or oral tests, supervisors' observations of an employee's performance both before and after the training, and notes regarding improvements or changes, plus measurable changes effectuated in the workplace.

Safety

Hazard Communication

The right-to-know standard (29 CFR 1910.1200) (HAZCOM) requires all employers to provide information to their employees about the hazardous chemicals to which they are exposed in the workplace, by means of five approaches:

1. Written hazard communication program
2. Hazardous chemical inventory listing (that is part of the written program)
3. Labels and other forms of warning
4. Material safety data sheets (MSDS)
5. Information and training

Information and Training

HAZCOM employee training must include:

- Methods and observations that may be used to detect the presence or release of a hazardous chemical in the work area—for example, monitoring conducted by the employer, continuous monitoring devices, visual appearance or odor of hazardous chemicals when being released
- Physical and health hazards of the chemicals in the work area
- Measures employees can take to protect themselves from these hazards, including specific procedures the employer has implemented to protect employees from exposure to hazardous chemicals, such as:
  - Appropriate work practices
  - Emergency procedures
  - Personal protective equipment (PPE) to be used
- Details of the hazard communication program developed by the employer, including:
  - Explanation of the labeling system used on workplace containers

- Explanation of MSDSs
- Explanation of how employees can obtain and use the appropriate hazard information

Evaluation of HAZCOM Training

OSHA only expects you to make a good-faith effort to train your employees regarding hazardous chemicals. In general, the most important aspects of training under HAZCOM are to ensure the following:

- Employees are aware that they are exposed to hazardous chemicals.
- They know how to read and use labels and MSDSs.
- They are following the appropriate protective measures established by the employer.

Fire

Regarding fire prevention plans (29 CFR 1910.39), an employer must:

- Inform employees upon initial assignment to a job of the fire hazards to which they are exposed.
- Review with each employee those parts of the fire prevention plan necessary for self-protection, including the preferred means of reporting emergencies, such as manual pull box alarms, public-address systems, radio, or telephones; and the procedures for sounding emergency alarms in the workplace.

Personal Protective Equipment

Minimum Requirements

OSHA's minimum PPE training requirements demand that employees be trained to know at least the following:

- When PPE is necessary
- What PPE is necessary

- How to properly don, doff, adjust, and wear PPE
- The limitations of the PPE
- The proper care, maintenance, useful life, and disposal of the PPE

Training Verification

The employer must verify that each affected employee has received and understands the required training through a written certification that contains:

- Name of each employee trained
- Dates of training
- Identification of the subject of the certification

Sexual Harassment

Due to the Supreme Court's landmark decisions in the *Burlington Industries v. Ellerth* and *Faragher v. The City of Boca Raton* sexual harassment cases, subsequent court decisions, and EEOC Guidelines, sexual harassment training is essential. (See Chapter 7, "Hot-Button Issues.") To be able to raise a defense or avoid punitive damages in sexual harassment lawsuits, employers need to show that they have provided periodic sexual harassment training to all employees.

Courts and EEOC guidelines have made clear that sexual harassment training should address not just sexual harassment but all forms of unlawful harassment, including race, religion, age, and national origin.

Managers and Supervisory Staff

Manager and supervisory staff training should run a minimum of two to three hours. At its conclusion, your management staff should be able to:

- Appreciate how devastating to an organization their own improper actions can be.
- Initiate steps to insulate the company from charges of sexual harassment.
- Analyze factual settings to determine if a sexual harassment charge is "quid pro quo" or "hostile environment."

- Undertake programs that will force sexual harassment claims to surface in a timely manner.
- Comprehend the seriousness of this topic to your organization.
- Participate in an effective investigation of sexual harassment allegations.
- Create an environment in which aggrieved employees can air their concerns without fear of retaliation.

General Staff

Employee sexual harassment training should run a minimum of two hours. At its conclusion, your staff should be able to:

- Understand what sexual harassment is—and what it's not.
- State your organization's posture toward this topic.
- Follow steps an aggrieved employee must take regarding real or perceived sexual harassment at your company.
- Appreciate the consequences of not reporting an alleged grievance related to discrimination or harassment.
- Avoid engaging in hostile environment harassment of other workers, clients, or visitors.

Training Records

Contents

At minimum, training records should contain:

- Name of individual trained with proof of attendance (e.g., signature, personal identification code)
- Date(s) of training
- Training content
- Name of trainer
- Test scores, supervisor's evaluation, or other evidence of successful course completion

Training Record Retention

Because OSHA injury and illness records must be retained for five years, and because the issue of whether or not an employee was properly trained may become relevant, it is recommended that training records be retained for five years.

CHAPTER 4

Benefits

Introduction: The Family and Medical Leave Act

The Family and Medical Leave Act (FMLA) is intended to help employees balance their work and family responsibilities by taking unpaid leave for certain reasons.

Basically, the FMLA entitles eligible employees to take up to twelve workweeks of unpaid, job-protected leave in a twelve-month period for specified family and medical reasons, during which time the employer must continue to pay its portion of the employee's health-care coverage.

In addition, there are two types of FMLA leave related to the relatives of military service members:

1. *On an Annual Basis*—Up to twelve weeks of leave for an exigency related to active duty service by the employee's immediate family member.

2. *Once During an Employee's Employment*—Up to twenty-six weeks of leave to care for a spouse, son, daughter, parent, or next of kin who is a member of the Armed Forces and who is undergoing medical treatment or who is medically unfit to perform military duties due to an injury or illness incurred while on active duty.

This chapter deals with federal FMLA. Some states have state family leave laws providing other or greater rights.

Covered Entities

Coverage Generally

According to the FMLA regulations, an employer covered by FMLA is any person engaged in commerce or in any industry or activity affecting commerce who employs fifty or more employees for each working day during each of twenty or more calendar workweeks in the current or preceding calendar year.

Engaged in Commerce

The terms *commerce* and *industry affecting commerce* are so broadly defined that they include virtually every employer.

Separate Entities

As a general rule, the legal entity that employs the employee is the employer under FMLA; for example, a corporation is a single employer rather than its separate establishments or divisions.

Where one corporation has an ownership interest in another corporation, these separate entities will be deemed to be parts of a single employer for purposes of FMLA if they meet the *integrated employer* test. Where this test is met, the employees of all entities making up the integrated employer will be counted in determining employer coverage and employee eligibility. Factors (none of which standing alone is definitive) considered in determining whether two or more entities are an integrated employer include:

- Common management
- Interrelation between operations
- Centralized control of labor relations
- Degree of common ownership/financial control

Fifty or More Employees

In "counting noses" to determine if you have fifty or more workers, count full- and part-time workers as well as temporary workers over whom you are exercising daily supervision.

If you hire a worker from a temporary employment agency and are directing not only what he or she is doing but also how it is being done, then you are exercising sufficient control over that employee so that he or she must be included in your FMLA head count. This temporary worker is engaged in *joint employment*. The primary (payroll) employer is the employment agency and your organization is the host employer.

Employees jointly employed by two employers must be counted by both employers, whether or not maintained on one of the employers' payrolls, in determining employer coverage and employee eligibility.

In joint employment relationships, only the primary employer is responsible for giving required notices to its employees, providing FMLA leave, and maintenance of health benefits. Also, job restoration is the primary responsibility of the primary employer. The secondary (host) employer is responsible for accepting the employee returning from FMLA leave in place of a replacement employee if the secondary employer continues to utilize an employee from the temporary or leasing agency, and the agency chooses to place the employee with the secondary employer.

> **EXAMPLE:** Your organization hires a temporary worker from the ABC Agency. ABC sends you George. George does an adequate job. George goes out on FMLA under his employment with ABC. ABC sends you Alana to replace George. Alana is terrific. George is ready to return from FMLA leave and ABC wishes to send him back to your company. If you are going to continue to employ someone from ABC for the job in question, then you must accept George back even though you would rather keep Alana.

Twenty or More Calendar Weeks

The "twenty or more calendar workweeks in the current or preceding calendar year" do not have to be consecutive. Many businesses are seasonal in nature and may have more than fifty workers for portions of a year and far fewer employees at other times.

Individuals as Employers

The term *employer*, as covered by FMLA, also includes any person acting, directly or indirectly, in the interest of a covered employer to any of the employees of the employer, any successor in interest of a covered employer, and any public agency. In plain terms, this means *you have personal liability* if you violate an employee's rights under the FMLA. (Also, see "Personal Liability" in Chapter 5, "Compensation.")

Public Agencies

Public agencies are covered employers without regard to the number of employees employed. Public as well as private elementary and secondary schools are also covered employers.

The federal government at large is a *covered employer* subject to the FMLA and, therefore, as a general rule, civilian federal employees can become eligible for FMLA leave. However, the FMLA provisions that apply to the federal government are not uniform.

Most federal employees are covered under Title II of the act. Certain federal agencies and federal employees are covered under Title I of the FMLA, which also applies to employees in the private sector and those working for state and local government. The FMLA rights of employees of the Senate and the House of Representatives are contained in the Congressional Accountability Act of 1995 (CAA), 2 USC 1301, et seq., which replaced Title V of the FMLA. Finally, the FMLA applies to employees of the Executive Office of the President through the Presidential and Executive Accountability Act (PEOAA), 3 USC 412.

This chapter takes the position that federal employees can become eligible for FMLA leave without going into the complex rules for when a worker may not be eligible for family leave.

The Twelve-Month Period

Methods

An employer may choose one of four methods for determining the twelve-month period in which the twelve weeks of leave entitlement occurs provided the alternative chosen is applied consistently and uniformly to all employees.

The Calendar Year

Under this method, an eligible employee would be entitled to up to twelve weeks of FMLA leave at any time between January 1 and December 31.

Basically, unused FMLA leave time, if any, is cancelled at the end of the calendar year with a grant of twelve workweeks occurring on January 1 of the next year.

A potential negative to this method for the employer is that an employee could take twelve weeks of leave at the end of the year and twelve weeks at the beginning of the following year. The employee could therefore take up to twenty-four straight weeks of job-protected leave during which the employer would have to continue to pay its portion of the worker's health-care coverage. This is a primary reason an employer may want to select a different method.

Any Fixed Twelve-Month "Leave Year"

Under this method, the employer can select any fixed time period such as a fiscal year, a year required by state law, or a year starting on an employee's anniversary date.

Basically, unused FMLA leave time, if any, is cancelled at the end of the fixed-year period with a grant of twelve workweeks occurring on the first day of the following fixed-year period.

Just as with the calendar year method, a potential negative to this method for the employer is that an employee could take twelve workweeks of leave at the end of the fixed twelve-month year and twelve workweeks at the beginning of the following year. The employee could therefore take up to twenty-four straight workweeks of job-protected leave during which the employer would have to continue to pay its portion of the worker's health-care coverage. This is a primary reason an employer may want to select a different method.

A Twelve-Month Period Measured Forward from the Date Any Employee's First FMLA Leave Begins

Under this method, an employee would be entitled to twelve weeks of leave during the year, beginning on the first date FMLA leave is taken, with the next twelve-month period beginning the first time FMLA leave is taken after completion of any previous twelve-month period.

Eventually, this third method will establish the same type of fixed twelve-month leave year as the fixed-year method previously discussed.

A "Rolling" Twelve-Month Period Measured Backward from the Date an Employee Uses Any FMLA Leave

Under this method, each time an employee takes FMLA leave, the remaining leave entitlement would be any balance of the twelve weeks that has not been used during the immediately preceding twelve months. Basically, unused time is never cancelled and used leave is not available until twelve months from when it was used.

> **EXAMPLE:** An eligible worker takes one workweek of FMLA leave in month one of a twelve-month period and one workweek during another month of that same twelve-month period. The remaining ten workweeks remain in the worker's FMLA leave bank, and the first week of leave taken returns to the leave bank twelve months after it was used. The same is true of the second week of leave taken.

Although the most difficult to track from an administrative standpoint, this is the most precise method, and the one that prevents an employee from being able to take two twelve-workweek periods consecutively.

Changing Methods

An employer can change methods. If it does, it must give at least sixty days' notice to all employees, and the transition must take place in such a way that the employees retain the full benefit of twelve weeks of leave under whichever method affords the greatest benefit to the employee. Under no circumstances may a new method be implemented in order to avoid the Act's leave requirements.

Notice

Notice from the Employer to the Employee

Posting

Every employer covered by the FMLA, including those that have no FMLA-eligible workers, must post a notice explaining the Act's provisions and providing information concerning the procedures for filing complaints of violations of the Act with the Wage and Hour Division.

The notice must be posted in a conspicuous place where your workers are likely to see it.

Where an employer's workforce is made up of a significant portion of workers who are not literate in English, the employer is responsible for providing the notice in a language in which the employees are literate.

Note: All of the federally required posters are available free, in both English and Spanish, on the Department of Labor's website (www .dol.gov).

There is a $100 per offense penalty for not posting the notice.

Written Notice

The FMLA contains a strong requirement that the employer provide the employee with written notice of the employer's policies and procedures and the employee's obligations related to the FMLA. Among other things, 29 CFR 825.301 says:

> If an FMLA-covered employer has any eligible employees and has any written guidance to employees concerning employee benefits or leave rights, such as in an employee handbook, information concerning FMLA entitlements and employee obligations under the FMLA must be included in the handbook or other document. For example, if an employer provides an employee handbook to all employees that describes the employer's policies regarding leave, wages, attendance, and similar matters, the handbook must incorporate information on FMLA rights and responsibilities and the employer's policies regarding the FMLA.

You must still provide this information in a written format even if you do not have an employee handbook. And, it must be provided to the employee in a language in which the worker is literate. This requirement could well force an employer to have its FMLA policies translated into a language the worker can read.

The type of information should include the specific expectations and obligations of the employee and explain any consequences of a failure to meet these obligations, such as the following examples:

- The leave will be counted against the employee's annual FMLA leave entitlement.
- Any requirements for the employee to furnish medical certification of a serious health condition and the consequences of failing to do so.
- The employee's right to substitute paid leave and whether the employer will require the substitution of paid leave, and the conditions related to any substitution.

- Any requirement for the employee to make any premium payments to maintain health benefits and the arrangements for making such payments, and the possible consequences of failure to make such payments on a timely basis (e.g., the circumstances under which coverage may lapse).

- Any requirement for the employee to present a fitness-for-duty certificate to be restored to employment.

- The key employee status and the potential consequence that restoration may be denied following FMLA leave for such employees, and explaining the conditions required for such denial.

- The employee's right to restoration to the same or an equivalent job upon return from leave.

- The employee's potential liability for payment of health insurance premiums paid by the employer during the employee's unpaid FMLA leave if the employee fails to return to work after taking FMLA leave.

You may also want to include in the specific notice other information such as if the employer will require periodic reports of the employee's status and intent to return to work, or if the worker can engage in other employment while on FMLA leave (perhaps during work hours or days the employee is not scheduled to work for you).

You should expressly state in your notice(s) that if and when the employer learns that an eligible employee has been away from work for an FMLA-qualifying event that the time away *will* be counted against the employee's FMLA allotment. This will serve to eliminate any argument that the employee would not have taken leave or other actions of one type or another if he or she had known that the time away would be counted against his or her FMLA leave entitlement. (See the *Ragsdale v. Wolverine World Wide, Inc.* discussion that follows.)

Ragsdale v. Wolverine World Wide, Inc. (00–6029) 535 U.S. 81 (2002)

A misconception is that only the employee can invoke FMLA, or that unless and until the employer provides the employee notice that leave is being counted against the worker's FMLA entitlement, FMLA leave does not start running.

The Equal Employment Opportunity Commission (EEOC) previously took the position and actually promulgated a regulation (now repealed) that if the employer did not provide the employee with written notice that time away was being counted against the employee's FMLA allotment, then the FMLA twelve-workweek time allotment would not start running until the written notice was given.

The Supreme Court flatly rejected this notion in the *Ragsdale* case. Twelve workweeks is both the minimum and the maximum amount of FMLA leave that the employer must grant or that the employee is legally entitled to. Organizations can, of course, offer more generous leave if they wish to.

If the employer fails to provide the required notice and the employee believes that he or she has suffered some sort of detriment because of the notice failure, then the worker can seek relief from the courts. The employee may be entitled to some sort of financial compensation, reinstatement, or attorney's fees; however, he or she is not entitled to and cannot receive more than twelve workweeks of FMLA leave.

Notice from the Employee to the Employer

Many employers feel they are the victims of FMLA leave abuse when employees do not give adequate notice of the need for leave, and especially when workers provide last-minute notice of the need to take intermittent leave. Employers should be explicit in their notice requirements and strictly enforce them.

Notice When the Need for Leave Is Foreseeable

An employee must provide the employer at least thirty days of advance notice before FMLA leave is to begin if the need for the leave is foreseeable based on an expected birth, placement for adoption or foster care, or planned medical treatment for a serious health condition of the employee or of a family member.

If an employee fails to give thirty days' notice for *foreseeable* leave with no reasonable excuse for the delay, the employer may delay the taking of FMLA leave until at least thirty days after the date the employee provides notice to the employer of the need for FMLA leave.

Notice When the Need for Leave Is Unforeseeable

If thirty days' notice is not practical because of a lack of knowledge of when leave will be required to begin, a change in circumstances, or a medical emergency, the employee is supposed to give notice "as soon as practicable." Ordinarily, this means at least verbal notification to the employer within one or two business days of when the need for leave becomes known to the employee.

Notice by Someone Other Than the Employee

Notice may be given by the employee's spokesperson, such as a spouse, adult family member, or other responsible party, if the employee is unable to do so personally.

Employer's Internal Notice Procedures

Usual and Customary Procedures An employer can require an employee to comply with the employer's usual and customary notice and procedural requirements for requesting leave.

> **EXAMPLE:** An employer may require that written notice set forth the reasons for the requested leave, the anticipated duration of the leave, and the anticipated start of the leave.

Medical Certification Employers may also require employees to provide:

- Medical certification supporting the need for leave due to a serious health condition affecting the employee or an immediate family member.
- Second or third medical opinions (at the employer's expense) and periodic recertification.
- Periodic reports during FMLA leave regarding the employee's status and intent to return to work. The employer can ask for recertification of a serious health condition no more often than once every thirty days, and the employee has fifteen days to provide the certification.

Note: Failure to comply with these requirements may result in a delay in the start of FMLA leave.

Second Medical Opinion

If you, the employer, have reason to doubt the validity of a medical certification you can require the employee to obtain a second opinion at the employer's expense.

The employer is permitted to designate the health-care provider to furnish the second opinion; however, the selected health-care provider may not be employed on a regular basis by the employer. An exception to this rule is if the employer is located in an area where access to health care is extremely limited, for example, a rural area where no more than one or two doctors practice in the relevant specialty in that vicinity.

Third Medical Opinion

If the opinions of the employee's and the employer's designated health-care providers differ, the employer may require the employee to obtain certification from a third health-care provider, again at the employer's expense. This third opinion shall be final and binding.

The third health-care provider must be designated or approved jointly by the employer and the employee.

The employer and the employee must each act in good faith to attempt to reach agreement on whom to select for the third-opinion provider. If the employer does not attempt in good faith to reach agreement, the employer will be bound by the first certification. If the employee does not attempt in good faith to reach agreement, the employee will be bound by the second certification.

> **EXAMPLE:** An employee who refuses to agree to see a doctor in the specialty in question may be failing to act in good faith. On the other hand, an employer who refuses to agree to any doctor on a list of specialists in the appropriate field provided by the employee and whom the employee has not previously consulted may be failing to act in good faith.

Employee's Rights Pending Receipt of Second or Third Medical Opinion(s)

Pending receipt of the second (or third) medical opinion, the employee is provisionally entitled to the benefits of the act, including maintenance of group health benefits.

If the certifications do not ultimately establish the employee's entitlement to FMLA leave, the leave shall not be designated as FMLA leave and may be treated as paid or unpaid leave under the employer's established leave policies.

Right to Copy of Each Medical Opinion

The employer is required to provide the employee with a copy of the second and third medical opinions, where applicable, upon request by the employee.

Requested copies should be provided within two business days unless extenuating circumstances prevent such action.

Out-of-Pocket Expenses

If the employer requires the employee to obtain either a second or third opinion, the employer must reimburse an employee or a family member for any reasonable out-of-pocket travel expenses incurred to obtain the second and third medical opinions. The employer may not require the employee or family member to travel outside normal commuting distance for purposes of obtaining the second or third medical opinions except in very unusual circumstances.

Serious Health Conditions Arising Out of the Country

In circumstances when the employee or a family member is visiting in another country, or a family member resides in another country, and a serious health condition develops, the employer shall accept a medical certification as well as second and third opinions from a health-care provider who practices in that country.

Fitness for Duty Releases Pursuant to a uniformly applied policy, the employer may also require that an employee present a certification of fitness to return to work when the absence was caused by the employee's serious health condition. The employer may delay restoring the employee to employment without such certificate relating to the health condition that caused the employee's absence.

Adequacy of Notice

The employee does not have to expressly assert rights under the FMLA or even mention the FMLA, but only needs to state that leave is needed. You, the employer, are expected to obtain any additional required information through informal means, such as asking the employee.

Note: When employees ask for time off, but do not expressly mention FMLA, supervisors need to ask employees sufficient questions to determine if the FMLA applies *without* asking about the nature or extent of the condition! Red-flag words to listen for and follow-up on are *hospitalization, multiple hospital visits*, and *incapacitation*. For example, if an employee calls in and says to his or her supervisor, "My child is sick and can't go to school today [incapacitation]." The supervisor must not ask, "What's wrong with her?" What the manager should ask is, "Will he or she be unable to go to school for more than three consecutive days and is he or she under a doctor's care?"

The employee or spokesperson is expected to provide more information when it can readily be accomplished as a practical matter, taking into consideration all of the circumstances of the situation.

Scheduling the Leave

Intermittent Leave and Reduced Workweek Schedule

Under some circumstances, employees may take FMLA leave intermittently, which means taking leave in blocks of time, or by reducing their normal weekly or daily work schedule.

If FMLA leave is for birth and care or placement for adoption or foster care, use of intermittent leave is subject to the employer's approval.

FMLA leave may be taken intermittently whenever medically necessary to care for a seriously ill family member, or because the employee is seriously ill and unable to work.

Employee Responsibilities

Employers often feel they are being victimized by FMLA leave abuse due to either inadequacy of the amount of notice provided or the uncertainty of when an employee will have to take time off on an intermittent basis when a serious health condition flares up.

To reduce disruption to the workplace to the greatest extent possible, employers should ensure that employees strictly adhere to the FMLA regulations requiring that when planning medical treatment, the employee must consult with the employer and make a reasonable effort to schedule the leave so as not to unduly disrupt the employer's operations (subject to the approval of the health-care provider).

Advise your employees that they are expected to consult with you prior to scheduling medical treatment in order to work out a treatment schedule that best suits the needs of both the employer and the employee.

If an employee who provides notice of the need to take FMLA leave on an intermittent basis for planned medical treatment neglects to consult with you to make a reasonable attempt to arrange the schedule of treatments so as not to unduly disrupt your operations, initiate discussions with the employee and require the employee to attempt to make such arrangements, subject to the approval of the health-care provider.

Stopping FMLA Abuse

Here are suggestions for stopping potential employee FMLA abuse.

- Require employees to comply with FMLA notice requirements and any notice requirements that the employer has in place regarding leave and absences.
- Require employees to obtain and submit a certification from their health-care provider.
- Require employees to submit recertification every thirty days.
- Do not pay for or reimburse the employee for recertification.
- Require employees to attempt (if possible) to take leave during times that cause the least disruption to the operation of the business.
- Require employees to use paid leave, such as sick leave and vacation days, concurrently with FMLA leave.
- Assign employees taking intermittent leave to alternative positions that cause less disruption, if possible.
- If you suspect an employee is abusing intermittent FMLA leave, place the person under private surveillance to check what he or she is doing when supposedly incapacitated.
- Put discreet influence on an employee's doctor to look harder at the person's FMLA intermittent leave recertification by including his or her attendance report, and if applicable, his or her FMLA treatment record, in the recertification paperwork.

The Workweek

Definition of a Workweek

Unlike under the Fair Labor Standards Act (FLSA), where a workweek is defined as a regularly recurring 168 hours or 7 consecutive 24-hour periods that can begin any hour of the day, any day of the week, there is no standard definition of a workweek under the FMLA.

For FMLA purposes, the workweek is the employee's regular schedule (hours/days per week) prior to the start of FMLA leave. This is very important in that the workweek will be the controlling factor in determining how much time the employee is entitled to use when taking intermittent FMLA leave or on a reduced workweek schedule. (See "Intermittent Leave and Reduced Workweek Schedule" in this chapter.)

Basically, if one worker regularly works a forty-hour workweek and another worker works a thirty-hour workweek, then one is entitled to the equivalent of twelve forty-hour workweeks and the other to twelve thirty-hour workweeks.

Workweek and the Impact of Overtime

If overtime hours are on an "as needed basis" and are not part of the employee's usual or normal workweek, or are voluntary, then these hours would not (1) be counted to calculate the amount of the employee's FMLA leave entitlement or (2) be charged to the employee's FMLA leave entitlement.

If the normal workweek is greater than forty hours, then hours worked over forty hours are included in determining the maximum amount of leave available to the employee under the FMLA.

> **EXAMPLE:** An employee normally works overtime in three of every four weeks. These overtime hours are part of the employee's normal workweek schedule and are included in calculating the amount of FMLA leave available to the employee.

Employees Whose Schedules Vary from Week to Week

The weekly average of the hours worked over the twelve weeks prior to the beginning of the leave period would be used to determine the workweek for employees whose work schedule varies from week to week.

Employee Eligibility

To be eligible for FMLA benefits, an employee *must* achieve all of the following items covered in this section.

Work for a Covered Employer

The employee must work for an employer that had fifty or more workers on its payroll each working day during twenty or more calendar weeks during the current or immediately preceding calendar year. (See "Covered Entities" in this chapter.) The twenty or more calendar weeks do not have to be consecutive.

Have Worked for the Employer for a Total of Twelve Months

The twelve months an employee must have been employed by the employer do not have to be consecutive months.

If an employee is maintained on the payroll for any part of a week, including any periods of paid or unpaid leave (e.g., sick leave or vacation) during which other benefits or compensation are provided (e.g., workers compensation, group health plan benefits) the week counts as a week of employment.

For purposes of determining whether intermittent, occasional, or casual employment qualifies as "at least twelve months," fifty-two weeks is deemed to be equal to twelve months.

If there has been a break in service, prior periods of employment are considered in determining the twelve-month threshold.

> **EXAMPLE:** If an employee worked for the employer for two months, moved away for three years, and then returned and worked for the same employer for another ten months, the twelve-month requirement would have been met.

Have Worked at Least 1,250 Hours in the Immediately Preceding Twelve Months

Hours Worked

The 1,250 hours are defined as actual hours worked as defined under the FLSA and must have been worked immediately preceding the commencement of the leave, that is, measured backward from the day before the leave began.

To determine eligibility, if at the time an employee requests FMLA leave he or she hasn't worked the 1,250 hours, the employer and the employee would review the worker's normal schedule to determine if it is probable that the required number of hours will have been worked prior to the commencement of the leave.

FLSA-Exempt Employees

In the case of exempt employees, if no record of their actual hours worked has been kept, the burden of proving the employee has not worked the required number of hours falls on the employer.

Full-Time Teachers

Full-time teachers of an elementary or a secondary school system, or institution of higher education, or other educational establishment or institution are deemed to meet the 1,250-hour test.

An employer would have to clearly demonstrate that such an employee did not work 1,250 hours during the previous twelve months in order to claim that the employee is not eligible for FMLA leave.

Work at a Location in the United States or in a Territory or Possession of the United States Where at Least Fifty Employees Are Employed by the Employer Within Seventy-Five Miles

The seventy-five-mile distance is not measured in a straight line, but rather by surface miles, using surface transportation over public streets, roads, highways, and waterways, by the shortest route from the facility where the eligible employee needing leave is employed.

The determination of how many employees are employed within seventy-five miles of the work site of an employee is based on the number of employees maintained on the payroll. Employees of educational institutions who are employed permanently or who are under contract are *maintained on the payroll* during any portion of the year when school is not in session.

Because of this seventy-five-mile rule, it is possible for a covered employer to have fifty or more workers and yet not have any workers eligible for FMLA leave.

> **EXAMPLE:** If an organization with eighty-five workers had three widely dispersed locations with one having thirty-five workers and the other two having twenty-five each, none of the workers would be eligible for FMLA benefits. An employer can, of course, voluntarily grant eligibility if it so desires.

Be a Relative of a Service Member

As of January 28, 2008, employees may also be eligible for FMLA leave if they meet all of the conditions set out previously and are the spouse, child, parent, or nearest blood relative of a member of the Armed Forces, including the National Guard or Reserves, requiring care for a serious injury or illness in the line of duty while on active duty that may render the service member medically unfit to perform the duties of his or her office, grade, rank, or rating.

Eligible Reasons for Leave

A covered employer must grant an eligible employee up to a total of twelve workweeks of unpaid leave during any twelve-month period for one or more of the following reasons outlined in this section.

Birth and Care of the Newborn Child of the Employee

Equal Gender Treatment for Birth and Care

The right to take leave under the FMLA applies equally to male and female employees. A father, as well as a mother, can take family leave for the birth of a child.

Birth and Care Within One Year

Leave for birth and care of the newborn must conclude within twelve months of the birth.

Placement with the Employee of a Son or Daughter for Adoption or Foster Care

Equal Gender Treatment for Adoption or Foster Care

The right to take leave under the FMLA applies equally to male and female employees. A father, as well as a mother, can take family leave for adoption or foster care of a child.

Placement for Adoption or Foster Care Within One Year

Leave for placement for adoption or foster care must conclude within twelve months of the placement.

Commencement of Leave Prior to Placement

FMLA leave must be granted before the actual placement or adoption of a child if an absence from work is required for the placement to proceed.

> **EXAMPLE:** The employee may be required to attend counseling sessions, appear in court, consult with his or her attorney or the doctor(s) representing the birth parent, or submit to a physical examination.

Note: A husband and wife who are eligible for FMLA leave and are employed by the same covered employer may be limited to a combined total of twelve weeks of leave during any twelve-month period if the leave is taken (1) for birth of the employee's son or daughter or to care for the child after birth; (2) for placement of a son or daughter with the employee for adoption or foster care, or to care for the child after placement; or (3) to care for the employee's parent with a serious health condition.

This limitation on the total weeks of leave only applies to leave taken for the reasons just stated. Where the husband and wife both use a portion of the total twelve-week FMLA leave entitlement for one of the purposes stated, they are each still entitled to the difference between the amount he or she has taken individually and twelve weeks for FMLA leave for other FMLA purposes.

> **EXAMPLE:** If each spouse took six weeks of leave to care for a healthy, newborn child, each could use an additional six weeks due to his or her own serious health condition or to care for a child with a serious health condition.

Care for an Employee's Spouse, Parent, or Son or Daughter with a Serious Health Condition

Spouse

Spouse means a husband or wife as defined or recognized under state law for purposes of marriage in the state where the employee resides, including common-law marriage in the states where it is recognized.

Note: The Defense of Marriage Act (DOMA), 28 USC 115.1738B, defines *spouse* for federal law purposes. DOMA does two things:

1. It legislates that no state is required to give effect to a law of any other state with respect to same-sex marriage.

2. It defines the word *marriage* as "only a legal union between one man and one woman as husband and wife," and the word *spouse* as a "person of the opposite sex who is a husband or wife."

Parent

Parent means a biological parent or an individual who stands or stood *in loco parentis* ("in place of a parent") to an employee when the employee was a son or daughter. This term does not include parents "in law" under federal FMLA, although it may under various states' family leave acts.

Son or Daughter

Son or daughter means a biological, adopted, or foster child, a stepchild, a legal ward, or a child of a person standing *in loco parentis* who is either under age 18, or age 18 or older, and "incapable of self-care because of a mental or physical disability."

Incapable of Self-Care *Incapable of self-care* means that the individual requires active assistance or supervision to provide daily self-care in three or more of the activities of daily living (ADLs) or instrumental activities of daily living (IADLs).

- *ADLs*—Activities of daily living include adaptive activities such as caring appropriately for one's grooming and hygiene, bathing, dressing, and eating.
- *IADLs*—Instrumental activities of daily living include cooking, cleaning, shopping, taking public transportation, paying bills, maintaining a residence, using telephones and directories, and using a post office.

Physical or Mental Disability *Physical or mental disability* means a physical or mental impairment that substantially limits one or more of the major life activities of an individual.

In Loco Parentis

1. **The Relationship**—Persons who are *in loco parentis* include those with day-to-day responsibilities to care for and financially support a child,

or in the case of an employee, who had such responsibility for the employee when the employee was a child (e.g., an employee who was raised by his or her aunt; a biological or legal relationship is not necessary).

2. *Proving the Relationship*—For purposes of confirmation of family relationship, the employer may require the employee to provide reasonable documentation or statement of family relationship. This documentation may take the form of a simple statement from the employee, or a child's birth certificate, a court document, and so on.

Serious Health Condition That Makes the Employee Unable to Perform the Functions of the Employee's Job

See "Serious Health Conditions" in this chapter.

Exigency Related to Active Duty Service by the Employee's Immediate Family Member

Employees are entitled to twelve workweeks of leave because of any *qualifying exigency* when the employee's spouse, child, or parent is on active duty (or has been notified of an impending call or order to active duty) in the Armed Forces in support of a *contingency operation.*

A contingency operation includes military actions as designated by the Secretary of Defense involving hostilities against an enemy of the United States or other calls to duty during times of war or national emergency. The term *qualifying exigency* is not defined in the statute.

Service Member Family Leave

Service member family leave entitles an eligible employee who is a spouse, child, parent, or next of kin—for example, nearest blood relative—of a covered service member to a total of twenty-six workweeks of leave during a single twelve-month period to care for a spouse, son, daughter, parent, or next of kin who is a member of the Armed Forces undergoing medical treatment or who is medically unfit to perform military duties due to an injury or illness incurred while on active duty.

With proper certification, an employee may take this type of leave on an intermittent basis or pursuant to a reduced leave schedule.

Unpaid Nature of Leave

FMLA Leave

Under the federal FMLA, employers are not required to pay for FMLA time. State family medical leaves acts may require that some or all state-mandated family leave be paid. For example, in New Jersey workers can receive two-thirds of their regular pay up to a maximum of $524 a week. As always, an employer may choose to pay for some or all FMLA time.

Use of Paid Time-Off Benefits (PTO)

The FMLA permits an eligible employee to choose to substitute paid leave for FMLA leave or for the employer to require the employee to substitute accrued paid leave for FMLA leave. In other words, accrued paid leave will run concurrently with the unpaid FMLA leave.

Where an employee has earned or accrued paid vacation or personal or family leave (allowed by the employer), that paid leave may be substituted for all or part of any (otherwise) unpaid FMLA leave relating to birth; placement of a child for adoption or foster care; or care for a spouse, child, or parent who has a serious health condition.

Substitution of paid accrued vacation, personal, or medical/sick leave may be made for any (otherwise) unpaid FMLA leave needed to care for a family member or the employee's own serious health condition.

Substitution of paid sick or medical leave may be elected to the extent the circumstances meet the employer's usual requirements for the use of sick or medical leave. In other words, you, the employer, are not required to allow substitution of paid sick or medical leave for unpaid FMLA leave "in any situation" where the employer's uniform policy would not normally allow such paid leave.

> **EXAMPLE:** An employee would have the right to substitute paid medical or sick leave to care for a seriously ill family member only if the employer's leave plan allows paid leave to be used for that purpose.

Paid vacation or personal leave, including leave earned or accrued under plans allowing for paid time off, may be substituted, at either the employee's or the employer's option, for any qualified FMLA leave. No limitations may be placed by the employer on substitution of paid vacation or personal leave for these purposes.

Short-Term Disability Programs

Because leave pursuant to a temporary disability benefit plan is not unpaid, the provision for substitution of paid leave is inapplicable. However, the employer may designate the leave as FMLA leave and count the leave as running concurrently for purposes of both the benefit plan and the FMLA leave entitlement.

Workers Compensation

The employee's FMLA twelve-week leave entitlement may run concurrently with a workers compensation absence when the injury is one that meets the criteria for a serious health condition. As the workers compensation absence is not unpaid leave, the provision for substitution of the employee's accrued paid leave is not applicable.

If the health-care provider treating the employee for the workers compensation injury certifies the employee is able to return to a "light-duty job" but is unable to return to the same or equivalent job, the employee may decline the employer's offer of a light-duty job. As a result, the employee may lose workers compensation payments but is entitled to remain on unpaid FMLA leave until the twelve-week entitlement is exhausted. As of the date workers compensation benefits cease, the substitution provision becomes applicable and either the employee may elect or the employer may require the use of accrued paid leave.

Basically, a workers compensation absence can run concurrently with FMLA leave, and unless the worker is receiving workers compensation payments, the employer can force the employee to use accrued paid leave concurrently with FMLA leave.

Exempt Workers Under the Fair Labor Standards Act

The employer may proportionately reduce the compensation of an employer exempt from the overtime provisions of the FLSA for FMLA leave taken intermittently or on a reduced work schedule without jeopardizing that employee's exempt status. (See Chapter 5, "Compensation.")

Maintaining Health Benefits

Employer's Portion

The employer must maintain employee coverage under any group health plan on the same conditions as coverage would have been provided if the employee had been continuously employed during the entire leave period.

Note: For FMLA purposes, the term *group health plan* does not include a health-care insurance program under which employees buy individual policies from insurers.

In addition, you must maintain the same group health plan benefits during the FMLA leave as you provided to the employee prior to the FMLA leave. And, the employer must provide new or changed plans or benefits to the same extent as if the employee were not on leave (this applies if you provide a new health plan, benefits, or changes in them while the employee is on FMLA leave).

The employer is not responsible for the employee's portion of health-care coverage, and, if the employee fails to make such payments, he or she will lose coverage under the plan. Where appropriate, arrangements will need to be made for employees taking unpaid FMLA leave to pay their share of health insurance premiums. Such payments may be made under any arrangement voluntarily agreed to by the employer and employee.

An employer's obligation to maintain health benefits under the FMLA stops if and when an employee informs the employer of intent not to return to work at the end of the leave period, or if the employee fails to return to work when the FMLA leave entitlement is exhausted.

The employer's obligation also stops if (1) the employee's premium payment is more than thirty days late *and* (2) the employer has given the employee written notice at least fifteen days in advance advising that coverage will cease if payment is not received.

Serious Health Conditions

A *serious health condition* is any or some combination of the following:

1. An illness, injury, impairment, or physical or mental condition that involves any period of incapacity or treatment connected with in-patient care (i.e., an overnight stay) in a hospital, hospice, or residential medical-care facility, and any period of incapacity or subsequent treatment in connection with such inpatient care.

2. Continuing treatment by a health-care provider that includes any period of incapacity (i.e., inability to work, attend school, or perform other regular daily activities) due to:
   - A health condition (including treatment therefore, or recovery therefrom) lasting more than three consecutive days, and any

subsequent treatment or period of incapacity relating to the same condition that also includes:

- Treatment two or more times by or under the supervision of a health-care provider.
- One treatment by a health-care provider with a continuing regimen of treatment.

3. Pregnancy or prenatal care. A visit to the health-care provider is not necessary for each absence.

4. A chronic serious health condition that continues over an extended period of time, requires periodic visits to a health-care provider, and may involve occasional episodes of incapacity (e.g., asthma, diabetes). A visit to a health-care provider is not necessary for each absence.

5. A permanent or long-term condition for which treatment may not be effective (e.g., Alzheimer's, a severe stroke, terminal cancer). Only supervision by a health-care provider is required, rather than active treatment.

6. Any absences to receive multiple treatments for restorative surgery or for a condition that would likely result in a period of incapacity of more than three days if not treated (e.g., chemotherapy or radiation treatments for cancer).

Health-Care Provider

A *health-care provider* is any of the following:

- Doctors of medicine or osteopathy authorized to practice medicine or surgery by the state in which the doctors practice
- Podiatrists, dentists, clinical psychologists, optometrists, and chiropractors (limited to manual manipulation of the spine to correct a subluxation as demonstrated by X-ray to exist) authorized to practice, and performing within the scope of their practice, under state law
- Nurse practitioners, nurse-midwives, and clinical social workers authorized to practice, and performing within the scope of their practice, as defined under state law; or Christian Science prac-

titioners listed with the First Church of Christ, Scientist in Boston, Massachusetts

- Any health-care provider recognized by the employer or the employer's group health plan benefits manager

Key Employees

Key Employee Defined

A *key employee* is a salaried FMLA-eligible employee who is among the highest paid 10 percent of all the employees (both salaried and non-salaried, eligible and noneligible) employed by the employer within 75 miles of the employee's work site.

Denial of Job Restoration

Under limited circumstances where restoration to employment will cause substantial and grievous economic injury to its operations, an employer may refuse to reinstate certain highly paid key employees after they use FMLA leave during which health coverage was maintained.

In order to do so, the employer must:

- Notify the employee of his or her status as a key employee in response to the employee's notice of intent to take FMLA leave.
- Notify the employee as soon as the employer decides it will deny job restoration, and explain the reasons for this decision.
- Offer the employee a reasonable opportunity to return to work from FMLA leave after giving this notice.
- Make a final determination as to whether reinstatement will be denied at the end of the leave period if the employee then requests restoration.

Consolidated Omnibus Budget Reconciliation Act of 1985

Introduction

The Consolidated Omnibus Budget Reconciliation Act of 1985 (COBRA) gives an employee or a former employee and his or her family the right to choose to temporarily keep the group health insurance benefits that he or she would otherwise lose after experiencing a *qualifying event*. (See "Qualifying Events" in this chapter.)

Before this law went into effect in 1986, when employees left a company or experienced some other event, such as a layoff, that would cause them to be ineligible for the employer's health-care plan, they and any covered family members lost their health insurance immediately. If the employee or a family member was ill, they were often not able to get new health insurance because they were already sick and had a preexisting health condition. COBRA allows an employee to buy health insurance through the employer even though the person no longer works there or no longer works full-time.

Like COBRA, many states have laws requiring that group insurance policies provide certain employees and their dependents with the opportunity to continue their health benefit coverage under the employer's plan or convert to an individual policy if, because of certain events, they would otherwise lose coverage under their employer's group health plan.

There are three basic requirements that must be met before a company is required to offer someone the option to elect COBRA continuation coverage:

1. The group health plan must be covered by COBRA.
2. A qualifying event must occur.
3. The individual must be a qualified beneficiary for that event.

Coverage

COBRA applies to employers who employ twenty or more workers on 50 percent of the business days during the preceding calendar year. The term *employees* includes all full-time and part-time employees, as well as self-employed individuals. For this purpose, the term *employees* also includes agents, independent contractors, and directors, but only if they are eligible to participate in a group health plan.

COBRA would preempt state law if the state provides a lesser level of rights to employees than those provided by COBRA; however, states are generally free to provide greater protection to employees, and many states require that group health plans offer continuation of coverage for employer groups with fewer than twenty employees.

Qualified Beneficiary

A *qualified beneficiary* is an individual who was covered by a group health plan on the day before a qualifying event occurred that caused him or her to lose coverage.

A qualified beneficiary must be:

- A covered employee.
- An employee's spouse or former spouse.
- An employee's dependent child.
- In certain cases involving the bankruptcy of the employer sponsoring the plan, a retired employee, the retired employee's spouse (or former spouse), and the retired employee's dependent children may be qualified beneficiaries.
- In addition, any child born to or placed for adoption with a covered employee during a period of continuation coverage is automatically considered a qualified beneficiary.
- Agents, independent contractors, and directors who participate in the group health plan may also be qualified beneficiaries.

Qualifying Events

Qualifying Events Defined

Qualifying events are certain types of events that would cause an individual to lose health coverage except for COBRA continuation coverage. The type of qualifying event will determine who the qualified beneficiaries are and the required amount of time that a plan must offer the health coverage to them under COBRA. A plan, at its discretion, may provide longer periods of continuation coverage.

Qualifying Events for Employees

The types of qualifying events for employees are:

- Voluntary or involuntary termination of employment for reasons other than *gross misconduct.*
  - If an employee is terminated for gross misconduct, the employer has the legal right to deny the employee the option to elect COBRA continuation coverage.

The COBRA legislation doesn't clearly define the term *gross misconduct* and the courts have not agreed on when it's appropriate to apply this exception. Generally, acts of gross misconduct are those that are intentional, willful, deliberate, reckless, or in deliberate indifference to an employer's interest. The acts most likely to lead to termination for gross misconduct are those done willfully and in deliberate violation of the employer's express standards. However, acts of simple negligence or incompetence are not enough.

- Employers who terminate workers for gross misconduct and deny continuation coverage run the risk of being sued for wrongfully denying COBRA benefits. If the former employee prevails, the employer may be liable for significant medical expenses.
- Reduction in the number of hours of employment below those required for plan eligibility.
- Employee becoming entitled to Medicare and the employer taking him or her off the health insurance plan.

Qualifying Events for Spouses of Employees

The types of qualifying events for spouses are:

- Termination of the covered employee's employment for any reason other than gross misconduct
- Reduction in the hours worked by the covered employee
- Covered employee's becoming entitled to Medicare and the employer taking him or her off the health insurance plan
- Divorce or legal separation of the covered employee
- Death of the covered employee

Qualifying Events for Dependent Children of Employees

The types of qualifying events for dependent children are:

- Termination of the covered employee's employment for any reason other than gross misconduct
- Reduction in the hours worked by the covered employee

- Covered employee's becoming entitled to Medicare and the employer taking him or her off the health insurance plan
- Divorce or legal separation of the covered employee
- Death of the covered employee
- Loss of dependent child status under the plan rules

Coverage Periods

The length of COBRA coverage depends on your qualifying event.

Qualifying Events	Beneficiary	Coverage
Termination	Employee	18 months
Reduced hours	Spouse	
	Dependent child	
Employee entitled to Medicare	Spouse	36 months
Divorce or legal separation	Dependent child	
Death of covered employee		
Loss of dependent child status	Dependent child	36 months

Note: Certain people with a disability are allowed to qualify for twenty-nine months (the original eighteen months plus an eleven-month extension) of COBRA continuation coverage. To qualify for this disability extension, the person must get a formal disability determination from the Social Security Administration that shows he or she was disabled at the time (or within sixty days) of the COBRA qualifying event. After getting the SSA decision, the employee must send a copy of the letter to the plan administrator.

COBRA Notices

Types of Notices

Summary Plan Description COBRA'S notification requirements arise out of the Employee Retirement Income Security Act (ERISA) in that

ERISA Part 1 of Title I requires the administrator of an employee benefit plan to furnish participants and beneficiaries with a written summary plan description (SPD) describing in understandable terms:

- The plan, including what benefits are available under the plan
- The rights and responsibilities of participants and beneficiaries under the plan
- How the plan works

Summary of Material Modifications If there are material changes to the plan, the plan administrator has to provide the beneficiary with a summary of material modifications (SMM) no later than 210 days after the end of the plan year when the changes become effective. If the change is a material reduction in covered services or benefits, the SMM has to be provided no later than 60 days after the reduction is adopted.

Note that a beneficiary can request a copy of the SPD and any SMM (or any other plan documents) and the plan administrator (or employer) must provide them within thirty days of a written request.

COBRA General Notice Each employee and each spouse covered under the plan must receive a general notice describing COBRA rights within the first ninety days of coverage.

You can satisfy this requirement by giving the beneficiary the plan's SPD within the ninety-day period as long as it contains the general notice information.

The general notice must contain the following information:

- Name of the plan and someone who can be contacted for more information
- General description of the continuation coverage provided under the plan
- Explanation of any notices the beneficiary must give the plan administrator to protect his or her COBRA rights

This information enables the beneficiary to protect his or her COBRA rights from the moment of coverage.

COBRA Qualifying Event Notices Before an employee is eligible for continuation coverage, a qualifying event must occur, and the group health plan administrator must be notified of the qualifying event. The responsibility for notifying the plan administrator depends on the type of qualifying event.

The *employer* must notify the group health plan administrator within thirty days following a qualifying event if the event is one of the following:

- Termination or reduction in hours of employment of the covered employee
- Death of the covered employee
- Covered employee becoming entitled to Medicare
- Employer filing for bankruptcy

The *covered employee* or *one of the qualified beneficiaries* must notify the plan administrator within sixty days of a qualified event if the event is:

- Divorce
- Legal separation
- Loss of a child's dependent status under the plan

As an employer, you need to communicate to employees what their responsibilities are for notifying the plan administrator and what the rules are for how to provide notice if a qualifying event occurs. This information should be described in both the general notice and the plan's SPD.

If a beneficiary doesn't adhere to the requirements for notification or election procedures and the timeframes, the beneficiary will lose his or her rights.

COBRA Election Notice Within fourteen days of receiving notice of a qualifying event, the administrator must provide the qualified beneficiary an election notice that:

- Describes the beneficiary's rights to continuation coverage
- Clearly explains how to make an election

The election notice should contain all of the information the beneficiary needs to understand continuation coverage and make an informed decision whether or not to elect continuation coverage. It should also include the name of the plan's COBRA administrator and tell the beneficiary how to get more information.

COBRA Notice of Unavailability of Continuation Coverage When a beneficiary requests continuation coverage and the plan administrator determines that the beneficiary isn't entitled to the continuation coverage, within fourteen days of receiving the request, the plan administrator must provide the beneficiary with a notice of unavailability that explains the reason for denying the request.

COBRA Notice of Early Termination of Continuation Coverage Continuation coverage must be available for a maximum period of eighteen, twenty-nine, or thirty-six months. However, the coverage can be terminated earlier for any of the following reasons:

- Premiums aren't paid in full or on time.
- The employer ceases to maintain a group health plan.
- A covered beneficiary begins coverage under another group health plan—but only if the new plan doesn't impose an exclusion or limitation that affects a preexisting condition of the beneficiary.
- A covered beneficiary becomes entitled to Medicare benefits after electing coverage.
- A covered beneficiary engages in conduct that justifies terminating the coverage—this is the type of conduct that would result in an *employee's* group health coverage being terminated (such as fraud).

When continuation coverage is terminated early, the plan administrator must give the beneficiary a notice of early termination. This notice needs to be given as soon as practical after the decision is made and must describe:

- Date coverage will terminate
- Reason for termination
- Any lawful rights the beneficiary has to elect alternative group or individual coverage—such as the right to convert to an individual policy

Timing of Notices

Notices should be sent out as follows:

- *General (or Initial) Notice*—Plan administrator to employee/beneficiary within ninety days after coverage begins
- *Summary Plan Description*—Employer/plan administrator to employee/beneficiary within ninety days after employee becomes a plan participant
- *Summary of Material Modifications*—Plan administrator to employee/beneficiary not later than 210 days after the end of plan year in which changes become effective; if a material reduction in covered services or benefits, then notice within sixty days after reduction is adopted
- *Qualifying Events Notice*
    - Employer to plan administrator within thirty days after qualifying event
    - Employee/beneficiary to plan administrator within sixty days after qualifying event
- *Election Notice*—Plan administrator to employee/beneficiary within fourteen days after notice of qualifying event or forty-four days if employer is the administrator
- *Notice of Unavailability of Continuation Coverage*—Plan administrator to employee/beneficiary within fourteen days or forty-four days if employer is the administrator and explain why
- *Notice of Early Termination of Continuation Coverage*—Plan administrator to employee/beneficiary ASAP

Election Timing

Employees have sixty days after receiving the qualifying notice to choose health insurance coverage for themselves or their dependents under COBRA. Employees must notify the plan administrator in writing if they wish to keep their health insurance.

Payment of First Premium

The beneficiary has forty-five days from the date he or she decided to continue health insurance coverage to pay the first bill. Neither the health plan nor the employer is required to send the beneficiary monthly premium notices.

Cost

The premium for COBRA coverage is equal to the full cost of your group health coverage—including the employer and employee share—plus up to 2 percent more for administrative costs.

This total premium cost is usually much more than the employee paid when he or she worked for the company, since the company probably paid for part of the premium.

If the beneficiary has already had the eighteen-month standard COBRA coverage and has started on the eleven-month disability extension, the premium may be much higher. In this situation, the employer may charge up to 150 percent of the actual insurance cost.

Health Insurance Portability and Accountability Act of 1996—Preexisting Conditions

Preexisting Condition Exclusion Reduction

The Health Insurance Portability and Accountability Act of 1996 (HIPAA) limits the circumstances under which coverage may be excluded for medical conditions present before an employee enrolls in a group plan.

Portability rules require any plan with a preexisting condition limitation (PCL) to count a person's prior coverage periods toward his or her PCL period. A preexisting condition exclusion generally may not be imposed for more than twelve months (eighteen months for a late enrollee). The twelve-month (or eighteen-month) exclusion period is reduced by one month for each month of an employee's prior health coverage. The employee is entitled to a certificate that will show evidence of prior health coverage. If the employee buys health insurance other than through an employer group health plan, a certificate of prior coverage may help the employee obtain coverage without a preexisting condition exclusion.

Documentation Required When Coverage Ends

To ensure that individuals receive proper credit for prior coverage, employers and carriers must provide:

- Certification of creditable coverage periods
- Certification for the individual's or family's active coverage period and COBRA coverage period
- Certification of prior coverage, which may be requested by individual or family anytime during twenty-four months after all coverage ends

Health-Related Discrimination Prohibited

Health plan eligibility, premium, and benefits for a group enrollee cannot be based on the enrollee's:

- Health status or health history
- Claim experience or receipt of health care
- Physical or mental medical condition
- Disability, genetic information, or evidence of risk (i.e., for domestic violence)

Guaranteed Renewability

Contracts for coverage must be renewable at the option of the covered individual. Carriers are allowed to terminate plans for only the following reasons:

- Nonpayment of group premium or fraud
- Termination of individual's membership in an association
- A network plan enrollee leaving the network service area
- Carrier withdrawal from the state market

CHAPTER 5

Compensation: The Fair Labor Standards Act

Introduction

The Fair Labor Standards Act of 1938 (FLSA), Title 29 United States Code Sections 201–219, provides for minimum standards for both wages and overtime entitlement and spells out administrative procedures by which covered work time must be compensated. Included in the Act are provisions related to child labor, equal pay, and portal-to-portal (home-to-work, work-to-home) activities. In addition, the Act exempts specified employees or groups of employees from the application of certain of its provisions.

Minimum Wage and Overtime

Basically, two types of employees exist under the FLSA—those who must be paid overtime for all time worked over forty hours in a workweek, called *nonexempt*, and workers who are not paid overtime, called *exempt*.

Misleading terms that are often used in connection with the FLSA are *hourly* and *salaried*. These words are (incorrectly) employed to denote nonexempt and exempt concepts. They do not. Although the word *hourly* suggests a worker who must be paid overtime, the term *salaried* is misleading. To be salaried implies that if an employee is paid a salary then he nor she is exempt from the overtime provisions of the Act. In reality, as a general rule, to be exempt an employee must *both* be paid a true salary of no less than $455 per week *and* pass a "duties" test. (See "Exempt vs. Nonexempt Status Under the FLSA" in this chapter.)

Minimum Wage

The federal minimum wage was increased to $6.55 per hour on July 24, 2008, and on July 24, 2009, to $7.25 per hour. If a state minimum wage is higher, a nonexempt employee must be paid no less than the higher minimum wage amount.

Workweek

Employees must be paid at the rate of time and one-half their regular hourly rate for compensable hours over forty during a workweek.

A workweek is made up of a fixed and regularly recurring period of 168 hours, or seven consecutive 24-hour periods. The workweek can begin any hour of the day and on any day of the week. The beginning of the workweek may be changed only if the change is intended to be permanent and not to circumvent the law.

Each workweek stands alone.

Calculating Overtime

Overtime pay for a nonexempt employee depends on the employee's *regular rate* of pay. Part 778 of the regulations contains all of the various ways to determine an employee's regular rate.

Under 29 CFR 778.109, an employee's regular rate of pay is an hourly rate. This is true no matter what pay method is used to determine an employee's pay.

In calculating overtime pay, the most important things to keep in mind are:

- Overtime pay depends on the employee's regular rate of pay for the workweek, which can vary from week to week, depending on exactly how the employee is paid.

- Regular rate of pay includes all components of the pay agreement, except for very narrowly defined premium pay outlined in Section 207(e) of the FLSA.
- For all but straight hourly pay or straight forty-hour per week salaries, the general method for calculating overtime is to divide total pay by total hours worked for the workweek, and then pay one-half of the resulting regular rate for each overtime hour worked.

Compensatory Time Off

Federal, state, and local government employers can provide compensatory time off in lieu of paying overtime to nonexempt employees—private employers cannot.

Private employers can provide a *time-off plan* to nonexempt employees. Time off must be:

- Granted at time and one-half for all hours worked over forty hours per workweek
- Taken within the pay period in which it is earned

EXAMPLE 1: A nonexempt employee works forty-four hours during week one of a two-week pay period. The employee must be paid four hours of overtime for week one. If the employer wishes to keep its overall payroll at a straight time level for the entire pay period, it must have the worker clock out and leave after thirty-four hours during week two of the pay period.

- *Week One*—For forty-four hours, the worker must be paid four hours of overtime.
- *Week Two*—Since four overtime hours equal six regular time hours (at time and one-half) the worker would need to clock out and leave after thirty-four hours in order for the overall payroll to equal eighty straight time hours during the two-week pay period.

EXAMPLE 2: A nonexempt employee works forty hours during week one of a two-week pay period and forty-four hours during week two. The employer cannot keep its overall payroll at a straight time level for that pay period. It must pay four hours of overtime and cannot pay for eighty hours and "make up" the four overtime hours during the next pay period.

Fluctuating Workweek

Many employees do not have fixed weekly schedules and will either (1) regularly work both long (more than forty-hour) and short (less than forty-hour) workweeks or (2) regularly work overtime each workweek, but the amount of overtime will vary from workweek to workweek. In situations where the employee has these types of fluctuating workweeks, the employer can potentially save itself money by using the fluctuating workweek method of calculating overtime.

Under this method, the employee is paid a fixed salary for all hours worked, whether the employee works fewer than forty hours or more than forty hours. In weeks in which the employee works more than forty hours, the employee is paid an overtime premium for the extra hours. Cost savings to the employer are derived from paying the employee a salary that involves fewer administrative costs, and *any overtime premiums are paid at 50 percent of the employee's regular rate of pay.*

To use this method of payment, an employer must conform to certain rules as outlined in 29 CFR 778.114, summarized as follows:

- There must be an understanding between the employer and the employee that the employee will be paid using the fluctuating workweek method. (*Suggestion:* Put the understanding in writing.)

- The workweek of the employee must be a fluctuating one.

- The employee must be paid a fixed salary regardless of the number of hours worked each week. Employees who are paid an hourly wage *do not* qualify.

- The salary must be sufficiently large enough so that the regular rate of pay will never drop below the minimum wage.

EXAMPLE: If the employee is paid a salary of $300 per week and works only thirty-five hours, then the regular rate of pay for that week is $8.57 per hour, which meets the federal minimum wage requirement. However, if the employee works forty-eight hours in the next week, then the regular rate of pay for that week would be $6.25 per hour, which would not meet the federal minimum wage after July 24, 2008, and the employer would have to make up the difference. In summary, the rate of pay cannot be less than either the federal or state minimum wage.

- In addition to his or her salary, the employee must be paid over-time premiums for any hours worked over forty in the workweek. The overtime premium rate is 50 percent of the regular rate of pay for the workweek.

In summary, payroll calculation under the fluctuating workweek method is as follows:

- The total number of hours worked is divided into the employee's weekly salary.
- The overtime premium is 50 percent of the regular rate of pay times the number of hours of overtime worked.

EXAMPLE: Assume a worker works alternating weeks of forty-eight hours and seventy-two hours and is paid $500 per week. The calculation of the biweekly pay would be as follows:

First Week

Regular rate of pay: ($500 ÷ 48 hr = $10.42/hr)
Overtime premium: (50 percent × 8 hr × $10.42/hr = $41.68)
Total pay: ($500 + $41.68 = $541.68)

Second Week

Regular rate of pay: ($500 ÷ 72 hr = $6.94/hr)
Overtime premium: (50 percent × 32 hr × $6.94/hr = $111.04)
Total pay: ($500 + $111.04 = $611.04)

Therefore, the employee's gross pay for the biweekly payroll period would be $1,152.72 ($541.68 + $611.04).

Suggestion: The fluctuating workweek rules are complex and you should obtain professional legal guidance if you are considering this method of determining employees' pay.

Tipped Employees

Characteristics

Tipped employees are those who customarily and regularly receive more than $30 a month in tips. Tips actually received by tipped employees may be counted as wages for purposes of the FLSA, but the employer must pay not less than $2.13 an hour in direct wages.

Requirements

If an employer elects to use the tip credit provision, the employer must:

- Inform each tipped employee about the tip credit allowance (including amount to be credited) before the credit is utilized.
- Be able to show that the employee receives at least the minimum wage when direct wages and the tip credit allowance are combined. If there is a workweek where tips are poor, the employer would have to increase direct pay to bring the combined total of tips and direct compensation up to at least the minimum wage level.
- Allow the tipped employee to retain all tips, whether or not the employer elects to take a tip credit for tips received, except to the extent the employee participates in a valid tip-pooling arrangement.

If an employee's tips combined with the employer's direct wages of at least $2.13 an hour do not equal the minimum hourly wage of $6.55 per hour effective July 24, 2008, and $7.25 per hour effective July 24, 2009, the employer must make up the difference per workweek.

Youth Minimum Wage

The 1996 Amendments to the FLSA allow employers to pay a youth minimum wage of not less than $4.25 an hour to employees who are under twenty years of age during the first ninety consecutive calendar days after initial employment by their employer. Employers may not take any action to displace any employee (including partial displacements such as a reduction in hours, wages, or employment benefits) for the purpose of employing someone at the youth wage. (See "Child Labor" in this chapter.)

Dual Jobs

When an employee is employed concurrently in both a tipped and a not tipped occupation, the tip credit is available only for the hours spent in the tipped occupation.

Retention of Tips

The law forbids any arrangement between the employer and the tipped employee whereby any part of the tip received becomes the property of the employer. A tip is the sole property of the tipped employee. Where an employer does not strictly observe the tip credit provisions of the Act, no tip credit may be claimed and the employees are entitled to receive the full cash minimum wage, in addition to retaining tips they may or should have received.

Service Charges

A compulsory charge for service, for example, 15 percent of the bill, is not a tip. Such charges are part of the employer's gross receipts. Where service charges are imposed and the employee receives no tips, the employer must pay the entire minimum wage and overtime required by the Act.

Tip Pooling

The requirement that an employee must retain all tips does not preclude a valid tip-pooling or sharing arrangement among employees who customarily and regularly receive tips, such as waiters, waitresses, bellhops, counter personnel (who serve customers), busboys or busgirls, and service bartenders.

Credit Cards

Where tips are charged on a credit card and the employer must pay the credit card company a percentage on each sale, the employer may pay the employee the tip less that percentage.

Compensable Hours

Employees "Suffered or Permitted" to Work

Compensable work time is time spent by a worker for the benefit of the employer, with the employer's actual or constructive knowledge, performing the worker's *principal* activity or functions integral to his or her principal activity.

- Employees must be paid for all work *suffered*—the employer made them do it.

- Employees must be paid for all work *permitted*—the employer let them do it.

According to Department of Labor (DOL) regulations, if an employer does not want work performed by an employee,

> It is the duty of management to exercise its control and see to it that the work is not performed. . . . It cannot sit back and accept the benefits without compensating for them. The mere promulgation of a rule against such work is not enough. Management has the power to enforce the rule and must make every effort to do so. (29 CFR 785.13—Duty of Management)

Note: Although you may not authorize it, if you allow a nonexempt employee to work through lunch, even if he or she clocks out, you must pay that employee for the time worked.

Early Clock-In—De Minimis Rule

In accordance with 29 CFR 785.47, in recording working time under the Act, insubstantial or insignificant periods of time beyond the scheduled working hours, which cannot as a practical administrative matter be precisely recorded for payroll purposes, may be disregarded. The courts have held that such trifles are de minimis.

This rule applies only where there are uncertain and indefinite periods of time involved of a few seconds' or minutes' duration, and where the failure to count such time is due to considerations justified by industrial realities.

An employer may not arbitrarily fail to count as hours worked any part, however small, of the employee's fixed or regular working time or practically ascertainable period of time he or she is regularly required to spend on duties assigned to him or her.

Waiting (On-Call) Time

Whether waiting time is time worked under the Act depends on the particular circumstances. Generally, the facts may show that the employee was engaged to wait (which is work time) or the facts may show that the employee was waiting to be engaged (which is not work time).

On-Duty Waiting Time

When your employee is waiting for work to do, for repairs to be made, and so forth, while on duty, he or she is engaged to wait and the time is hours worked.

Off-Duty Waiting Time

Off-duty waiting time or layover time is a period during which the employee is waiting to be engaged and is *not* hours worked if:

- Your employee is completely relieved from duty.
- The periods are long enough to enable your employee to use the time effectively for his or her own purposes (e.g., more than thirty minutes).
- Your employee is told in advance that he or she may leave the job.
- Your employee is advised of the time that he or she is required to return to work.

Rest and Meal Periods

Rest and meal periods are not required under the FLSA, although they may be under state laws.

Rest Periods

Rest periods of short duration, usually twenty minutes or less, are common in industry and are customarily paid as working time.

Unauthorized extensions of authorized work breaks need not be counted as hours worked when the employer has expressly and unambiguously communicated to the employee that the authorized break may last for only a specific length of time, that any extension of the break is contrary to the employer's rules, and that any extension of the break will be punished.

Bona Fide Meal Periods

Bona fide meal periods (typically thirty minutes or more) generally need not be compensated as work time. The employee must be completely relieved from duty for the purpose of eating regular meals. The employee is *not* relieved if he or she is required to perform any duties, whether active or inactive, while eating, such as answering telephone calls.

Sleeping Time and Certain Other Activities

An employee who is required to be on duty for fewer than twenty-four hours is working even though he or she is permitted to sleep or engage in other personal activities when not busy.

An employee required to be on duty for twenty-four hours or more may agree with the employer to exclude from hours worked bona fide regularly scheduled sleeping periods of not more than eight hours provided adequate sleeping facilities are furnished by the employer and the employee can usually enjoy an uninterrupted night's sleep. No reduction is permitted unless at least five hours of sleep are taken.

Lectures, Meetings, and Training Programs

Attendance at lectures, meetings, training programs, and similar activities need not be counted as working time only if the following four criteria are met:

1. It is outside normal work hours.
2. It is voluntary.
3. It is not job related.
4. No other work is concurrently performed.

Travel Time

The principles that apply in determining whether time spent in travel is compensable time depends on the kind of travel involved.

Home-to-Work Travel

An employee who travels from home before the regular workday and returns to his or her home at the end of the workday is engaged in ordinary home-to-work travel, which is not work time.

Home to Work on a Special One-Day Assignment in Another City

This is a situation where an employee who regularly works at a fixed location in one city is given a special one-day assignment in another city and returns home the same day. The time spent in traveling to and returning from the other city is work time except that the employer may deduct/

not count that time the employee would normally spend commuting to the regular work site.

Travel That Is All in the Day's Work

Time spent by an employee in travel as part of his or her principal activity, such as travel from job site to job site during the workday, is work time and must be counted as hours worked.

Travel Away from Home Community

Travel that keeps an employee away from home overnight is called *travel away from home*.

Travel away from home is clearly work time when it cuts across the employee's workday. The time is not only hours worked on regular working days during normal working hours but also during corresponding hours on nonworking days.

As an enforcement policy, the division will not consider as work time that time spent in travel away from home outside of regular working hours as a passenger on an airplane, train, boat, bus, or automobile (29 CFR 785.39—Travel away from home community).

Equal Pay for Men and Women (Equal Pay Act)

Men and women who perform the same job at the same levels of skill, experience, and responsibility must be paid the same.

Child Labor

Overview

Generally, children younger than age 14 may not work for an employer.

Children ages 14 and 15 may work, but only in nonhazardous occupations and only during nonschool hours, and there is a substantial limitation on the number of hours they can work each day and week.

Children ages 16 and 17 may work any hours they want but may not work in hazardous occupations.

Once a person reaches age 18, there is no limitation on either hours or duties (other than whatever rules may apply pursuant to regulations promulgated under the Occupational Safety and Health Act [OSHA]).

Nonagricultural Jobs (Child Labor)

Regulations governing youth employment in nonfarm jobs differ somewhat from those pertaining to agricultural employment. In nonfarm work, the permissible jobs and hours of work, by age, are as follows:

- Youths age 18 years or older may perform any job, whether hazardous or not, for unlimited hours.

- Youths ages 16 and 17 may perform any nonhazardous job for unlimited hours.

- Youths ages 14 and 15 may work outside school hours in various nonmanufacturing, nonmining, and nonhazardous jobs under the following conditions: no more than three hours on a school day, eighteen hours in a school week, eight hours on a nonschool day, or forty hours in a nonschool week. Also, work may not begin before 7 A.M. or end after 7 P.M. except from June 1 through Labor Day, when evening hours are extended to 9 P.M. Under a special provision, youths ages 14 and 15 years enrolled in an approved Work Experience and Career Exploration Program (WECEP) may be employed for up to twenty-three hours in school weeks and three hours on school days (including during school hours).

Fourteen is the minimum age for most nonfarm work. However, at any age, youths may deliver newspapers; perform in radio, television, movie, or theatrical productions; work for parents in their solely owned nonfarm business (except in manufacturing or on hazardous jobs); or gather evergreens and make evergreen wreaths.

Farm Jobs (Child Labor)

In farm work, permissible jobs and hours of work, by age, are as follows:

- Youths age 16 years and older may perform any job, whether hazardous or not, for unlimited hours.

- Youths ages 14 and 15 may perform any nonhazardous farm job outside of school hours.

- Youths ages 12 and 13 may work outside of school hours in nonhazardous jobs, either with a parent's written consent or on the same farm as the parent(s).

- Youths under age 12 may perform jobs on farms owned or operated by parent(s), or with a parent's written consent, outside of school hours in nonhazardous jobs on farms not covered by minimum wage requirements.

Minors of any age may be employed by their parents at any time in any occupation on a farm owned or operated by their parents.

Coverage

As a practical matter, all organizations are covered by the FLSA in that the Act provides two different ways for coverage to apply:

1. *Individual Coverage*—An individual whose work affects interstate commerce is covered as an individual.

   Note: Interstate commerce is so broadly defined that practically anything fits, such as purchasing or using supplies from out of state or accepting payments from customers based on credit cards issued by out-of-state banks.

2. *Enterprise Coverage*—For most businesses, enterprise coverage applies if the business is involved in interstate commerce and the gross annual business volume is at least $500,000. If those two conditions exist, all employees working for the business are covered.

   - Coverage is automatic for:
     - Schools, hospitals, nursing homes, or other residential care facilities.
     - All governmental entities at whatever level of government, no matter how big or small.
   - Coverage does not apply to certain entities that are not organized for a business purpose, such as churches and eleemosynary (charitable) institutions.

Benefits and Payroll Practices Not Covered by the FLSA

Breaks

Some states require breaks, but most do not. Federal law has no break requirement.

Note: OSHA regulations relating to highly hazardous occupations such as high-altitude steel erection workers or nuclear plant workers do require breaks.

Premium, Holiday, and Weekend Pay

This is extra pay for unusual hours, such as double time or triple time pay for working extra overtime or during times when most employees take off. This type of pay is not required under the FLSA.

Shift Differentials

This type of compensation is defined as higher hourly pay for second or third shifts, as opposed to the normal hourly rate given to workers on the daytime shift. The FLSA does not require this type of pay.

Raises

Pay increases are not required under state or federal laws unless the minimum wage is increased on either the federal or the state level.

Note: Once a raise goes into effect, the employer must pay it until it is withdrawn. Raises may be withdrawn only prospectively, never retroactively. A retroactive pay cut will always violate the FLSA.

Pensions

Pension or retirement plans are not required.

Exempt vs. Nonexempt Status Under the FLSA

The FLSA has many exemptions. Some are extremely broad—for example, exemptions from the definition of *employee*—while others are narrower, such as various exemptions from overtime pay. Other exemptions apply to two or more protections normally afforded by the FLSA.

Total Exemption—Exemptions from the Definition of *Employee*

The following categories of workers are excluded from the definition of *employee* under the Fair Labor Standards Act and thus do not have the benefit of any of the provisions of the FLSA:

- Congressional interns. (Section 203(e)(2)(A), in conjunction with Section 203(a)(2) of the Congressional Accountability Act of 1995, made most employees of Congress subject to the FLSA.)

- Employees of the U.S. Postal Service or the Postal Rate Commission—Section 203(e)(2)(B).

- Employees of states, political subdivisions of states, or interstate governmental agencies who are exempt from the civil service laws of their states and who are either elected officeholders of the state or subdivision or else are selected by such officeholders to serve on their personal staff, are appointed by such officeholders to a policymaking position, serve as an immediate adviser to such officeholders regarding constitutional or legal powers of the office in question (such as a general counsel), or are employed by the legislature of the state or political subdivision (except for employees of the legislative library of such a state or political subdivision)—Section 203(e)(2)(C).

- Independent contractors.
  The Supreme Court has said that there is no definition that solves all problems relating to the employer-employee relationship under the FLSA. The Court has also said that determination of the relationship cannot be based on isolated factors or upon a single characteristic, but depends upon the circumstances of the whole activity. Factors the Court has considered significant, although no single one is regarded as controlling, are:

  - Extent to which the worker's services are an integral part of the employer's business

  - Permanency of the relationship

  - Amount of the worker's investment in facilities and equipment

  - Nature and degree of control by the principal

  - Worker's opportunities for profit and loss

  - Level of skill required in performing the job and the amount of initiative, judgment, or foresight in open market competition with others required for the success of the claimed independent enterprise

- Volunteers for public agencies of states, political subdivisions of states, or interstate governmental agencies under certain conditions—Section 203(e)(4).
- Volunteers at community food banks who are paid with groceries—Section 203(e)(5).
- Volunteers for nonprofit religious, charitable, and civic organizations.
- Certain trainees.

  Although certain types of trainees are completely excluded from FLSA coverage, the requirements for such total exclusion are quite stringent. In an administrative letter ruling dated February 22, 1974 (WH-254, BNA WHM 99:1152), the Department of Labor (DOL) gave the following criteria for the designation of a person as a trainee:

  1. The training, even though it includes actual operation of the facilities of the employer, is similar to that which would be given in a vocational school.
  2. The training is for the benefit of the trainees.
  3. The trainees do not displace regular employees, but work under close observation.
  4. The employer that provides the training derives no immediate advantage from the activities of the trainees, and on occasion his operations may actually be impeded.
  5. The trainees are not necessarily entitled to a job at the completion of the training period.
  6. The employer and the trainees understand that the trainees are not entitled to wages for the time spent in training.
     Note: The courts find it important that there be a written agreement to the effect that payment for the services is neither intended nor expected.
  7. Prisoners in jail or correctional institutions.
  8. Church members performing religious duties.

Exemptions—Minimum Wage, Overtime, Child Labor, and Record Keeping

The following categories of employees are exempt from the minimum wage, overtime, child labor, and record-keeping provisions of the FLSA:

- Employees who work in foreign countries or in certain territories under the jurisdiction of the United States—Section 213(f).

- Employees of nonappropriated fund instrumentalities under the jurisdiction of the Armed Forces who serve in foreign countries or in certain territories under the jurisdiction of the United States—Section 213(f), in conjunction with Sections 218(b) and 218(b)(2).

Exemptions—Minimum Wage, Overtime, and Child Labor

The following categories of employees are exempt from the minimum wage, overtime, and child labor provisions of the FLSA:

- Employees who deliver newspapers to consumers—Section 213(d)
- Homeworkers who make wreaths from evergreens—Section 213(d)

Exemptions—Minimum Wage and Overtime

The following categories of employees are exempt from both minimum wage and overtime pay requirements of the FLSA:

- White-collar exempt employees—executive, administrative, professional, computer professional, and outside sales representative employees—Section 213(a)(1).

- Section 213(a)(17) relates to the computer employee exemption. To be exempt the following tests must be met:

  1. The employee must be compensated *either* on a salary or fee basis (as defined in the regulations) at a rate not less than $455 per week *or,* if compensated on an hourly basis, at a rate not less than $27.63 an hour.

  2. The employee must be employed as a computer systems analyst, computer programmer, software engineer, or other similarly skilled worker in the computer field performing the following duties

  3. The employee's primary duty must consist of:
     - The application of systems analysis techniques and proce-

dures, including consulting with users, to determine hardware, software or system functional specifications

- The design, development, documentation, analysis, creation, testing, or modification of computer systems or programs, including prototypes, based on and related to user or system design specifications

- The design, documentation, testing, creation, or modification of computer programs related to machine operating systems

- A combination of the aforementioned duties, the performance of which requires the same level of skills

- Employees of certain amusement or recreational establishments—Section 213(a)(3).

- Employees involved in cultivation, propagation, catching, harvesting, or first processing at sea of aquatic forms of animal or vegetable life—Section 213(a)(5).

- Certain agricultural employees of small farms or family-owned farms—Section 213(a)(6)—does not apply to farms operating in conjunction with other establishments, the combined business volume of which exceeds $10 million.

- Employees principally engaged in the range production of livestock—Section 213(a)(6).

- Employees exempt under special certificates issued under Section 214—Section 213(a)(7). The 213(a)(7) exemption encompasses the following categories:

  - *Learners* under special certificates issued by the Secretary of Labor—Section 214(a).

  - *Apprentices* under special certificates issued by the Secretary of Labor—Section 214(a).

  - *Messengers* under special certificates issued by the Secretary of Labor—Section 214(a).

  - *Students employed in retail or service establishments* under special certificates issued by the Secretary of Labor—significant limitations on hours—Section 214(b)(1).

  - *Students employed in agriculture* under special certificates issued by the Secretary of Labor—in compliance with child labor laws—Section 214(b)(2).

- *Students in institutions of higher education who are employed by their institutions* under special certificates issued by the Secretary of Labor—significant limitations on hours—Section 214(b)(3).

- *Handicapped workers* under special certificates issued by the Secretary of Labor—Section 214(c).

- *Students of elementary or secondary schools who are employed by their schools as part of the curriculum* in compliance with child labor laws—Section 214(d).

- Employees of certain small local newspapers—Section 213(a)(8).

- Switchboard operators for certain independently owned public telephone companies—Section 213(a)(10).

- Seamen on vessels other than American vessels—Section 213(a)(12).

- Certain babysitters or companions for the elderly—Section 213 (a)(15).

- Criminal investigators paid on an availability pay basis—Section 213(a)(16).

- Computer software professionals—Section 213(a)(17). (Also noted at the beginning of this list.)

Exemptions—Minimum Wage Only

The following categories of employees are exempt from minimum wage only:

- Employees in Puerto Rico or the Virgin Islands (special rates apply)—Section 206(a)(2).

- Employees in American Samoa (special rates apply)—Section 206(a)(3).

- Domestic service employees who are not covered by the Social Security Act or who work eight or less hours per week in such service—Section 206(f).

- New employees younger than age 20 who are within their first ninety days on a job—Section 206(g).

Exemptions—Overtime Only

The following categories of employees are exempt from overtime pay, but not from the minimum wage; some of the exemptions from overtime pay are very limited and need to be studied carefully:

- Employees working under a collective bargaining agreement that limits hours worked to 1,040 in any period of twenty-six consecutive weeks—Section 207(b)(1).

- Employees working under a collective bargaining agreement that imposes certain minimums and maximums on hours worked in a fifty-two-week period—Section 207(b)(2).

- Employees of certain smaller wholesale or bulk distributors of petroleum products that are engaged primarily in intrastate operations if such employees receive at least 1.5 times the minimum wage for hours worked between forty and fifty-six in a workweek and 1.5 times their regular rate for hours in excess of twelve in a day or fifty-six in a workweek—Section 207(b)(3).

- Employees working irregular hours under a bona fide individual contract or collective bargaining agreement that specifies a guaranteed regular rate not less than minimum wage for purposes of calculating overtime pay and guarantees such pay for not more than sixty hours in a workweek—Section 207(f).

- Certain employees paid on a piece rate basis—Section 207(g).

- Retail or service establishment employees whose regular rates are at least 1.5 times minimum wage and who earn at least half their income in a representative period from commissions—Section 207(i).

- Employees of hospitals or other types of residential care facilities—exemption from the forty-hour workweek rule—two-week period may be used for overtime computation if employees are paid time and a half for hours worked in excess of eight in a day or eighty in a two-week period—Section 207(j).

- Fire protection or law enforcement employees of public agencies—a period of seven to twenty-eight days may be used for overtime computation if time and a half is paid for hours in excess of a certain number set by regulation—Section 207(k).

- Certain employees who are engaged in activities related to the auction sale of certain types of tobacco as long as such employees get time and a half for hours worked over ten in a day or forty-eight in a workweek—exemption good for up to fourteen weeks in a fifty-two-week period—Section 207(m).

- Employees of local electric railways, trolleys, or bus carriers—limited exclusion from overtime computation of hours spent in charter activities—Section 207(n).

- Public agency employees working under a compensatory time agreement—Section 207(o).

- Fire protection and law enforcement employees who volunteer for a special detail in the employ of a separate and independent public agency—Section 207(p)(1).

- Public agency employees who work part-time for the same agency in some other capacity or who substitute for other workers—under certain conditions, hours in excess of forty may be paid at straight time—Section 207(p)(2,3).

- Employees receiving certain types of remedial education in connection with the employment—overtime exclusion is limited to ten hours per workweek (i.e., straight time is paid for up to fifty hours per workweek)—Section 207(q).

- Certain employees of motor carriers regulated by the U.S. Department of Transportation—Section 213(b)(1).

- Employees of certain rail carriers (as defined in 49 USC 10102)—Section 213(b)(2).

- Employees of certain air carriers—Section 213(b)(3).

- Outside buyers of poultry, eggs, cream, or milk in their raw or natural state—Section 213(b)(5).

- Any employee employed as a seaman on any vessel—Section 213(b)(6).

- Certain employees of small local radio or television stations—Section 213(b)(9).

- Certain employees of automobile, truck, farm implement, trailer, boat, or aircraft dealerships—Section 213(b)(10).

- Local delivery drivers or driver's helpers compensated on a trip rate or other delivery payment basis—Section 213(b)(11).

- Any agricultural employee—Section 213(b)(12).

- Employees who operate or maintain ditches, canals, reservoirs, or waterways for agricultural purposes—Section 213(b)(12).

- Employees who are primarily engaged in agricultural work, but who occasionally perform livestock auction duties that are paid at minimum wage or more—Section 213(b)(13).

- Certain employees of small country grain elevators and related establishments—Section 213(b)(14).

- Employees who process maple sap into unrefined sugar or syrup—Section 213(b)(15).

- Employees who prepare and transport fruits or vegetables from the farm to the place of first processing or first marketing within the same state—Section 213(b)(16).

- Employees who transport fruit or vegetable harvest workers within a state—Section 213(b)(16).

- Drivers employed by taxicab companies—Section 213(b)(17).

- Firefighting and law enforcement employees of certain very small fire or police departments—Section 213(b)(20).

- Domestic service employee who resides in the household in which the work is performed—Section 213(b)(21).

- Certain married houseparents in nonprofit educational institutions for children enrolled in and residing at such facilities who either are orphans or else have at least one natural parent who is deceased—Section 213(b)(24).

- Employees of motion picture theaters—Section 213(b)(27).

- Certain employees of small forestry or lumbering operations—Section 213(b)(28).

- Employees of amusement or recreational facilities located in national parks, forests, or refuges—Section 213(b)(29).

- Criminal investigators who are paid on an availability pay basis—Section 213(b)(30).

- Certain minimum wage employees whose minimum wage rates are set by the Secretary of Labor—Section 213(e).

- Certain employees engaged in cotton ginning, processing of raw cotton or cottonseed, or processing of sugarcane or sugar beets in certain facilities as long as such employees get time and a half for hours worked over ten in a day or forty-eight in a workweek—exemption good for up to fourteen weeks in a calendar year—Section 213(h).

- Certain employees who are engaged in cotton ginning for market in a county where cotton is grown in commercial quantities as long as such employees get time and a half for hours worked over ten in a day or forty-eight in a workweek—exemption good for up to fourteen weeks in a fifty-two-week period—Section 213(i).

- Certain employees who process sugar beets, sugar beet molasses, or sugar cane into sugar (other than refined sugar) or syrup as long as such employees get time and a half for hours worked over ten in a day or forty-eight in a workweek—exemption good for up to fourteen weeks in a fifty-two-week period—Section 213(j).

Focus on White-Collar Exemptions

Quick Basics

The executive, administrative, and professional exemption categories each have a salary test (minimum salary is $455/week; computer professionals can be paid $27.63/hour or more in straight time pay for each hour worked in lieu of the minimum salary) and a duties test.

Employees who meet the tests for their categories do not have to be paid overtime pay, regardless of how much overtime they work.

A salary alone does not make an employee exempt. A title alone does not make an employee exempt.

Salary Test

In order for an employee to be exempt from the minimum wage and overtime requirements, with only minor exceptions relating to persons paid a fee, he or she must be paid on a *salary basis*.

DOL regulations at 29 CFR 541.602(a) state that a person is paid a salary if he or she receives at each pay period a set amount constituting all or part of the compensation, the amount of which is "not subject to reduction because of variations in the quality or quantity of the work performed."

The minimum salary amount is $455 per week. Generally, an employee "must receive his full salary for any week in which he performs any work without regard to the number of days or hours worked." However, the regulation recognizes "the general rule that an employee need not be paid for any workweek in which he performs no work."

Further guidance on the salary test is found in DOL's Field Operations Handbook, Section 22b01: "Extra compensation may by paid for OT to an exempt employee on any basis. The overtime payment need not be at time and one-half, but may be at straight time, or flat sum, or on any other basis." "Any other basis" would presumably include compensatory time.

Almost No Partial-Day Deductions from Salary Allowed Under DOL interpretations and the U.S. Supreme Court's decision in *Auer v. Robbins*, 519 U.S. 452 (1997), if an employer has a clear policy that creates a substantial likelihood that an exempt employee's salary will be docked under circumstances not allowed in 29 CFR 541.118, the salary test is not met, and the employee would be considered an hourly employee potentially entitled to back overtime pay. The Court felt that since salaried exempt employees often put in substantial overtime for no additional compensation, it is unfair to make them subject to monetary penalties for missing a nominal amount of work on isolated occasions, especially if, as is usually the case, the few hours missed are made up by extra hours within the same week.

Allowable Deductions There are seven exceptions to the *no pay-docking* rule:

1. Absence from work for one or more full days for personal reasons other than sickness or disability.
2. Absence from work for one or more full days due to sickness or disability if deductions made under a bona fide plan, policy, or practice of providing wage replacement benefits for these types of absences.

    Employers may require salaried exempt employees who miss partial days or partial weeks to apply paid leave time to such absences. In a letter ruling dated April 9, 1993 (BNA, WHM 99:8003), the DOL stated, "Where an employer has bona fide vacation and sick time benefits, it is permissible to substitute or reduce the accrued benefits for the time an employee is absent from work, even if it is less than a full day, without affecting the salary basis of payment, if by substituting or reducing such benefits, the employee receives in payment an amount equal to his or her guaranteed salary." DOL has affirmed this position in several letter rulings issued since then.

3. To offset any amounts received as payment for jury fees, witness fees, or military pay.

4. Penalties imposed in good faith for violating safety rules of *major significance*.

5. Unpaid disciplinary suspension of one or more full days imposed in good faith for violations of workplace conduct rules.

6. Proportionate part of an employee's full salary may be paid for time actually worked in the first and last weeks of employment.

7. Unpaid leave taken pursuant to the Family and Medical Leave Act.

Special Rules for Governmental Employers Special rules apply for governmental employers with personal leave and sick leave accrual policies.

Generally, due to principles of public accountability for tax money, governmental employers may dock salaried employees' pay for absences of less than a day without losing the salary basis for the exemption as long as the absences are due to personal or health-related reasons, assuming that (1) the employee is either out of paid leave or chooses not to use it, or (2) has been denied permission to use paid leave (29 CFR 541.710; DOL administrative letter rulings of January 9, 1987, and July 17, 1987).

Duties Tests

The DOL has set forth special tests for the executive, administrative, and professional exemption categories.

Primary Duty In each category, the employee's primary duty must be exempt in nature. *Primary duty* is defined in 29 CFR 541.700 as a duty in which the employee spends "more than 50 percent" of his or her work time, which is presumed to be the primary duty. However, the same regulation notes that in cases where the employee happens to spend 50 percent or less of the workweek in exempt duties, the exempt duties may still be the primary duties depending on the following criteria:

1. Relative importance of the managerial duties as compared with other types of duties

2. Amount of time spent performing exempt work

3. Employee's relative freedom from direct supervision

4. Relationship between the employee's salary and the wages paid to other employees for the kind of nonexempt work performed by the supervisor (or other type of exempt employee)

These criteria have been widely accepted by courts around the country. Some courts have related the second criterion to the frequency with which the employee exercises discretionary powers.

Executive Exemption

Effective August 23, 2004, DOL regulation 29 CFR 541.100, all parts of which must be satisfied, defines an executive exempt employee as any employee:

1. Who is compensated on a salary basis at a rate of not less than $455 per week (or $380 per week, if employed in American Samoa by employers other than the federal government), exclusive of board, lodging, or other facilities

2. Whose primary duty is management of the enterprise in which the employee is employed or of a customarily recognized department or subdivision thereof

3. Who customarily and regularly directs the work of two or more other employees

4. Who has the authority to hire or fire other employees or whose suggestions and recommendations as to the hiring, firing, advancement, promotion, or any other change of status of other employees are given particular weight

EXAMPLES: Examples include the president of the company or the head of a major division of an enterprise, a general manager with hiring and firing authority, and department heads who have hiring and firing authority.

Administrative Exemption

DOL regulation 29 CFR 541.200 defines an administrative exempt employee as one:

1. Who is compensated on a salary or fee basis at a rate of not less than $455 per week (or $380 per week, if employed in American Samoa by employers other than the federal government), exclusive of board, lodging, or other facilities

2. Whose primary duty is the performance of office or nonmanual work directly related to the management or general business operations of the employer or the employer's customers

3. Whose primary duty includes the exercise of discretion and independent judgment with respect to matters of significance

EXAMPLES: Examples include the vice president of operations, general manager, department heads, personnel director, payroll director, chief financial officer, comptroller, head buyer, and head dispatcher.

Professional Exemption

Under regulation 29 CFR 541.300, the Department of Labor distinguishes between two categories of exempt professional employees: *learned professionals* and *creative professionals*.

The exemption applies to any employee:

- Who is compensated on a salary or fee basis at a rate of not less than $455 per week (or $380 per week, if employed in American Samoa by employers other than the federal government), exclusive of board, lodging, or other facilities

- Whose primary duty is the performance of work:
  1. Requiring knowledge of an advanced type in a field of science or learning customarily acquired by a prolonged course of specialized intellectual instruction
  2. Requiring invention, imagination, originality, or talent in a recognized field of artistic or creative endeavor

Learned Professionals As 29 CFR 541.301 notes, the primary duty test for learned professionals includes three elements:

1. The employee must perform work requiring advanced knowledge.
2. The advanced knowledge must be in a field of science or learning.

3. The advanced knowledge must be customarily acquired by a prolonged course of specialized intellectual instruction.

Creative Professionals Regarding creative professionals, 29 CFR
541.302(a) notes that "to qualify for the creative professional exemption,
an employee's primary duty must be the performance of work requiring
invention, imagination, originality, or talent in a recognized field of artistic
or creative endeavor as opposed to routine mental, manual, mechanical,
or physical work. The exemption does not apply to work which can be
produced by a person with general manual or intellectual ability and
training."

> **EXAMPLES:** Examples include physicians, attorneys, CPAs, engineers,
> architects, scientists (chemists, physicists, astronomers, geologists, zoolo-
> gists, biologists, and so on), registered nurses, pharmacists, dentists, teach-
> ers, artists, writers, and other creative professionals.

Other Types of White-Collar Exemptions

*   *Outside Salespeople.* Outside salespeople fall into a special category of exempt employees who do not have to receive either a salary or
fee or minimum wage or overtime pay.

Many such employees receive only a commission, while others receive
that plus occasional bonuses, dividends, or overrides, depending on the
individual pay agreement in effect.

Under 29 CFR 541.500, an *outside sales employee* is someone who is
"customarily and regularly engaged" away from the employer's place of
business in making sales or obtaining orders for the sale of goods or services, and such person's pay is determined by a compensation agreement.

*   *Computer Professionals.* Another white-collar exemption that
does not necessarily require a salary to be valid is an exempt *computer professional*. The definitions found in 29 CFR 541.400 apply the exemption to
any computer employee paid on a salary or fee basis at least $455 per week,
exclusive of board, lodging, or other facilities, or else paid an hourly wage
of not less than $27.63 an hour. In addition, the exemptions apply only to
computer employees whose primary duty consists of:

*   The application of systems analysis techniques and procedures, including consulting with users, to determine hardware, software, or
system functional specifications

- The design, development, documentation, analysis, creation, testing, or modification of computer systems or programs, including prototypes, based on and related to user or system design specifications

- The design, documentation, testing, creation, or modification of computer programs related to machine operating systems

- A combination of the aforementioned duties, the performance of which requires the same level of skills

Wage and Hour Violations

Significant Financial Exposure

Under the FLSA, plaintiffs can recover double the amount of actual damages and attorneys' fees. If a willful violation of the FLSA is found, a three-year statute of limitations applies to all plaintiff claims. Since FLSA litigation often involves large groups of employees, liability exposure is often significant. And, most insurance policies exclude coverage for FLSA claims.

Common Errors

Wage and hour violations commonly resulting in litigation include:

- Misclassifying employees as exempt and failing to pay them overtime (the requirements for exempt status are set forth in the FLSA and often misapplied)

- Failing to pay nonexempt employees for overtime, including overtime not approved in advance

- Failing to pay for time worked off the clock (e.g., requiring or allowing employees to arrive early to perform necessary preparations for work or stay late to perform duties such as "closing up")

- Granting compensatory time off to nonexempt employees in lieu of overtime pay

- Making automatic wage deductions, such as from:
  - Exempt employees' salaries for partial-day absences
  - Nonexempt employees' pay for meal breaks when they do not clock in or out for those breaks

Minimizing Liability

Organizational Liability

To minimize liability exposure under wage and hour laws employers should:

- Perform an internal audit of the company's wage and hour practices with the assistance of legal counsel.
- Keep an accurate record of nonexempt employees' work time.
- Require nonexempt employees to clock in and clock out at the beginning and end of the workday and before and after unpaid lunch periods and pay for all hours worked.
- Prevent employees from taking breaks in work areas.
- Pay fixed, predetermined salaries to exempt employees without improper deductions.
- Train managers on the FLSA and state wage and hour laws.

Personal Liability

It is a well-settled American law that if you are acting within the scope of your employment, your employer is liable for your actions. Generally, you are not personally liable. That is not true with regard to the FLSA.

The definition of *employer* in FLSA section 3(d) includes "any person acting directly or indirectly in the interest of an employer" in relation to an employee. Under the FLSA, individuals such as corporate officers "acting in the interest of an employer" are individually liable for any violations of the requirements of FMLA. Be very cautious about changing an employee's time card or time sheet or denying the payment of overtime for any work "permitted or suffered" by nonexempt workers even if the time wasn't authorized.

CHAPTER 6

Employment Laws

Introduction

The subject of employment law deals with all aspects of the employer-employee relationship. It includes not only relationships between employers and current employees but also job applicants and former employees.

Employment relationships are complex and span a gamut of situations arising out of recruitment, hiring, benefits, taxation, management, discipline, and discharge. Other chapters of this book deal with many of these issues. This chapter is focused on employment laws dealing with discrimination.

Major federal antidiscrimination laws are enforced by the Equal Employment Opportunity Commission (EEOC). Most states have fair employment practice acts enforced by state fair employment practice agencies (FEPAs). State enforcement measures, by and large, follow those practiced by the EEOC.

Key Federal Employment Laws

Key federal employment laws establish a structure in which individuals with characteristics that place them into protected groups cannot be discriminated against in any aspect of the employment relationship because of being, or perceived as being, a member of the protected group.

Protected groups under federal law are those based on race/color, religion, national origin, sex, pregnancy, age (age 40 and over), disability, and genetic predisposition (effective November 2009) (see "Genetic Predispositions: Genetic Information Nondiscrimination Act" in this chapter). Various state and local laws create protection for groups based on sexual orientation; gender identification (e.g., transsexualism); marital status; genetic predisposition; age at levels below 40 years; and off-premise/off-duty use of lawful products, such as tobacco and alcohol. Various federal and state laws protect those in the military.

If someone is not a member of a protected group, he or she can be disadvantaged even if the employer's actions are clearly discriminatory. For example, sex discrimination under the 1964 Civil Rights Act is gender based—that is, it is based on someone being male or female. It has nothing to do with sexual orientation such as heterosexuality, homosexuality, or bisexuality. Therefore, an employer could refuse to hire an individual solely based on the employer's belief that the applicant is homosexual. That employer's action may be homophobic, biased, and discriminatory; however, one thing it is not is illegal under federal law as it exists at the time of this writing. However, many state laws and county and city ordinances create the protected class of *sexual orientation,* and if the same event took place in one of those jurisdictions, the action would be unlawful.

Some of the more significant federal employment laws are:

Federal Law	Employment-Related Prohibition	Employers Subject to the Law
Title VII, 1964 Civil Rights Act	Prevents discrimination against employees on the basis of race, color, religion, sex, or national origin	Employers having fifteen or more employees
Age Discrimination in Employment Act	Prevents discrimination on the basis of age against employees who are age 40 or older	Employers having twenty or more employees
Pregnancy Discrimination Act	Prevents discrimination on the basis of pregnancy or related conditions	Employers having fifteen or more employees

Federal Law	Employment-Related Prohibition	Employers Subject to the Law
Americans with Disabilities Act	Prevents discrimination on the basis of disability	Employers having fifteen or more employees
Immigration Reform and Control Act (claims of national origin discrimination handled by EEOC; general enforcement of this law is by Immigration, Customs Enforcement, Department of Homeland Security)	Prevents discrimination on the basis of national origin or citizenship	Employers having four or more employees
Occupational Safety and Health Act (enforced by the Occupational Safety and Health Administration)	Protects employees against unsafe working conditions and prohibits retaliation against workers who report unsafe working conditions or work practices	Employers having one or more employees
Equal Pay Act (enforced by the Wage and Hour Division, Department of Labor)	Provides that women must be paid no less than a man for equal work unless the difference in pay is caused by differences in seniority, merit, or some other factor that is not based on sex	Employers having one or more employees

Prohibited Acts

Under the employment structure created by the referenced laws, an employer cannot:

- Fail or refuse to hire because an individual is a member of a protected class.
- Discharge an individual because he or she is a member of protected class.
- Deprive an individual of employment opportunities because he or she is a member of a protected class. Employment opportunities

include not only hiring and firing issues but also working hours, working conditions, rates of pay, training, and advancement opportunities.

- Fail to provide training to an individual because he or she is a member of a protected class.

- Retaliate because an individual made a charge, testified, assisted, or participated in any manner in an action protected by this law (Title VII).

- Print or publish, or cause to be printed or published, an ad that may adversely affect a member of a protected class.

- Fail to post and keep posted in an obvious place a notice concerning the contents of this law. Most of the federal civil rights laws require that a poster notifying employees of their rights and responsibilities under that law be posted in a conspicuous place on a 24/7 basis, with various penalties attaching if you don't have them up. These posters can be ordered or downloaded without charge from the Department of Labor website: www.dol.gov.

The primary required posters are:

Poster	Who Must Post	Citations/Penalty	Other Information
Job Safety and Health Protection Occupational Safety and Health Administration. 29 USC 657(c), 29 CFR 1903.2	Private employers engaged in a business affecting commerce. Does not apply to federal, state, or political subdivisions of states.	Any covered employer failing to post the poster may be subject to citation and penalty.	Employers in states operating OSHA–approved state plans should obtain and post the state's equivalent poster.
Equal Employment Opportunity Is the Law Employment Standards Administration, Office of Federal Contract Compliance	Private employers with fifteen or more employees; entities holding federal contracts or subcontracts or federally assisted construction contracts of $10,000 or more;	Appropriate contract sanctions may be imposed for uncorrected violations.	Post copies of the poster in conspicuous places available to employees, applicants for employment, and representatives of labor organizations with which there is

Programs. Executive Order 11246, as amended; Section 503 of the Rehabilitation Act of 1973, as amended; 38 USC 4212 of the Vietnam Era Veterans' Readjustment Assistance Act of 1974, as amended; 41 CFR Chapter 60-l.42; 41 CFR 60-250.4(k); 41 CFR 60-74 1.5(a)4	financial institutions that are issuing and paying agents for U.S. savings bonds and savings notes; depositories of federal funds or entities having government bills of lading.		a collective bargaining agreement. Also, nonconstruction contractors or subcontractors with fifty or more employees and a contract of $50,000 or more [otherwise required by 41 CFR 60-2.1(a)] should develop an equal opportunity policy as part of an affirmative action plan and post the policy on company bulletin boards. 41 CFR 60-2.2 1 (a)(9).
Fair Labor Standards Act (FLSA) Minimum wage poster Employment Standards Administration, Wage and Hour Division	Every private, federal, state, and local government employer employing any employee subject to the Fair Labor Standards Act, 29 USC 211, 29 CFR 516.4 posting of notices.	No citations or penalties for failure to post.	Any employer of employees to whom Section 7 of the Fair Labor Standards Act does not apply may alter or modify the poster legibly to show that the overtime provisions do not apply.
Employee Right for Workers with Disabilities/ Special Minimum Wage Poster Employment Standards Administration, Wage and Hour Division. 29 CFR 525.14	Every employer having workers employed under special minimum wage certificates authorized by Section 14(c) of the Fair Labor Standards Act.	No citations or penalties for failure to post.	Where an employer finds it inappropriate to post such a notice, the employer may provide the poster directly to all employees subject to its terms.

Poster	Who Must Post	Citations/Penalty	Other Information
Your Rights Under the Family and Medical Leave Act Employment Standards Administration, Wage and Hour Division. 29 CFR 825.300, .402	Public agencies (including state, local, and federal employers); public and private elementary and secondary schools; as well as private sector employers who employ fifty or more employees in twenty or more workweeks and who are engaged in commerce or in any industry or activity affecting commerce, including joint employers and successors of covered employers.	Willful refusal to post may result in a civil money penalty by the Wage and Hour Division not to exceed $100 for each separate offense.	Where an employer's workforce is not proficient in English, the employer must provide the notice in the language the employee speaks. The poster must be posted prominently where it can be readily seen by employees and applicants for employment.
Uniformed Services Employment and Reemployment Rights Act (Notice for use by private and state employers) Veterans' Employment and Training Service 38 USC 4334, 20 CFR 1002	The full text of the notice must be provided by each employer to persons entitled to rights and benefits under USERRA.	No citations or penalties for failure to notify. An individual could ask DOL to investigate and seek compliance, or file a private enforcement action to require the employer to provide the notice to employees.	Employers may provide the notice by posting it where employee notices are customarily placed. However, employers are free to provide the notice in other ways that will minimize costs while ensuring that the full text of the notice is provided (e.g., by distributing the notice by direct handling, mailing, or via electronic mail).

Notice to All Employees Working on Federal or Federally Financed Construction Projects (Davis-Bacon Act) Employment Standards Administration, Wage and Hour Division. 29 CFR 5.5(a)(l)	Any contractor/ subcontractor engaged in contracts in excess of $2,000 for the actual construction, alteration/repair of a public building or public work or building or work financed in whole or in part from federal funds, federal guarantee, or federal pledge that is subject to the labor standards provisions of any of the acts listed in 29 CFR 5.1.	No citations or penalties for failure to post.	The contractor or subcontractor is required to insert in any subcontract the poster requirements contained in 29 CFR 5.5(a)(l). The poster must be posted at the site of work in a prominent and accessible place where it can easily be seen by workers.
Notice to Employees Working on Government Contracts (Service Contracts Act) Employment Standards Administration, Wage and Hour Division. 29 CFR 4.6(e), .184	Every contractor or subcontractor engaged in a contract with the United States or the District of Columbia in excess of $2,500 the principal purpose of which is to furnish services in the United States through the use of service employees.	No citations or penalties for failure to post.	Contractors and any subcontractors engaged in federal service contracts exceeding $2,500 shall notify each service employee or post the minimum monetary wage and any fringe benefits required to be paid pursuant to the contract.
Notice: Employee Polygraph Protection Act Employment Standards Administration, Wage and Hour Division. 29 CFR 801.6	Any employer engaged in or affecting commerce or in the production of goods for commerce. Does not apply to federal, state, and local governments, or to	The Secretary of Labor can bring court actions and assess civil penalties for failing to post.	The Act extends to all employees or prospective employees regardless of their citizenship status. Foreign corporations operating in the United States must

			comply or will receive penalties for failing to post. The poster must be displayed where employees and applicants for employment can readily observe it.
Notice Migrant and Seasonal Agricultural Worker Protection Act Employment Standards Administration, Wage and Hour Division. 29 CFR 500.75, .76	Agricultural employers, agricultural associations, and farm labor contractors.	A civil money penalty may be assessed.	Each employer covered by the Act who provides housing to migrant agricultural workers shall post in a conspicuous place throughout the occupancy period information on the terms and conditions of occupancy of such housing.

Enforcement Mechanisms

With the exception of the Equal Pay Act (EPA) and the Immigration Reform and Control Act, each of the antidiscrimination laws requires anyone (whether employee or applicant) who believes that he or she has been discriminated against to exhaust *administrative remedies* prior to bringing a lawsuit.

Many state FEPAs allow a claimant to proceed to court without exhausting administrative remedies; however, bringing the court action usually precludes the claimant from then also filing the claim with the FEPA. If the aggrieved party first exhausts his or her administrative remedies, they can then go to court if they are dissatisfied with the FEPA's findings.

Statutes of Limitation

Under the Title VII structure, in states without a FEPA, the aggrieved party must file his or her claim with the EEOC within 180 days of the last time the discriminatory action took place or 300 days in states with a FEPA.

These time limits do not apply to claims under the EPA, because under that Act, employees do not have to first file a charge with EEOC in order to have the right to go to court. However, since many EPA claims also raise Title VII sex discrimination issues, lawyers will advise the aggrieved party to file charges under both laws within the time limits indicated.

If (1) the EEOC finds there was no discriminatory action or (2) it does and chooses not to litigate on the claimant's behalf, it will issue a "Right to Sue Letter" to the claimant, and the aggrieved party will then have ninety days to file a court action.

Missing these deadlines will bar the claim forever.

Also see Chapter 7, "Hot-Button Issues," for a discussion of summary judgments based on the *Ellerth/Faragher Defense*.

Federal employees have a shorter time frame in which to act. Aggrieved individuals who believe they have been discriminated against must contact their agency EEO counselor prior to filing a formal complaint. The person must initiate counselor contact within forty-five days of the matter alleged to be discriminatory [29 CFR Section 1614.105(a)(1)]. This time limit can be extended if the aggrieved person shows: he or she was not notified of the time limits and was not otherwise aware of them; he or she did not and reasonably could not have known that the discriminatory matter occurred; or despite due diligence, he or she was prevented by circumstances beyond his or her control from contacting the counselor within the time limits [29 CFR Section 1614.105(a)(2)].

Complaint Procedures

Other than federal employees (see "Federal Employee Equal Employment Opportunity Complaint Processing Procedures" in this chapter), the EEOC process works as follows:

Complainant

Any individual who believes that his or her employment rights have been violated may file a charge of discrimination with the EEOC. In addition, in order to protect a claimant's identity, an individual, organization, or agency may file a charge on behalf of another person.

Filing the Charge

The aggrieved party fills out and submits an intake questionnaire by mail, in person, or online. Other correspondence can also constitute a charge under the statutes enforced by the EEOC if it contains the following information:

- The complaining party's name, address, and telephone number
- The name, address, and telephone number of the respondent employer, employment agency, or union that is alleged to have discriminated, and number of employees (or union members), if known
- A short description of the alleged violation (the event that caused the complaining party to believe that his or her rights were violated)
- The date(s) of the alleged violation(s)

Charges Also Covered by State or Local Law

Through the use of *work-sharing agreements*, the EEOC and FEPAs avoid duplication of effort while ensuring that a charging party's rights are protected under both federal and state law. Therefore:

- If a charge is filed with a FEPA and is also covered by federal law, the FEPA "dual files" the charge with the EEOC to protect federal rights. The charge usually will be retained by the FEPA for handling.
- If a charge is filed with the EEOC and also is covered by state or local law, the EEOC dual files the charge with the state or local FEPA, but ordinarily retains the charge for handling.

Claim Handling

The employer is notified within ten days that the charge has been filed. Then there are a number of ways a charge may be handled:

- If the facts of the initial charge strongly indicate that there has been a violation of law, the EEOC can make the investigation a priority. Where the initial evidence is weaker, the charge may be assigned for follow-up investigation to determine whether it is likely that a violation has occurred.

- The EEOC can seek to settle a charge at any stage of the investigation if the parties are interested in doing so. If settlement efforts are not successful, the investigation continues.

- In investigating a charge, the EEOC may make written requests for information; interview people; review documents; and, as needed, visit the facility where the alleged discrimination occurred. When the investigation is complete, the EEOC will discuss the evidence with the charging party or employer, as appropriate.

- The charge may be selected for the EEOC's mediation program if both parties express an interest in this option. Mediation is offered as an alternative to a lengthy investigation. Participation in the mediation program is confidential, voluntary, and requires consent from both the charging party and the employer. If mediation is unsuccessful, the charge is returned for investigation.

- A charge may be dismissed at any point if, in the agency's best judgment, further investigation will not establish a violation of the law.

When a charge is dismissed, a right to sue notice is issued giving the charging party ninety days in which to file a lawsuit on his or her own behalf.

If the evidence obtained in an investigation does not establish that discrimination occurred, this will be explained to the charging party and a right to sue letter issued.

If the evidence establishes that discrimination has occurred, the employer and the charging party will be informed of this situation in a letter of determination that explains the finding. The EEOC will then attempt conciliation with the employer to develop a remedy for the discrimination.

If the case is successfully conciliated, or if a case has earlier been successfully mediated or settled, neither the EEOC nor the charging party may go to court unless the conciliation, mediation, or settlement agreement is not honored.

If the EEOC is unable to successfully conciliate the case, the agency will decide whether to bring suit in federal court. If the EEOC decides not to sue, it will issue a right to sue notice closing the case and giving the charging party ninety days in which to file a lawsuit on his or her own behalf.

The Department of Justice handles Title VII and Americans with Disabilities Act (ADA) cases against state or local governments.

Federal Employee Equal Employment Opportunity Complaint-Processing Procedures

Equal Employment Opportunity Counselor Contact

Aggrieved persons must contact an agency EEO counselor prior to filing a formal complaint. As stated earlier, the person must initiate counselor contact within forty-five days of the matter alleged to be discriminatory.

EEO counselors provide information to the aggrieved individual concerning how the federal sector EEO process works, including time frames and appeal procedures, and attempts to informally resolve the matter.

At the initial counseling session, counselors must advise individuals in writing of their rights and responsibilities in the EEO process, including the right to request a hearing before an EEOC administrative judge or an immediate final decision from the agency following its investigation of the complaint.

Counseling must be completed within thirty days of the date the aggrieved person contacted the agency's EEO office to request counseling. If the matter is not resolved in that time period, the counselor must inform the individual in writing of the right to file a discrimination complaint. This notice ("Notice of Final Interview") must inform the individual that a complaint must be filed within fifteen days of receipt of the notice, identify the agency official with whom the complaint must be filed, and explain that it is the individual's duty to inform the agency if he or she is represented.

Alternative Dispute Resolution

Federal agencies are required to establish or make available an alternative dispute resolution (ADR) program for both the pre-complaint process and the formal complaint process.

At the initial counseling session, counselors must advise individuals that where an agency agrees to offer ADR in a particular case, the individual may choose between participation in the ADR program and EEO counseling.

If the matter is not resolved in the ADR process within ninety days of the date the individual contacted the agency's EEO office, a notice of final interview must be issued to the individual giving him or her the right to proceed with a formal complaint.

Complaints

A complaint must be filed with the agency that allegedly discriminated against the complainant within fifteen days of receipt of the notice of final interview.

The agency must acknowledge receipt of the complaint in writing and inform the complainant of the date on which the complaint was filed and of the address of the EEOC office where a request for a hearing should be sent. The complainant has the right to appeal the agency's final action or dismissal of a complaint. The agency must investigate the complaint within 180 days of the filing date.

Dismissals of Complaints Prior to a request for a hearing, in lieu of accepting a complaint for investigation an agency may dismiss an entire complaint for any of the following reasons:

- Failure to state a claim, or stating the same claim that is pending or has been decided by the agency or the EEOC
- Failure to comply with the time limits
- Filing of a complaint on a matter that has not been brought to the attention of an EEO counselor and that is not similar or related to the matters counseled
- Filing of a complaint that is the basis of a pending civil action or that was the basis of a civil action already decided by a court
- Where the complainant has already elected to pursue the matter through either the negotiated grievance procedure or in an appeal to the Merit Systems Protection Board
- Where the matter is moot or merely alleges a proposal to take a personnel action
- Where the complainant cannot be located

- Where the complainant fails to respond to a request to provide relevant information

- Where the complaint alleges dissatisfaction with the processing of a previously filed complaint

- Where the complaint is part of a clear pattern of misuse of the EEO process for a purpose other than the prevention and elimination of employment discrimination

Investigations Investigations are conducted by the respondent agency.

The investigation must be completed within 180 days from the filing of the complaint. A copy of the investigative file must be provided to the complainant, along with a notification that within 30 days of receipt of the file, the complainant has the right to request a hearing and a decision from an EEOC administrative judge or may request an immediate final decision from the agency.

Final Action by Agencies

When an EEOC administrative judge has issued a decision (either a dismissal, a summary judgment decision, or a decision following a hearing), the agency must take final action on the complaint by issuing a final order within forty days of receipt of the hearing file and the administrative judge's decision.

The final order must notify the complainant whether or not the agency will fully implement the decision of the administrative judge and must contain notice of the complainant's right to appeal to EEOC or to file a civil action.

A complainant may appeal an agency's final action or dismissal of a complaint within thirty days of receipt. Appeals must be filed with the EEOC's Office of Federal Operations (OFO).

Civil Actions

Prior to filing a civil action under Title VII of the Civil Rights Act of 1964 or the Rehabilitation Act of 1973, a federal sector complainant must first exhaust the administrative process set out at 29 CFR Part 1614.

The regulations provide that civil actions may be filed in an appropriate federal court:

- Within ninety days of receipt of the final action where no administrative appeal has been filed

- After 180 days from the date of filing a complaint if an administrative appeal has not been filed and final action has not been taken

- Within ninety days of receipt of the EEOC's final decision on an appeal

- After 180 days from the filing of an appeal with the EEOC if there has been no final decision by the EEOC

Under the Age Discrimination in Employment Act (ADEA), a complainant may proceed directly to federal court after giving the EEOC notice of intent to sue.

Under the Equal Pay Act, a complainant may file a civil action within two years (three years for willful violations), regardless of whether he or she has pursued an administrative complaint. Filing a civil action terminates the EEOC's processing of an appeal.

Proof of Discrimination

The burden of proof in showing that discrimination occurred begins with the plaintiff and the proof required depends on the type of discrimination being complained of. There are two primary forms of discrimination: *disparate treatment* and *disparate impact*.

Disparate Treatment

Employers may not treat applicants or employees differently because of their membership in a protected class. The fact that someone was treated differently from individuals not in the protected class by itself is not evidence of discrimination. The central issue is whether the employer's actions were motivated by discriminatory intent.

The McDonnell Douglas *Tripartite Burden-Shifting Analysis*

The basic evidentiary approach taken by the courts when dealing with disparate treatment cases was established by the Supreme Court in *McDonnell Douglas Corp. v. Green*, 411 U.S. 792 (1973). The Supreme Court has elaborated on and modified the "McDonnell Douglas Standard" many times since 1973.

The approach is a *burden-shifting* procedure that (1) begins with the plaintiff having to prove a prima facie ("on its face") case of discrimination, (2) then the defendant having to prove that it acted for a legitimate nondiscriminatory reason, and (3) the plaintiff then having to prove that the defendant's stated reason(s) is a pretext and that it actually acted with the intent to discriminate.

To rebut the inference of discrimination the employer must articulate, through admissible evidence, a legitimate, nondiscriminatory reason for its actions. The employer's burden is one of production, not persuasion. The ultimate burden of persuasion always remains with the plaintiff, as seen in *St. Mary's Honor Center v. Hicks*, 509 U.S. 502 (1993).

Plaintiff's Prima Facie Case   To establish a prima facie case of discrimination, the plaintiff must show he or she was:

- A member of a protected class
- Qualified for the position sought
- Rejected for the position
- Treated less favorably than a similarly situated candidate outside his or her protected class

A common variation would be where the plaintiff shows the following:

- He or she is a member of a protected class.
- His or her actions were no different from similarly situated employees' not in the protected class.
- He or she was treated less favorably than similarly situated employees not in the protected class.

As stated previously, if the plaintiff makes a prima facie showing of discrimination, the burden shifts to the defendant to articulate a legitimate, nondiscriminatory reason for its decision. If the employer does so, it rebuts the presumption of discrimination, and the burden shifts back to the employee to show that the proffered reason was pretextual.

Example of Tripartite Burden-Shifting Analysis

Alana, Betsy, and Maya, who are white women, and Bertha, who is an African-American woman, all work for the RachLyd Manufacturing Company. They are all accounting clerks. The ladies are direct reports of Charlene, the controller, who is a white woman.

Charlene does not like Bertha and decides to "get her." She notices that Bertha consistently comes in several minutes late for work. Although each incident standing alone is minor, since there is a consistent pattern of tardiness, Charlene decides to confront Bertha.

Bertha asks why she is being treated differently from Alana, Betsy, and Maya. Charlene asks her what she means. Bertha replies that since all of the women in question carpool together and all arrive at work at the same time—which is always late—why is she the only one being disciplined?

Bertha can establish a prima facie case by showing that she is a member of a protected class (race), that her actions were no different from those not in the protected group, and that she is being treated less favorably than the women not in the protected group.

Charlene responds, "Oh, I know you all carpool together and arrive at the same time; however, your actions are different once you all clock in. The other women immediately go to their workstations and begin to work. You, Bertha, consistently clock in and then walk around gossiping with your friends for five or ten minutes." Charlene has articulated a business-related nondiscriminatory reason for her actions.

Bertha would now have to prove that Charlene's statements are really a pretext for treating African Americans less favorably than whites.

Employers must be very careful when they treat similarly situated employees differently because discriminatory intent can be proved by either direct or circumstantial evidence.

Direct Evidence

In attempting to establish that membership in the protected class was a motivating factor in the adverse job action, the plaintiff may offer any one or a combination of the following:

1. Defendant admits that it was motivated by discriminatory intent. (Obviously, this type of evidence is generally not available since few, if any, employers will openly admit that they discriminate.)

2. Defendant acted pursuant to a policy that is discriminatory on its face—for example, a dress designer only hires women to model its clothes. Facially discriminatory policies *are* permissible if gender, national origin, or religion is a bona fide occupational qualification (BFOQ) for the position in question. Race or color cannot be a BFOQ. (See "Legal Discrimination—Bona Fide Occupational Qualifications" in this chapter.)

Indirect Evidence

The plaintiff could try to prove disparate treatment by offering any or all of the following three types of circumstantial evidence:

1. Showing "suspicious timing, ambiguous statements oral or written, behavior toward or comments directed at other employees in the protected group, and other bits and pieces from which an inference of discriminatory intent might be drawn" (*Troupe v. May Department Stores*, 20 F.3d 734, 736 [7th Circuit, 1994])

2. Evidence that other, similarly situated employees not in the protected class received systematically better treatment (*Marshall v. American Hospital Assoc.*, 157 F.3d 520 [7th Circuit, 1998])

3. Evidence that the plaintiff was qualified for the job, a person not in the protected class got the job, and the employer's stated reason for its decision is unworthy of belief (The *McDonnell Douglas* analysis)

Disparate Impact

An employer cannot use an employment practice that is neutral on its face but that has an unjustified adverse impact on members of a protected class. The practice doesn't have to negatively impact every member of the protected class(es), just most of them.

Intent is not a necessary element in proving a disparate impact case, and compensatory and punitive damages, in addition to a trial by jury, are not available with this type of claim.

The Supreme Court first described the disparate impact theory in *Griggs v. Duke Power Co.*, 401 U.S. 424, 431–2 (1971). The Court said that Title VII "proscribes not only overt discrimination but also practices that are fair in form, but discriminatory in operation. The touchstone is business necessity. . . . [G]ood intent or absence of discriminatory intent does not redeem employment procedures or testing mechanisms that operate as 'built-in headwinds' for minority groups and are unrelated to measuring job capability." In that case, Duke Power required each employee to have a high school diploma although having a high school diploma did not have any direct relationship to someone's being capable of performing the jobs in question. That policy disproportionately impacted African Americans who had been denied educational opportunities in the South for many years. The policy measured people in the abstract and not by their ability to perform the jobs in question.

The types of practices where disparate impact challenges arise include pre-employment tests; height and weight requirements; educational requirements; no facial hair policies (may conflict with religious observances or African-American men with ingrown hairs that make shaving painful); subjective procedures, such as interviews; and referrals from the current workforce if the current workforce is predominantly of one race, gender, and so forth.

Allocation of Proof in Disparate Impact Cases

Plaintiff's Prima Facie Case To make out a prima facie case of disparate impact the plaintiff must prove, generally through statistical comparisons, that the challenged practice or selection device has a substantial adverse impact on a protected group. See 42 USC Section 2000e-2(k)(1)(A)(i).

Several methods of proving disparate impact are available to the plaintiff, including:

• *Scored Tests*—The EEOC's *Uniform Guidelines on Employee Selection Criteria* states that there is an adverse impact if members of a protected class are selected at rates less than four-fifths (80 percent) of that of another group where applicants take a written test—for example, if 50 percent of white applicants receive a passing score on a test, but only 30 percent of African-Americans pass, the relevant ratio would be 30/50, or 60 percent, which would violate the 80 percent rule; 29 CFR Sections 1607.4 (D) and 1607.16 (R). The 80 percent rule is not law—it is merely a rule of thumb.

An often used measurement is where courts find an adverse impact if the difference between the number of members of the protected class selected and the number that would be anticipated in a random selection system is more than two or three standard deviations.

If the plaintiff is successful in making out a prima facie case, then the defendant can rebut by demonstrating that the scored test is job related and consistent with business necessity by showing that the test is validated, although a formal validation study is not necessarily required; 29 CFR Section 1607.5(B).

• *Nonstatistical Criteria*—The statistical imbalances brought up in the *Uniform Guidelines* are also applicable to other measures of employee qualifications (e.g., educational, experience, and licensing requirements as in the *Griggs v. Duke Power* case). The employer can rebut the prima facie case by showing business relatedness or necessity.

• *Subjective Criteria*—The use of subjective decision making is subject to challenge under a disparate impact theory, particularly when used to make employment decisions regarding blue-collar or more entry-level types of jobs. Company procedures that allow supervisors to make hiring and disciplinary decisions simply based on their "gut feelings" invite litigation.

Business Necessity If the plaintiff establishes disparate impact, the employer must prove that the challenged practice is "job-related for the position in question and consistent with business necessity"; 42 USC Section 2000e-2(k)(1)(A)(i).

Alternative Practice with Lesser Impact The plaintiff may still prevail even if the employer proves business necessity by showing that the employer has refused to adopt an alternative employment practice that would satisfy the employer's legitimate interests without having a disparate impact on a protected class; 42 USC Section 2000e-2(k)(1)(A)(ii).

Legal Discrimination—Bona Fide Occupational Qualifications

Must a company hire someone who is blind to drive a forklift or risk being charged with violating the Americans with Disabilities Act? Of course not.

The ability to see at some minimum level is a bona fide occupational qualification. That type of requirement is the rationale behind allowing organizations to discriminate on the basis of a BFOQ.

By definition, a BFOQ is an employment practice that would constitute discrimination as to certain individuals of a particular religion, gender, national origin, or age range (but not race or color) when the otherwise illegal discrimination is a qualification reasonably necessary for the normal performance of the duties of that particular occupation.

Under Title VII, religious organizations and schools are allowed to hire only members of that religion even if religion is not a bona fide occupational qualification for that position, such as a requirement that all teachers in a parochial school be Catholic, even though they teach subjects that do not require a Catholic background.

A BFOQ cannot be based on the preferences of customers, coworkers, or the organization itself, unless there is something like a legitimate desire for personal privacy on the part of the customer, client, or coworker—for example, being touched by a member of the opposite sex (patients in a hospital, people getting a massage, and so on) or performing bodily functions in proximity to members of the opposite gender (restrooms, locker rooms, and so on). The airlines once argued that they only wanted to hire flight attendants who were female because that was what their customers preferred. That argument went nowhere. See *Diaz v. Pan Am. World Airways, Inc.*, 442 F.2d 385, 387 (5th Circuit, 1971).

Arrest and Conviction Records

The EEOC takes the position that "since the use of arrest records as an absolute bar to employment has a disparate impact on some protected groups, such records alone cannot be used to routinely exclude persons from employment. However, conduct that indicates unsuitability for a particular position is a basis for exclusion. Where it appears that the applicant or employee engaged in the conduct for which he was arrested and that the conduct is job-related and relatively recent, exclusion is justified." See *Policy Guidance on the Consideration of Arrest Records in Employment Decisions* under Title VII of the Civil Rights Act of 1964, as amended, 42 USC Section 2000e et seq. (1982).

The EEOC's position is based on both case law and FBI statistics showing that African Americans are arrested at a much higher rate than whites and, therefore, using an arrest record alone to make a hiring decision has a disparate impact based on race.

The commission takes a different view when it comes to convictions, however. The EEOC's *Policy Guidance* states, "Conviction records constitute reliable evidence that a person engaged in the conduct alleged since the criminal justice system requires the highest degree of proof ('beyond a reasonable doubt') for a conviction. In contrast, arrests alone are not reliable evidence that a person has actually committed a crime."

The bottom line is that a blanket policy excluding any applicant who has been arrested for any reason whatsoever will be viewed as discriminatory by the EEOC. However, not hiring when you can show relevance of a recent arrest to the job in question would pass the test of acting for a nondiscriminatory, business-related reason.

A number of states forbid using arrest records in the hiring process, and some prohibit using conviction records unless the crime in question bears a reasonable relationship to the job in question.

Title VII Remedies

According to Title VII, 1964 Civil Rights Act, Section 706(g):

> If the Court finds that the organization has intentionally engaged in or is intentionally engaging in an unlawful employment practice charged in the complaint, the Court may prevent the organization from engaging in such unlawful employment practice and order such affirmative action as may be appropriate, which may include, but is not limited to, reinstatement or hiring of employees, with or without back pay, or any other equitable relief the Court deems appropriate.

What this section of the law did not allow for were compensatory or punitive damages or trial by jury. However, the Civil Rights Act of 1991 (CRA91) does permit these types of damages and trial by jury in cases where the plaintiff can prove unlawful intentional discrimination. These damages and trial by jury are only available in cases of disparate treatment discrimination, where a showing of intent is required. They are not allowed in cases of disparate impact discrimination where intent to discriminate is not an element of the action. (See "Disparate Treatment" and "Disparate Impact" in this chapter.)

Reinstatement

For reinstatement, an employee is placed back into the same or an equivalent position he or she had prior to the discriminatory act. Reinstatement may also include retroactive seniority.

Back Pay

Back pay consists of wages, salary, and fringe benefits the employee would have earned during the period of discrimination from the date of termination (or failure to promote) to the date of trial. Back pay is the most common form of relief.

Interest on the back pay can also be awarded.

Compensatory Damages

Compensatory damages are allowed for the loss of future earning capacity, emotional distress, pain and suffering, inconvenience, mental anguish, and loss of enjoyment of life.

Caps are placed on compensatory damages according to the size of the employer. The limits on damages are as follows:

Up to 100 employees:	$50,000
101–200 employees:	$100,000
201–500 employees:	$200,000
500+ employees:	$300,000

These caps apply only to individuals. In a class action situation, each plaintiff can be awarded the maximum amount specified for the size of the company.

Punitive Damages

Punitive damages are meant to punish the wrongdoer and to deter others from engaging in the same unlawful behavior.

Punitive damages are limited to cases where the "employer has engaged in intentional discrimination and has done so with malice or reckless indifference to the federally protected rights of an aggrieved individual." See *Kolstad v. American Dental Association*, 527 U.S. 526 (1999). These damages are capped according to the size of the employer and are the same as those for compensatory damages.

Front Pay

Front pay is an equitable remedy to make the victim of discrimination "whole." *Make whole relief* includes all actions necessary to place the individual as near as possible in the situation he or she would have occupied if the wrong had not been committed. See *Albemarle Paper Co. v. Moody*, 422 U.S. 405 (1975).

The remedy of front pay compensates a victim in situations where reinstatement or nondiscriminatory placement would be an available remedy, but is denied for reasons peculiar to the individual claim. The compensation of front pay makes the victim of discrimination whole generally until such nondiscriminatory placement can be accomplished.

> **EXAMPLE:** A sixty-eight-year-old man is fired based on his age. At the time of the termination, he was making $80,000 per year. It takes two years for his litigation to end. During the two years, he diligently seeks a job with equal compensation but is only able to secure a $60,000-per-year position. If reinstatement to his former job is impracticable because he no longer has the skill set required for the job or there has been significant ill will between the victim and the former employer, then front pay would be the $20,000-a-year difference in compensation until he is able to find another job at the $80,000 level. If he is unsuccessful in that effort, then front pay would continue through the remainder of his working life. (Experts would testify regarding what that remaining term would be.)

There is a distinction between front pay, which is an equitable remedy, and the loss of future earning capacity, which is in the nature of compensatory damages.

Attorney's Fees

Attorney's fees can be awarded to a prevailing plaintiff.

Injunction

An injunction is a court-ordered action to be taken or to be refrained from.

Federally Protected Classes

Race and Color

It is a violation of Title VII to discriminate on the basis of an immutable characteristic associated with race, such as skin color, hair texture, or certain facial features (such as full lips or high cheekbones), even though not all members of the race share the same characteristic.

All races are protected, because it is just as easy to discriminate against someone who is white as someone of color.

Title VII also prohibits employment decisions based on stereotypes and assumptions about abilities, traits, or the performance of individuals of certain racial groups.

In addition, equal employment opportunity cannot be denied because of marriage to or association with an individual of a different race, membership in or association with ethnic-based organizations or groups, or attendance or participation in schools or places of worship generally associated with certain minority groups.

Furthermore, Title VII prohibits discrimination on the basis of a condition that predominantly affects one race unless the practice is job related and consistent with business necessity—for example, because sickle cell anemia predominantly occurs in African Americans, a policy that excludes individuals with sickle cell anemia must be job related and consistent with business necessity. This prohibition against the use of genetic predisposition will almost certainly be impacted by the Genetic Information Nondiscrimination Act (GINA). See "Genetic Predisposition: Genetic Information Nondiscrimination Act" in this chapter.

Religion

Title VII prohibits discrimination based on an employee's religious beliefs. This discrimination applies not only to hiring and firing but to all terms, conditions, and privileges of employment.

Under Title VII, the term *religion* is broadly defined to include "all aspects such as religious observance and practice, as well as belief." See 42 USC Section 2000z(j). The EEOC defines religious practice to include "moral or ethical beliefs as to what is right and wrong which are sincerely held with the strength of traditional religious views. . . . The fact that no religious group establishes such beliefs or the fact that the religious group to which the individual professes to belong may not set the beliefs will not determine whether the belief is a religious belief of the employee. . . ." (See *Guidelines on Discrimination Because of Religion,* 29 CFR Section 1605.1.) Title VII protects individual religious practices even though the practice is not mandated by the religious institution to which the employee belongs.

According to information published by the EEOC, under Title VII:

- Employers may not treat employees or applicants more or less favorably because of their religious beliefs or practices except to the extent a religious accommodation is warranted. For example, an employer may not refuse to hire individuals of a certain religion, may not impose stricter promotion requirements for persons of a certain religion, and may not impose more or different work requirements on an employee because of that employee's religious beliefs or practices.

- Employees cannot be forced to participate—or not participate—in a religious activity as a condition of employment.

- Employers must reasonably accommodate employees' sincerely held religious practices unless doing so would impose an undue hardship on the employer. A reasonable religious accommodation is any adjustment to the work environment that will allow the employee to practice his or her religion. An employer might accommodate an employee's religious beliefs or practices by allowing flexible scheduling, voluntary substitutions or swaps, job reassignments and lateral transfers, modification of grooming requirements, and other workplace practices, policies, or procedures.

- An employer is not required to accommodate an employee's religious beliefs and practices if doing so would impose an undue hardship on the employer's legitimate business interests. An employer can show undue hardship if accommodating an employee's religious practices requires more than ordinary administrative costs, diminishes efficiency in other jobs, infringes on other employees' job rights or benefits, impairs workplace safety, causes coworkers to carry the accommodated employee's share of potentially hazardous or burdensome work, or if the proposed accommodation conflicts with another law or regulation.

- Employers must permit employees to engage in religious expression unless the religious expression would impose an undue hardship on the employer. Generally, an employer may not place more restrictions on religious expression than on other forms of expression that have a comparable effect on workplace efficiency.

- Employers must take steps to prevent religious harassment of their employees. An employer can reduce the chance that employees will engage in unlawful religious harassment by implementing an antiharassment policy and having an effective procedure for reporting, investigating, and correcting harassing conduct.

It is also unlawful to retaliate against an individual for opposing employment practices that discriminate based on religion or for filing a discrimination charge, testifying, or participating in any way in an investigation, proceeding, or litigation under Title VII.

National Origin

The EEOC defines national origin discrimination broadly as including, but not being limited to, the denial of equal employment opportunity because of the place of origin of an individual, or his or her ancestors, or because an individual has the physical, cultural, or linguistic characteristics of a national origin group.

Examined will be charges alleging that individuals have been denied equal employment opportunity for reasons that are grounded in national origin considerations, such as:

- Marriage to or association with persons of a national origin group.
- Membership in, or association with, an organization identified with or seeking to promote the interests of national origin groups.
- Attendance or participation in schools, churches, temples, or mosques generally used by persons of a national origin group.
- An individual's name or spouse's name being associated with a national origin group. Employers may be liable not only for harassment by supervisors but also by coworkers or by nonemployees under their control.

National Security Exception

It is not an unlawful employment practice to deny employment opportunities to any individual who does not fulfill the national security requirements stated in Section 703(g) of Title VII:

Notwithstanding any other provision of this subchapter, it shall not be an unlawful employment practice for an employer to fail or refuse to hire and employ any individual for any position, for an employer to discharge any individual from any position, or for an employment agency to fail or refuse to refer any individual for employment in any position, or for a labor organization to fail or refuse to refer any individual for employment in any position, if:

(1) the occupancy of such position, or access to the premises in or upon which any part of the duties of such position is performed or is to be performed, is subject to any requirement imposed in the interest of the national security of the United States under any security program in effect pursuant to or administered under any statute of the United States or any Executive order of the President; and

(2) such individual has not fulfilled or has ceased to fulfill that requirement.

National Origin Harassment

National origin harassment violates Title VII when it is so severe or pervasive that the individual being harassed reasonably finds the work environment to be hostile or abusive. See *Meritor Sav. Bank v. Vinson*, 477 U.S. 57 (1986). Harassment based on national origin can take many different forms, including ethnic slurs, workplace graffiti, or other offensive conduct directed toward an individual's birthplace, ethnicity, culture, or foreign accent. A hostile environment may be created by the actions of supervisors, coworkers, or even nonemployees, such as customers or business partners. Relevant factors in evaluating whether national origin harassment rises to the level of creating a hostile work environment may include any of the following:

- Whether the conduct was physically threatening or intimidating
- How frequently the conduct was repeated
- Whether the conduct was hostile and/or patently offensive
- The context in which the harassment occurred
- Whether management responded appropriately when it learned of the harassment

Language Issues

Accent and English Fluency Linguistic characteristics are a component of national origin and, therefore, an employer cannot take an adverse action against a worker solely based on the employee's accent.

An employment decision based on foreign accent does not violate Title VII if an individual's accent materially interferes with his or her ability to perform job duties. The question an employer must ask itself is, "Is the individual's foreign accent merely discernible or one that materially interferes with the communication skills necessary to perform job duties?"

As a general rule, a fluency requirement is permissible if it is actually required for the effective performance of the position for which it is imposed. Because the degree of fluency that may be required varies from one position to the next, employers should avoid fluency requirements that apply uniformly to a broad range of dissimilar positions.

Speak English–Only Rules Some employers have instituted workplace policies restricting communication in languages other than English, often called *English-only rules.*

Title VII permits employers to adopt English-only rules when they are adopted for legitimate, work-related business reasons, such as safety or efficiency, and not with the intent to discriminate against any protected group. Likewise, a policy that prohibits some but not all of the foreign languages spoken in a workplace, such as a no-Arabic rule, would be unlawful.

Some justifications for English-only rules are:

- Evidence of safety justifications for the rule
- Evidence of other business justifications for the rule (e.g., effective supervision or communication with customers)
- Likely effectiveness of the rule in carrying out business objectives
- English proficiency of workers affected by the rule

Before adopting an English-only rule you, the employer, should consider whether there are any alternatives to an English-only rule that would be equally effective in promoting safety or efficiency and whether these policies should restrict the employee only when the business purpose is impacted—for example, the rule probably should not apply during on-premise but off-duty breaks.

An employer should ensure that affected employees are notified about an English-only rule and the consequences for its violation.

Sex

As used in Title VII, the term *sex* is gender based. It does not refer to sexual orientation—for example, heterosexuality, homosexuality, or bisexuality—or to gender identity. See "Gender Identity" in this chapter.

Gender-Based Discrimination

Fundamentally, a policy will be deemed to be discriminatory if it disadvantages women or men because of gender. Asking a female applicant about children but not male applicants and measuring job capabilities based on stereotypes—for example, men can't assemble intricate devices or women aren't aggressive enough to be good salespeople—are examples of measuring people in the abstract rather than assessing their abilities to perform the essential functions of the job in question.

Disadvantaging both genders equally may be poor management but not sex discrimination. For example, if a supervisor promotes his or her paramour over more qualified applicants, he or she is disadvantaging both sexes equally. Most courts (with the exception of California's) would not find this treatment of all other employees to be sex discrimination.

The refusal to hire an individual because of the preferences of coworkers, the employer, clients, or customers (except where customers or clients' desire for personal privacy creates a BFOQ) would be sex discrimination.

Where it is necessary for the purpose of authenticity or genuineness, the EEOC will consider sex to be a bona fide occupational qualification—for example, an actor or actress.

The BFOQ defense will not stand up where you are trying to protect women from injury but not men. The well-known case of *United Auto Workers v. Johnson Controls*, 499 U.S. 187 (1991) dealt with this issue. Some men working in the production of lead acid batteries suffered damage to their reproductive organs due to lead exposure. The company then formulated a fetal protection policy that prohibited women capable of bearing children from working in jobs involving lead exposure, but allowing fertile men to work in such jobs. The employer attempted to show that the policy was justified by a bona fide occupational qualification. The Supreme Court held that the employer could not defend the policy as a BFOQ, because the BFOQ defense is available only with respect to qualifications that affect an employee's ability to do the job, and the job qualification at issue must relate to the essence or central mission of the employer's business. The fact that the employer feared prenatal injury, no matter how sincere, did not prove that substantially all of its fertile women employees were incapable of doing the jobs in question, and therefore the BFOQ defense failed.

Sexual harassment is a form of sex discrimination. See Chapter 7, "Hot-Button Issues."

Pregnancy

The Pregnancy Discrimination Act (PDA) forbids treating a pregnant worker or job applicant less favorably than nonpregnant employees or applicants. The Supreme Court has stated that the PDA does not prohibit employment practices favoring pregnant employees, but rather sets a floor beneath which pregnancy disability benefits cannot drop. See *California Fed. Savings & Loan Assn. v. Guerra*, 479 U.S. 272 (1987).

Basically, you can treat a pregnant person better than other individuals with short-term disabilities (both men and women, not just men)—you just can't treat them worse.

It is a prima facie violation of Title VII to have a written or unwritten employment policy or practice that excludes from employment applicants or employees because of pregnancy, childbirth, or related medical conditions.

Disabilities caused or contributed to by pregnancy, childbirth, or related medical conditions for all job-related purposes must be treated the same as disabilities caused or contributed to by other medical conditions under any health or disability insurance or sick leave plan available in connection with employment.

Written or unwritten employment policies and practices involving matters such as the commencement and duration of leave, the availability of extensions, the accrual of seniority and other benefits and privileges, reinstatement, and payment under any health or disability insurance or sick leave plan, formal or informal, have to be applied to disability due to pregnancy, childbirth, or related medical conditions on the same terms and conditions as they are applied to other disabilities.

The EEOC's position is that health insurance benefits for abortion except where the life of the mother would be endangered if the fetus were carried to term or where medical complications have arisen from an abortion are not required to be paid by an employer; however, nothing precludes an employer from providing abortion benefits or otherwise affects bargaining agreements in regard to abortion.

Equal Pay Act

The Equal Pay Act states that an employer cannot discriminate, within any establishment in which it employs workers, between employees on the basis of sex by paying wages at a rate less than the rate at which the employer pays wages to employees of the opposite sex in that workplace for equal work on jobs that require equal skill, effort, and responsibility, and that are performed under similar working conditions except where such payment is made pursuant to (1) a seniority system, (2) a merit system, (3) a system that measures earnings by quantity or quality of production, or (4) a differential based on any factor other than sex.

A woman pursuing a claim under the EPA must have an actual male comparator, not a hypothetical or composite male.

Skill—Measured by factors such as the experience, ability, education, and training required to perform the job. The key issue is what skills are required for the job, not what skills the individual employees may have.

Effort—The amount of physical or mental exertion needed to perform the job.

Responsibility—The degree of accountability required in performing the job.

Working Conditions—This encompasses two factors: (1) physical surroundings like temperature, fumes, and ventilation; and (2) hazards.

Establishment—The prohibition against compensation discrimination under the EPA applies only to jobs within any establishment.

An employer who is paying a wage rate differential in violation of the EPA cannot reduce the wage rate of any employee in order to comply with the provisions of the law.

The EPA applies to all employers, regardless of the number of employees who engage in interstate commerce (basically all employees). Aggrieved individuals can file claims under Title VII or the EPA.

Some plaintiffs choose to file under the EPA because:

- The EPA covers more employers than Title VII does. Title VII covers employers with fifteen or more workers, while the EPA applies to all employers.

- Aggrieved parties can file a lawsuit under the EPA without first filing a complaint with the EEOC and receiving a right to sue letter. See "Enforcement Mechanisms" in this chapter.

- The EPA has a longer statute of limitations than Title VII. EPA wage discrimination claims must be brought within two years of the first act of discrimination; however, the statute of limitations is extended to three years if the employer's EPA violation is willful or intentional.

- Under the EPA, the plaintiff can collect liquidated damages. Double back pay can be awarded as liquidated damages unless the employer can show that the wage discrimination was in good faith. However, under the EPA, the claimant cannot collect punitive damages such as pain and suffering. Also, Title VII does not require that the claimant's job be substantially equal to that of a higher-paid person of the opposite sex or require the claimant to work in the same establishment.

It is a common practice for people to file claims under both the EPA and Title VII in order to preserve their sex discrimination claims under both laws.

The EPA does not establish a system of *comparable worth* because the Act specifically applies to *equal work*. See *EEOC v. Madison Community Unit School District* No. 12, 818 F.2d 577 (7th Circuit, 1987). Therefore, courts generally compare the wages of men and women performing the same jobs for the same company when considering a complaint brought under the EPA. The jobs do not have to be identical, but they must just be substantially equal. Job content (what duties are actually being performed), not job title, determines whether the jobs are substantially equal.

To make a discrimination claim under the Equal Pay Act, an employee (male or female) must show that (1) in the same establishment (2) the employer pays different wages to employees of the opposite sex (3) who perform equal work on jobs requiring equal skill, effort, and responsibility, and (4) the jobs are performed under similar working conditions. If there are no employees of the opposite sex currently performing the same job as the worker who has filed a claim, he or she can point to pay received by his or her immediate predecessors or successors in the position.

EPA claims are hard to prove since employers can defeat the claims by showing that the pay disparities were based on factors other than gender, such as education, experience, responsibilities, quality, throughput rates, and error rates.

Age Discrimination

The Age Discrimination in Employment Act of 1967 protects applicants and employees who are age 40 or older from employment discrimination based on age. Under the ADEA, it is unlawful to discriminate against a person because of his or her age with respect to any term, condition, or privilege of employment, including hiring, firing, promotion, layoff, compensation, benefits, job assignments, and training, or to retaliate against an individual for opposing employment practices that discriminate based on age or for filing an age discrimination charge, testifying, or participating in any way in an investigation, proceeding, or litigation under the ADEA.

The ADEA applies to employers with twenty or more employees, including state and local governments. It also applies to employment agencies and labor organizations, as well as to the federal government.

The ADEA is somewhat unusual in that claims of discrimination often state that the aggrieved worker was replaced by someone within the same protected group—for example, over age 40. As a general rule, in order to prevail, the claimant must show that he or she was replaced by someone who is seven or more years younger. See *Grosjean v. First Energy Corp.*, 349 F.3d 332 (2003).

Discrimination in favor of older workers is not prohibited by the ADEA. See *General Dynamics Land Sys., Inc. v. Cline*, 540 U.S. 581 (2004). In the *General Dynamics* case, a collective bargaining agreement provided full health benefits only to employees who were age 50 or older on the day the agreement was adopted. Employees age 40 to 49 filed an ADEA action, claiming unlawful discrimination against them on the basis of age. On appeal from the Sixth Circuit, the Supreme Court overturned the Sixth Circuit's holding that discrimination in favor of older workers was prohibited by the ADEA, stating that the ADEA's text, structure, purpose, history, and relationship to other federal statutes indicate that the ADEA does not stop an employer from favoring an older employee over a younger one. The Court stated that the ADEA's prohibitions against discrimination cover employment actions and policies that help younger workers by hurting older workers.

Some state age discrimination laws have lower age thresholds than the federal statute. For example, age protection starts at age 18 in several states. Therefore, in a situation where a younger worker is passed over for a promotion simply because of his or her age, the aggrieved employee would have a viable claim under state law, but not the ADEA.

Apprenticeship Programs

It is generally unlawful for apprenticeship programs, including joint labor-management apprenticeship programs, to discriminate on the basis of an individual's age.

Job Notices and Advertisements

The ADEA generally makes it unlawful to include age preferences, limitations, or specifications in job notices or advertisements.

You, the employer, should be very careful in publishing job advertisements that directly mention age or age ranges. Have a legitimate, business-related reason (BFOQ) for including such language, such as "must be of legal age to serve liquor," or leave these references out altogether. When help-wanted notices or advertisements contain terms or phrases such as "age 25 to 35," "young," "college student," "recent college graduate," "boy," "girl," or others of a similar nature, such terms or phrases deter older persons from applying and are a violation of the ADEA unless one of the business necessity exceptions applies. Similarly, phrases such as "age 40 to 50," "age over 65," "retired person," or "supplement your pension" discriminate against others within the protected group and, therefore, are prohibited unless one of the exceptions applies.

The use of the phrase "state age" in help-wanted notices or advertisements is not, in itself, a violation of the ADEA; however, because the request may tend to deter older applicants or otherwise indicate discrimination based on age, employment notices or advertisements that include the phrase "state age," or any similar term, raise a bright red flag and will be closely scrutinized by the EEOC.

Benefits

The Older Workers Benefit Protection Act of 1990 (OWBPA) amended the ADEA to specifically prohibit employers from denying benefits to older employees.

Congress recognized that the cost of providing health benefits to older workers is greater than the cost of providing those same benefits to younger workers. Those greater costs would create a disincentive to hire older workers. Therefore, the OWBPA allows an employer to reduce benefits based on age as long as the cost of providing the reduced benefits to older workers is the same as the cost of providing benefits to younger workers.

Waivers of ADEA Rights

An employer may ask an employee to waive his or her rights or claims under the ADEA. This might happen in the context of a settlement of an ADEA administrative or court claim or in connection with an exit incentive program or other employment termination program. The ADEA, as amended by the OWBPA, sets out specific minimum standards that must be met for a waiver to be considered knowing and voluntary and, therefore, valid.

Among other requirements, a valid ADEA waiver must:

- Be part of a written agreement that is easily understandable by the employee.
- Refer specifically to claims under the ADEA.
- Not encompass future ADEA claims.
- Be given in exchange for consideration beyond any benefit to which the employee is already entitled.
- Provide in writing that the employee is advised to consult with an attorney before signing the waiver.
- Give the employee adequate time to consider the waiver before signing it.
  - For individual terminations, the employee has twenty-one days to consider the waiver before signing it.
  - For a group exit-incentive program, he or she has at least forty-five days.
  - In either case, the employee has seven days after signing in which to revoke the waiver.

- In cases of a group-incentive program, the employer must also disclose in writing:
  - The groups of employees eligible for the program.
  - The program requirements.
  - Any time limitations under the program.
  - The job titles and ages of all employees eligible or selected for the program and the same information for those not eligible or selected.

The Americans with Disabilities Act

The Americans with Disabilities Act (ADA) is a federal antidiscrimination statute designed to remove barriers that prevent qualified individuals with disabilities from enjoying the same employment opportunities that are available to persons without disabilities. Title I of the ADA deals with the hiring, treatment, and accommodation of applicants and employees with disabilities. The ADA seeks to ensure access to equal employment opportunities based on merit, but it does not guarantee equal results, establish quotas, or require preferences favoring individuals with disabilities over those without disabilities.

The ADA is a very difficult law to understand and comply with because its definitions are vague and recent legislation, the ADA Amendments Act of 2008, overturns a number of Supreme Court decisions that limited the impact of the law's actual wording. Determining whether or not someone is even covered by the law, and is therefore within a protected class, is driven by the facts of the specific circumstances of the applicant or employee in question. Hard-and-fast rules of thumb don't really exist.

The ADA applies to employers with fifteen or more employees, employment agencies, labor organizations, joint labor management committees, and state and local governments.

Executive agencies of the U.S. Government are exempt from the ADA, but these agencies are covered by similar nondiscrimination requirements and additional affirmative employment requirements under Section 501 of the Rehabilitation Act of 1973. Also exempted from the ADA (as they are from Title VII of the Civil Rights Act) are corporations fully owned by the U.S. Government, Indian tribes, and bona fide private membership clubs that are not labor organizations and that are exempt from taxation under the Internal Revenue Code.

Protections

The ADA prohibits employment discrimination against *qualified individuals with disabilities*. A qualified individual with a disability is an individual with a disability who meets the skill, experience, education, and other job-related requirements of a position held or desired, and who, with or without reasonable accommodation, can perform the essential functions of a job.

ADA-Protected Individuals Protected are qualified individuals:

- With physical or mental impairment that substantially limits one or more major life activities
- With a record of such impairment
- Who are regarded as having such an impairment, but who are able to perform the essential functions of a job with or without reasonable accommodation

Physical or Mental Impairment:
"Any physiological disorder, or condition, cosmetic disfigurement, or anatomical loss affecting one or more of the following body systems: neurological, musculoskeletal, special sense organs, respiratory (including speech organs), cardiovascular, reproductive, digestive, genito-urinary, hemic and lymphatic, skin, and endocrine"

Mental Impairment:
"Any mental or psychological disorder, such as mental retardation, organic brain syndrome, emotional or mental illness, and specific learning disabilities"

Individuals Specifically Not Covered by the ADA Individuals who currently use drugs illegally (including those who use prescription drugs illegally) are not individuals with disabilities protected under the Act. However, people who have been rehabilitated and do not currently use drugs illegally, or who are in the process of completing a rehabilitation program, may be protected by the ADA as having a history of a disability.

Homosexuality and bisexuality are not impairments and therefore are not disabilities covered by the ADA. The Act also states that the term *disability* does not include the following sexual and behavioral disorders:

- Transvestism, transsexualism, pedophilia, exhibitionism, voyeurism, gender identity disorders not resulting from physical impairments, or other sexual behavior disorders
- Compulsive gambling, kleptomania, or pyromania
- Psychoactive substance use disorders resulting from current illegal use of drugs

"Substantially Limits"

An impairment is a disability under the ADA only if it substantially limits one or more major life activities.

The ADA Amendments Act of 2008:

- Overturned a number of Supreme Court decisions that eroded protections under the ADA.
- Rejects strict interpretation of the definition of disability, and makes it clear that the ADA is intended to provide broad coverage to protect anyone who faces discrimination on the basis of disability.
- Prohibits the consideration of mitigating measures such as medication, prosthetics, and assistive technology in determining whether an individual has a disability.
- Covers people who experience discrimination based on a perception of impairment regardless of whether the individual experiences disability.
- Provides that reasonable accommodations are only required for individuals who can demonstrate they have an impairment that substantially limits a major life activity or have a record of such impairment. Accommodations need not be provided to an individual who is only "regarded as" having an impairment.

Factors to Consider Regarding Substantial Limitations The regulations provide three factors to consider in determining whether a person's impairment substantially limits a major life activity:

1. Its nature and severity
2. How long it will last or is expected to last
3. Its permanent or long-term impact, or expected impact

Record of a Substantially Limiting Condition

This part of the definition protects people who have a history of a disability from discrimination, whether or not they currently are substantially limited in a major life activity. For example, it protects people with a history of cancer, heart disease, or other debilitating illness whose illnesses are either cured, controlled, or in remission. It also protects people with a history of mental illness.

This part of the definition also protects people who may have been misclassified or misdiagnosed as having a disability. For example, it protects a person who may at one time have been erroneously classified as having mental retardation or having a learning disability.

Regarded as Substantially Limited

This part of the definition protects people who are not substantially limited in a major life activity from discrimination because they are perceived as having such a limitation. This part of the definition is supposed to protect people from a range of discriminatory actions based on "myths, fears, and stereotypes" about disability, which occur even when a person does not have a substantially limiting impairment.

An individual may be protected under this part of the definition in three circumstances:

1. The individual may have an impairment that is not substantially limiting, but is treated by the employer as having such an impairment—for example, an employee has controlled high blood pressure, which does not substantially limit his work activities. If an employer reassigns the individual to a less strenuous job because of unsubstantiated fear that the person would suffer a heart attack if he or she continues in the present job, the employer has *regarded* this person as disabled.

2. The individual has an impairment that is substantially limiting because of the attitudes of others toward the condition—for example, an experienced assistant manager of a convenience store who has a prominent port wine birthmark on his or her face gets passed over for promotion to store manager because the employer believes that customers and vendors would not want to look at this person.

3. The individual may have no impairment at all but is regarded by an employer as having a substantially limiting impairment—for example, an employer discharges an employee based on a rumor that the individual has HIV.

Qualified Individual with a Disability

An employer is not required to hire or retain an individual who is not qualified to perform a job. The regulations define a qualified individual with a disability as a person with a disability who:

> Satisfies the requisite skill, experience, education, and other job-related requirements of the employment position such individual holds or desires, and who, with or without reasonable accommodation, can perform the essential functions of such position.

There are two basic steps in determining whether an individual is *qualified* under the ADA:

1. Determine if the individual meets necessary prerequisites for the job, such as:
   • Education
   • Work experience
   • Training
   • Skills
   • Licenses
   • Certificates
   • Other job-related requirements, such as good judgment or ability to work with other people
2. Determine if the individual can perform the essential functions of the job, with or without reasonable accommodation. This second step, a key aspect of nondiscrimination under the ADA, has two parts:
   1. Identifying "essential functions of the job"
   2. Considering whether the person with a disability can perform these functions, unaided or with a "reasonable accommodation"

The ADA requires an employer to focus on the essential functions of a job to determine whether a person with a disability is qualified.

When a qualified individual with a disability requests an accommodation, the employer must make a reasonable effort to provide an accommodation that is effective for the individual (gives the individual an equally effective opportunity to apply for a job, perform essential job functions, or enjoy equal benefits and privileges).

For assistance in formulating reasonable individualized accommodations, you can contact, without cost, the Job Accommodation Network, http://www.jan.wvu.edu.

ADA and Hiring

See Chapter 1, "Hiring."

State and Local Protected Classes

Some states, counties, and cities recognize some or all of the groups set out next as being protected classes.

Marital Status Discrimination

Marital status refers to the state of being married, single, separated, divorced, widowed, a partner in a civil union as recognized under state law, or a partner in a domestic partnership as recognized under state law. An employer cannot take any adverse employment action based on the applicant's or employee's marital status—for example, assigning longer hours to single workers or not hiring someone because of his or her marital status.

Marital status discrimination is not covered by Title VII; however, many federal government employees are covered by provisions in the Civil Service Reform Act of 1978 (CSRA) that prohibit marital status discrimination.

In the federal government the CSRA, as amended, prohibits federal employees who have authority to take—or to direct others to take, recommend, or approve—any personnel action discriminating against applicants and employees on the basis of race, color, sex, religion, national origin, age, disability, marital status, or political affiliation, and from discriminating against an applicant or employee on the basis of conduct that does not adversely affect the performance of the applicant or employee. The Office of Personnel Management (OPM) has interpreted the prohibition of discrimination based on *conduct* to include discrimination based on sexual orientation.

The Office of Special Council (OSC) and the Merit Systems Protection Board (MSPB) enforce the prohibitions against federal employment discrimination codified in the CSRA. The OSC will defer those bases of discrimination under EEOC's jurisdiction to the respective federal agency and its EEO process.

The overwhelming majority of courts interpreting these local or state marital discrimination statutes have ruled that they prohibit discrimination on the basis of marital status, not the identity of the person one is marrying. Therefore, an employer probably could refuse to hire someone who is married to someone already in the organization, while not being able to refuse to hire someone whose ex-spouse works for the company.

In addition, in states where marital status is a protected class, most courts will allow a company to have an antinepotism policy barring spouses from working for one another in a direct superior-subordinate reporting relationship.

Where marital status is a protected class, employers should not:

- Give different fringe benefits to married employees as opposed to single employees.

- Make available fringe benefits for wives of male employees that are not made available to single female employees.

- Make available fringe benefits for the husbands of female employees that are not made available to single male employees.

- Condition fringe benefits upon whether an employee is the head of household, principal wage earner, secondary wage earner, or other similar status.

- Deny equal access to training programs and promotion opportunities to married or single employees.

Sexual Orientation

Sexual orientation refers to heterosexuality, homosexuality, and bisexuality. It does not refer to gender identity, such as transsexualism.

Although Title VII does not protect against discrimination based on sexual orientation, homosexuals, heterosexuals, and bisexuals alike enjoy the same protections against discrimination because of their sex, race, religion, national origin, disability, and age.

Gender Identity

Transgender is an umbrella term used to describe people whose gender identity (sense of themselves as male or female) or gender expression differs from that usually associated with their birth sex.

A small number of states have recognized gender identity as a protected class. Some of these states recognize both transsexuals and cross-dressers as being protected, while others protect only transsexuals.

Transsexuals are transgender people who live or wish to live full-time as members of the gender opposite to their birth sex. Transsexuals often seek medical interventions, such as hormones and surgery, to make their bodies as congruent as possible with their preferred gender.

The process of transitioning from one gender to the other is called sex reassignment or gender reassignment.

Cross-dressers or transvestites, who wear the clothing of the other sex, comprise the most numerous transgender group. The great majority of cross-dressers are biological males, most of whom are sexually attracted to women.

People generally experience gender identity and sexual orientation as two different things. Sexual orientation refers to one's sexual attraction to men, women, both, or neither, whereas gender identity refers to one's sense of oneself as male, female, or transgender.

An area of litigation in this area surrounds the issue of a preoperative transsexual wishing to use the restroom of the gender with which he or she identifies. Some states allow for this while others have taken the position that the individual must use the restroom associated with the anatomical sex he or she presents at that time. Employers facing this issue often provide unisex restrooms to resolve the problem.

Lifestyle Laws

More than twenty states have some form of lifestyle law protecting off-premise/off-duty behavior. The majority of these laws protect only smokers, but a few are broader and cover the use of all lawful products—for example, alcohol. A few states ban discrimination based on any form of legal off-duty behavior, including Colorado, North Dakota, and New York.

Genetic Predisposition: Genetic Information Nondiscrimination Act

Genetic Predisposition in the Workplace

The Human Genome Project and other medical advances allow for a better understanding of the genetic compositions that contribute to various diseases and predispose those with a certain genetic makeup to those diseases.

Along with the positive aspects of these advances is the reality that employers are increasingly basing their hiring and firing decisions on the results of genetic tests that disclose which employees are at a higher risk of having medical problems down the road. And insurers are using the results of genetic testing to deny insurance coverage and raise premium rates.

A federal law that will go into effect in 2009 will dramatically impact employer-employee rights in this area.

Genetic Information Nondiscrimination Act

The Genetic Information Nondiscrimination Act (GINA) prohibits discrimination against individuals on the basis of their genetic information in both employment (effective November 2009) and health care (effective May 2009).

The legislation contains the following provisions:

State Genetic Law Preemption GINA will allow state laws that are more stringent in the requirements, standards, or implementations than those contained in GINA to supersede the new federal law.

Nondiscrimination in Employment GINA will prohibit an employer from discriminating against an individual in the hiring, firing, compensation, terms, or privileges of employment on the basis of genetic information of the individual or a family member of the individual.

Definition of Family Member GINA defines a family member as the:

- Spouse of the individual
- Dependent child of the individual, including a child who is born to or placed for adoption with the individual
- Parent, grandparent, or great-grandparent

Restrictions on Collecting Genetic Information GINA forbids an employer from requesting, requiring, or purchasing genetic information on the individual or family member except for the following:

- When the employer inadvertently requests or requires the information
- When genetic services are offered by the employer (including wellness programs)
- For purposes of complying with the Family and Medical Leave Act
- When the employer purchases documents that are commercially available

Genetic Monitoring in the Workplace Exception GINA does allow for genetic monitoring of biological effects of toxic substances in the workplace, but only if:

- Employer provides written notice of the monitoring to the employee.
- Employee agrees to the monitoring in writing or the monitoring is required by federal, state, or local law.
- Employee is informed of the results of the test.
- Monitoring conforms to any federal or state law, including rules promulgated by OSHA.
- Employer receives the results of the tests in aggregate terms.

Health–Care Coverage Protections GINA will prohibit an insured or self-insured health-care plan from denying eligibility to enroll for health-care coverage or from adjusting premiums or contribution rates under a plan based on an individual or family member's genetic information. Health-care plans would also be prevented from requiring a plan participant to undergo a genetic test to be eligible for coverage under a health-care plan.

Exceptions for Genetic Testing for Health–Care Treatment GINA will allow a health-care professional to request that a patient undergo a genetic test or advise a patient on the provision of a genetic test or services through a wellness program.

Remedies for Violations of the Health-Care Coverage Provisions GINA will allow plan participants to receive injunctive relief under the Employee Retirement Income Security Act (ERISA) and have health-care coverage reinstated back to the date of loss of coverage.

Plan administrators could be personally liable for discriminating in coverage decisions and be assessed a penalty of $100 per day for the period of noncompliance. Plans could be fined a minimum penalty of $2,500 to $15,000 for more than de minimis violations up to a total of $500,000 for multiple violations.

Confidentiality of Genetic Health-Care Information GINA requires that the disclosure of protected genetic health-care information be governed by the Health Insurance Portability and Accountability Act of 1996 (HIPAA). The law would also provide participants with injunctive and equitable relief for violations of the confidentiality provisions of GINA.

For violations of the privacy provisions of the law, civil monetary penalties of $100 per day up to $250,000 and ten years in prison for egregious violations could be assessed.

CHAPTER 7

Hot-Button Issues: Sexual Harassment and Workplace Violence

Sexual Harassment: Introduction

Sexual harassment became a legitimate theory of discrimination when the Supreme Court ruled in *Meritor Savings Bank v. Vinson*, 477 U.S. 57 (1986) that sexual harassment is a violation of Title VII of the 1964 Civil Rights Act.

It has developed into a complex and broad area of law costing U.S. businesses approximately $50 million per year in *settled* payouts, according to statistics from the Equal Opportunity Employment Commission (EEOC).

A common misconception is that innocent flirtation, horseplay, and other forms of social interaction are actionable sexual harassment if the victim does not like the harasser's words or actions. Also incorrect is the belief that isolated incidents of inappropriate conduct are enough to constitute sexual harassment—for example, a single sexually oriented remark, although offensive, probably isn't enough, unless really serious, to be sexual harassment. In reality, as stated in the Supreme Court case of *Oncale v.*

Sundowner Offshore Services, Inc., 523 U.S. 75 (1998), Title VII is not a "general civility code."

Basically, for words or actions to constitute sexual harassment, the victim must suffer some tangible employment action—for example, demotion, termination, or loss of pay—or they must be severe or pervasive enough to permeate the workplace and actually affect the victim's terms of employment—that is, unreasonably interfere with his or her working environment.

Sexual harassment is not limited to men-women or women-men situations. The *Oncale* case stands for the proposition that there can be same-sex sexual harassment, and that same-sex sexual harassment can exist without any of the parties involved being homosexual. All that the victim must prove is that the unwelcome conduct was based on the sex of the victim and disadvantaged him or her because of gender.

> **EXAMPLE:** In a work environment, if a man and a woman are continually flirting with one another, sexually touching each other, and otherwise engaging in conduct of a sexual nature in close physical proximity to the victim, and if their actions are severe and pervasive enough to interfere with the victim's ability to do his or her job, then (1) the conduct is unwelcome, (2) it is based on sex, and (3) it has the purpose or effect of unreasonably interfering with the victim's ability to do his or her job. That's sexual harassment.

Unlawful harassment is not limited to sex but can also involve discriminatory treatment on the basis of race, color, religion, national origin, age 40 or older, disability, or protected class under other antidiscrimination statutes.

Sexual Harassment Defined

Unwelcome sexual advances, requests for sexual favors, and other verbal or physical conduct of a sexual nature constitute sexual harassment when this conduct explicitly or implicitly affects an individual's employment, unreasonably interferes with an individual's work performance, or creates an intimidating, hostile, or offensive work environment.

There are two basic types of sexual harassment: *quid pro quo* and *hostile environment.* The lines between these two have blurred in recent years with the key issues now being (1) whether or not the victim suffered a significant change in working conditions, such as a tangible job action, or (2) whether the working environment is hostile, intimidating, or offensive because of sexual harassment even if the alleged victim has not suffered any job loss.

Quid Pro Quo ("This for That" or "Something for Something") Sexual Harassment

The most obvious form of sexual harassment is where a supervisor requires some sort of sexual trade-off from an employee as a condition for job benefits. In other words,

- Submission to such conduct is a term or condition of employment.
- Submission to or rejection of such conduct is a basis for employment decisions affecting the worker.

EXAMPLE: If a supervisor discussed the employee's performance review shortly before requesting that the worker perform oral sex on the manager, the close proximity in time between these two discussions would lead a reasonable person to believe a quid pro quo has been offered—that is, if the victim submits, he or she will gain a benefit or if he or she does not, he or she will suffer a job detriment.

Supervisor Status and Quid Pro Quo

Quid pro quo harassment requires that the harasser be a supervisor or other person in the organization who has the authority to (1) direct the employee's daily work activities, or (2) undertake or recommend tangible employment decisions affecting the employee. In other words, the individual is in a position to give or deny a benefit, or otherwise change working conditions such as hiring, firing, demotions, promotions, working hours, working conditions, and training opportunities.

The harasser does not have to have the final say over employment decisions. As long as the individual's recommendation is given substantial weight by the final decision maker(s), that individual meets the definition of supervisor.

Temporary Supervisory Status

An individual who is temporarily authorized to direct another employee's daily work activities does qualify as a supervisor during that time period.

However, someone who merely relays other officials' instructions regarding work assignments and reports back to those officials does not have true supervisory authority.

Harasser Outside Supervisory Chain of Command

Someone can also be a supervisor even if he or she is outside of the victim's chain of command if the alleged victim reasonably believed the alleged harasser had authority to undertake or recommend tangible employment decisions affecting the employee.

Tangible Job Action—Vicarious Liability

In the highly significant cases of *Burlington Industries, Inc. v. Ellerth*, 524 U.S. 742 (1998), and *Faragher v. City of Boca Raton*, 524 U.S. 775 (1998), the Supreme Court made clear that if a supervisor engages in quid pro quo sexual harassment and it results in a tangible job action for or against the victim, the employer is strictly liable and has no legal defense.

Prior to *Ellerth* and *Faragher*, sexual harassment complaints were analyzed as quid pro quo or hostile work environment cases. These decisions hold that these legal theories remain valid; however, courts will no longer focus on the technical distinction between hostile environment and quid pro quo allegations. Now a distinction will be drawn between cases where:

- Any tangible job action is taken against the plaintiff-victim by the offending supervisor.
- No tangible job action is taken (e.g., the plaintiff-victim either remains employed or quits).

Where a harassing supervisor takes a tangible job action, the employer is strictly liable. Where no tangible job action is taken, the employer remains vicariously liable for the supervisor's sexual harassment but may assert an affirmative defense relating to its efforts to prevent the harassment from occurring.

The employer's *vicarious* liability is appropriate because supervisors are aided in their misconduct by the authority the employer delegated to them. Basically, the standard of liability set forth in these decisions is based on two principles: (1) an employer is responsible for the acts of its supervisors, and (2) employers should be encouraged to prevent harassment and employees should be encouraged to avoid or limit the harm from harassment.

Although the *Faragher* and *Ellerth* decisions dealt with sexual harassment, the Court's analysis drew on standards set forth in cases involving harassment on other protected bases, and the EEOC has always taken the position that the same basic standards apply to all types of prohibited harassment, such as race, religion, age, national origin, or physical disability. Because of this vicarious liability standard, employers should establish antiharassment policies and complaint procedures covering *all* forms of unlawful harassment.

Examples of Tangible Job Actions An employment action qualifies as *tangible* if it results in a significant change in employment status. Unfulfilled threats are not enough.

According to the EEOC, characteristics of a tangible employment action are:

1. A tangible employment action is the means by which the supervisor brings the official power of the enterprise to bear on subordinates, as demonstrated by the following:
   - It requires an official act of the enterprise.
   - It usually is documented in official company records.
   - It may be subject to review by higher-level supervisors.
   - It often requires the formal approval of the enterprise and use of its internal processes.
2. A tangible employment action usually inflicts direct economic harm.
3. A tangible employment action, in most instances, can be caused only by a supervisor or other person acting with the authority of the company.

Examples of tangible employment actions include the following:

- Hiring and firing
- Promotion and failure to promote
- Demotion
- Undesirable reassignment

- Decision causing a significant change in benefits
- Compensation decisions
- Work assignment

An instructive case as to the nature of what constitutes a tangible job action is *Jin v. Metropolitan Life Ins. Co.,* 295 F.3d 335 (2nd Circuit, June 27, 2002). In *Jin,* a supervisor forced the victim to perform sexual acts each week to keep her job. The court ruled that a plaintiff who is forced to submit to sexual acts to keep her job has been subjected to a tangible employment action. A plaintiff who has paychecks withheld or has a paycheck delayed—for example, temporarily withheld—has suffered a tangible employment action. It also ruled that a lower court erred when it instructed a jury that a Title VII plaintiff alleging sexual harassment must be subjected to a "tangible adverse action." Some sexual harassment victims receive "benefits." For example, in this case the defendant argued that the victim received the benefit of keeping her job in return for submitting to sexual acts. (Notice that this reasoning is consistent with that part of the definition of sexual harassment that reads, "Submission to or rejection of such conduct is a basis for employment decisions affecting the worker.")

No Tangible Job Action—Hostile Environment

When a supervisor engages in sexual harassment that does not result in a tangible job action, the sexual harassment is deemed to be hostile environment harassment no different from that perpetrated by anyone else, such as a coworker or someone external to the organization.

If it is hostile environment harassment, the employer can raise an affirmative defense (the *Ellerth/Faragher Defense*) to liability or damages. (See "The *Ellerth/Faragher Defense*" in this chapter.)

Hostile Environment Sexual Harassment

Hostile environment sexual harassment occurs when the plaintiff can show that the work environment is hostile, intimidating, or offensive due to sexual harassment, even when no tangible job loss occurs because of the harassment. Basically, the harasser's conduct must have the purpose or effect of unreasonably interfering with the plaintiff's ability to do his or her job.

For the harasser's words or actions to rise to the level of actually being actionable, they must be sufficiently severe or pervasive to alter the victim's conditions of employment and to create an abusive working environment. The burden of proof is heavier in hostile environment lawsuits than in quid pro quo cases. For example, in a quid pro quo case a single incident could be enough; however, in hostile environment situations, it generally takes the plaintiff showing that his or her injury resulted from multiple incidents, comments, or conduct that occurred with some frequency.

In deciding whether or not an environment is hostile or abusive, all of the circumstances must be considered. Some of the criteria the courts have used include:

- Totality of the physical environment of the plaintiff's work area
- Lexicon (vocabulary) of obscenity that pervaded the environment both before and after the plaintiff's introduction into it
- Reasonable expectation of the plaintiff on entering the environment
- Nature of the unwelcome sexual acts or words
- Frequency of the offensive encounters (e.g., a small number of isolated incidents will not support a hostile environment claim)
- Total number of days over which the offensive meetings occurred
- Context in which the sexual harassment occurred
- Whether the conduct unreasonably interferes with an employee's work performance

Conduct Must Be Unwelcome

The EEOC and the Supreme Court have said that a key part of a sexual harassment claim is that the alleged sexual advances were *unwelcome*. For example, if everyone in a working environment continually uses foul and vulgar language and no one cares, then no one cares and it's not a hostile environment.

Sexual attraction often plays a role in the day-to-day social exchange between employees. In its various *Guidances* relating to sexual harassment, the EEOC has acknowledged that it is sometimes difficult to make a distinction among invited, uninvited-but-welcome, offensive-but-tolerated, and flatly rejected sexual advances. However, because sexual conduct is only unlawful when it is unwelcome, the distinction is essential. The Eleventh Circuit federal court provided a general definition of *unwelcome conduct* in *Henson v. City of Dundee*, 682 F.2d at 903: The challenged conduct must be unwelcome "in the sense that the employee did not solicit or incite it, and in the sense that the employee regarded the conduct as undesirable or offensive." Also, the conduct must be unwelcome through the eyes of a reasonable person—not necessarily from the viewpoint of the alleged victim. (See "Reasonable Person Standard.")

The employer will often be confronted with conflicting evidence as to welcomeness—for example, the parties may have had a prior consensual relationship. You must evaluate each situation on a case-by-case basis and look at the total circumstances. (See "The Investigation" in this chapter.)

Reasonable Person Standard

For sexual harassment to arise, the action must be unwelcome to a reasonable person under similar circumstances.

The *reasonable person* concept is a mainstay of U.S. jurisprudence; however, it is a very difficult standard to actually apply. Acknowledging that this test is not and cannot be mathematically precise, the Supreme Court emphasized that whether a work environment is hostile or abusive can be determined only by looking at all the circumstances.

According to the Supreme Court in *Harris v. Forklift Systems, Inc.*, 510 U.S. 17 (1993), some factors that could be part of the circumstances of the case include the following:

- Frequency of the discriminatory conduct
- Severity of that conduct
- Whether it is physically threatening or humiliating or a mere offensive utterance
- Whether it unreasonably interferes with an employee's work performance

The *Ellerth/Faragher* Defense

In 1998, when the Supreme Court decided *Burlington Industries, Inc. v. Ellerth*, 524 U.S. 742 (1998) and *Faragher v. City of Boca Raton*, 524 U.S. 775 (1998), it set forth an affirmative defense that may be used by an employer to avoid liability for sexual harassment based on a hostile work environment when no adverse employment action has been suffered by the employee.

The defense consists of two necessary elements:

1. Employer exercised reasonable care to prevent and correct promptly any harassment.
2. Employee unreasonably failed to take advantage of any preventive or corrective opportunities provided by the employer or to avoid harm otherwise.

Basically, if the employer can prove that it acted in a reasonable manner and that the employee could have avoided being harmed but unreasonably failed to do so, the employer will avoid liability for unlawful harassment.

As a practical matter, the *Ellerth/Faragher Defense* means that if the employee doesn't avail himself or herself of the employer's internal administrative procedures in a timely manner, the courts will grant the employer a summary judgment against the worker.

Note: Because of the wording of its state Fair Employment Practices Act, California does not recognize the *Ellerth/Faragher Defense*. However, California follows an *avoidable consequences* rule. Basically, in California there will not be a summary judgment against the plaintiff; however, the amount of damages will be reduced by the degree to which the harm could have been avoided if the employee had timely followed the employer's internal remedies.

Employer's Duty to Exercise Reasonable Care

In order for the employer to position itself to use the *Ellerth/Faragher Defense,* it must show that it undertook reasonable care to prevent and promptly correct harassment. Generally, the employer must establish, disseminate, and enforce an antiharassment policy and complaint procedure and take other reasonable steps to prevent and correct harassment.

It is clear from the *Ellerth* case that if an employer does not have a written policy, it will probably not be able to prove that it exercised reasonable care. And, simply having a written policy is not enough. You, the employer, should:

• Provide every employee with a copy of the policy and complaint procedure,

- Redistribute the policy and complaint procedure periodically,
- Post the policy and complaint procedure in central locations,
- Incorporate the policy and complaint procedure into employee handbooks, and
- Provide training to all employees to ensure that they understand their rights and responsibilities.

Because of the differences in levels of responsibilities, liabilities, and perspectives between supervisors and general staff, training should be separated into sessions for each respective category.

Simply having a written and widely distributed policy and procedure against sexual harassment (or discrimination generally) does not create a *safe harbor*—the employer must actually follow and enforce the policy in an effective manner.

Employer's Discrimination/Harassment Policy

An antiharassment policy and complaint procedure should contain, at a minimum, the following elements.

Clear Explanation of Prohibited Conduct

An employer's policy should make clear that it will not tolerate harassment by *anyone* in the workplace—supervisors, coworkers, or nonemployees—based on sex (with or without sexual conduct), race, color, religion, national origin, age, disability, and protected activity—for example, opposition to prohibited discrimination or participation in the statutory complaint process.

Although simply using the EEOC's definition of sexual harassment, found in the *Meritor* case and discussed in "Sexual Harassment Defined" in this chapter, and often used in sexual harassment policies, you may wish to expand on what your prohibitions are. For example, you may want to explain that there are four basic types of sexual harassment:

1. *Verbal Harassment*—Sexually suggestive comments (e.g., about a person's clothing, body, or sexual activities; sexually provocative compliments about a person's clothes or the way his or her clothes fit; comments of a sexual nature about weight, body shape, size, or figure; comments or questions about the sensuality of a person or his or her spouse or significant

other; repeated unsolicited propositions for dates or sexual intercourse; pseudo-medical advice such as "You might be feeling bad because you didn't get enough" or "A little TLC will cure your ailments"; continuous idle chatter of a sexual nature and graphic sexual descriptions; telephone calls of a sexual nature; derogatory comments or slurs; verbal abuse or threats; sexual jokes; suggestive or insulting sounds such as whistling, wolf calls, or kissing sounds; homophobic insults)

2. *Physical Harassment*—Assault, coerced sexual intercourse, attempted rape or rape; sexual gestures such as licking lips or teeth, holding or eating food provocatively, and lewd gestures such as hand or sign language to denote sexual activity; sexual looks such as leering and ogling with suggestive overtones; sexual innuendoes; cornering, impeding or blocking movement, or any physical interference with normal work or movement; touching that is inappropriate in the workplace such as patting, pinching, stroking, or brushing up against the body, mauling, attempted or actual kissing or fondling

3. *Visual Harassment*—Showing and distributing derogatory or pornographic posters, cartoons, drawings, books, or magazines; writing or distributing in any manner or medium, including but not limited to e-mail or text messaging, material whose purpose or effect is to create an offensive, intimidating, or hostile working environment

4. *Sexual Favors*—Persistent pressure for dates; unwanted sexual advances that condition an employment benefit upon an exchange of sexual favors

Assurance That Employees Who Make Complaints of Harassment or Provide Information Related to Such Complaints Will Be Protected Against Retaliation

In *Burlington Northern & Santa Fe (BNSF) Railway Co. v. White*, 548 U.S. 53 (2006), the Supreme Court substantially enhanced legal protection against retaliation for employees who complain about discrimination or harassment on the job.

The 9-to-0 decision adopted a broadly worded and employee-friendly definition of the type of retaliation that is prohibited by Title VII of the Civil Rights Act of 1964. Prior to this case, it had been almost impossible to win a retaliation case unless the retaliation resulted in dismissal. In this case, a worker was transferred to a less desirable job after complaining of discrimination.

By contrast, under the standard the justices adopted in the *BNSF v. White* case, any "materially adverse" employment that "might have dissuaded a reasonable worker" from complaining about discrimination will count as prohibited retaliation.

Depending on the context, retaliation might be found in an unfavorable annual evaluation, an unwelcome schedule change, or other action well short of losing a job.

Clearly Described Complaint Process That Provides Accessible Avenues of Complaint

A harassment complaint procedure should be easy for the (alleged) victim to use. Although the procedure should have some step-by-step structure, it should not create any unreasonable obstacles to someone coming forward. Also, it should not be rigid. In other words, if an employee complains to management about alleged harassment, the employer is obligated to investigate the allegation even if it doesn't conform to a particular format or is not made in writing.

It is important that the procedure provide accessible points of contact for the initial complaint. That is, if a complaining worker must always go to his or her immediate supervisor first about the alleged harassment, then the procedure is not effective (because that supervisor might be the harasser). Your procedure should allow employees to approach any supervisor, who, in turn, is obligated to report the complaint to appropriate officials.

The procedure should allow the worker to bypass his or her chain of command. This privilege would provide additional assurance that the complaint will be handled in an impartial manner.

Your antiharassment policy and complaint procedure should also contain information about the time frames for filing charges of unlawful harassment with the EEOC or state fair employment practice agencies (FEPAs). The statute of limitations for most FEPAs varies from 180 to 365 days. The deadline for filing with the EEOC is 300 days in states that have a FEPA, and 180 days for the few states that do not. Alert employees that the deadline runs from the last date of unlawful harassment.

Note: If an aggrieved worker wants to take advantage of Title VII protections, he or she must exhaust his or her administrative remedies with the EEOC before going to court. Whether or not an aggrieved worker can go straight to state court and bypass his or her state FEPA is a matter of the individual state's law.

Assurance That the Employer Will Protect the Confidentiality of Harassment Complaints to the Extent Possible

Do not promise total confidentiality! An employer must effectively investigate complaints of discrimination or harassment and cannot do so without revealing at least some relevant information to the alleged harasser or potential witnesses.

Of course, information about the harassment allegation should be shared only with those who need to know about it, and records relating to harassment complaints should be kept confidential on the same basis.

A supervisor who agrees not to reveal any information about a harassment complaint sets the stage for the victim to be revictimized, for others to be harmed by the harasser, and denies the alleged wrongdoer any opportunity to defend himself or herself. In fact, if the supervisor takes no action and the harasser later harms someone else, that knowledge coupled with inaction will almost certainly result in a charge that the organization condones discrimination.

Complaint Process That Provides a Prompt, Thorough, and Impartial Investigation

You, the employer, should set up a mechanism for a prompt, thorough, and impartial investigation into alleged harassment. See "The Investigation" in this chapter.

Assurance That the Employer Will Take Immediate and Appropriate Corrective Action When It Determines That Harassment Has Occurred

The employer must take action that is "reasonably calculated to end the harassment"—it doesn't necessarily actually have to be successful in its efforts. For example, in *Austin v. Norfolk Southern Corp.*, 158 Fed. Appx. 374 (3d Circuit, 2005), the railroad (the "company") undertook an investigation of the complaint, interviewed witnesses, reissued its sexual harassment policy, and took other steps to stop the harasser(s) from putting offensive graffiti around company property. The company was never able to identify the harasser(s) and the harassment periodically reoccurred. The court felt that the company had acted in a reasonable manner and was not liable for the occasional continued acts.

Also, the company's corrective actions should be proportionate to the harm done. Job death for the harasser may be inappropriate in every situation. Corrective actions could include one or more of the following:

- Oral and written warning
- Remedial training
- Reprimand
- Suspension
- Probation
- Transfer
- Demotion
- Discharge

Do not overreact! An accused who has been severely disciplined based on an incomplete or inconclusive investigation could sue for alleged wrongful termination, slander, or defamation.

The Investigation

Internal investigations, including sexual harassment investigation, should be triggered when the employer learns of possible misconduct by employees involving violations of rules, regulations, or law that, even if proved, will not likely result in criminal prosecution. Don't rush out and act impulsively; however, launch the investigation as soon as possible. We've all heard or read the old saying, "Justice delayed is justice denied."

A complaint is not always the event that triggers a company's duty to investigate. The duty to investigate doesn't arise only after a complaint has been made. When an employer observes acts or statements that suggest prohibited activity or even becomes aware of rumors regarding such acts or events, it must take effective action. Recent legal decisions have made certain that employers have an unequivocal duty to investigate promptly and thoroughly as soon as the employer is put on notice of possible wrongdoing.

Privacy matters related to internal investigations in the workplace in general are discussed in Chapter 8, "Privacy Issues."

Choosing Your Investigator

An immediate concern for an employer is what party will undertake the investigation.

Potential candidates include HR personnel, internal security, and non-lawyer third-party investigators. Lawyers, either outside counsel or in-house counsel, should also be considered.

HR Personnel

Investigating workplace complaints is a common function of an HR department. HR personnel are often perceived as objective and nonthreatening and have generally had experience in investigating a number of different issues within the company. Also, the HR department is usually the most familiar with the organization's history, policies, and procedures, as well as with its employees.

A feeling among workers that the HR department is too closely linked to management to be impartial and fair could work against using someone from that department. Also, if the alleged harasser is superior to the HR investigator in the investigator's chain of command—for example, the harasser can take or recommend tangible employment decisions affecting the investigator—the appearance of undue influence will be almost impossible to overcome.

Internal Security

Using in-house security personnel is advantageous because they often have some sort of law enforcement background and therefore possess investigation experience and, generally, exhibit a more assertive investigative demeanor than someone in HR.

Unfortunately, in-house security personnel are often viewed as being intimidating. Their approach may be, or at least could be, viewed as being too aggressive or inquisitorial. And, once again, if the alleged harasser is superior to the investigator in the investigator's chain of command, the appearance of undue influence will be almost impossible to overcome.

Nonlawyer Third-Party Investigators

The perceived lack of objectivity that using internal staff might bring up is somewhat overcome by using nonlawyer third-party investigators.

Organizations sometimes use former or retired employees to conduct investigations into workplace complaints because of their knowledge of the business and its employees.

Other times, and more commonly when outside resources are used, actual investigators are hired to conduct the investigation because of their knowledge of investigatory methods and techniques.

In the past, a major disadvantage associated with using outside investigators emanated from statutory restrictions on an employer's ability to anonymously obtain certain information about an employee who was the subject of a complaint. For example, up until 2003, the Fair Credit Reporting Act of 1970 (FCRA) and the Consumer Credit Reporting Act of 1996 precluded companies seeking to use third-party investigators from maintaining anonymity in the investigation of employee complaints.

Those statutes required that notice be given to the employee under investigation, that the employee consent to have his or her credit report disclosed to the investigator, and that the findings of the investigation be disclosed to the employee upon completion of the investigation. This created situations where the alleged wrongdoer could destroy evidence, intimidate witnesses, etc.

The Fair and Accurate Credit Transactions Act of 2003 (the FACT Act), which became effective on March 31, 2004, amended the FCRA. The new law clarified the application of the FCRA to employers' investigations of employee misconduct. The FACT Act allows an employer to use a third party to conduct any type of workplace investigation without having to comply with the FCRA's consent and disclosure requirements at the outset of the investigation.

Specifically, the FACT Act excludes certain employer investigations conducted by outside organizations from the FCRA's definition of *consumer report*, which was the designation that previously triggered the onerous notification and authorization obligations under the Federal Trade Commission's view. The law explicitly exempts these investigations from the FCRA if they concern "suspected misconduct related to employment" and likewise exempts investigations concerning "compliance with federal, state, or local laws and regulations" and compliance with "the rules of a self-regulatory organization, or any preexisting written policies of the employer."

The new law does not completely eradicate all FCRA-related obligations. Under the FACT Act, an employer that uses an outside organization to investigate allegations of employee misconduct, legal compliance, or other issues, and that later plans to take adverse action against an employee as a result of information received from the investigation, must provide the employee with a summary containing the nature and substance of the report after taking the adverse action. Employers are not required to disclose the sources of the information acquired in preparing the report. This summary need not be provided until after the adverse action takes place.

Attorney Investigators

Ethical and privilege issues arise when lawyers, both in-house and outside, act as internal investigators. Specifically, lawyers should always disclose to witnesses that the company, not the accused employee, is the attorney's client.

The use of outside counsel brings objectivity to an investigation. This is essential in situations where allegations are too sensitive for an employee-investigator to be objective—for example, when a high-level executive is accused of harassment. A negative is that outside counsel often lacks knowledge of the organization, its culture, and its employees.

There are some real benefits to using in-house counsel as your investigator. He or she has knowledge of employment laws, the company, its corporate culture, and its employees. Furthermore, in-house counsel benefits from the attorney-client privilege. Note, however, the attorney-client privilege will probably be waived, in whole or in part, when an employer asserts the defense that it exercised reasonableness in conducting a prompt and thorough investigation. The in-house counsel would be forced to discuss what he or she did, whom he or she talked to, etc.

Whether in-house or outside counsel, lawyer-investigators can be perceived as intimidating, which could prevent complaining parties and other witnesses from being completely forthright and honest.

There's no reason that you have to choose only one person to investigate an employee complaint. In fact, if you have the necessary resources, using a team consisting of, for example, an outside attorney and an HR employee is often particularly effective. The team approach also offers the essential element of corroboration should the complaining employee, the accused, or witnesses alter their earlier statements.

Witnesses

Do not simply rush out and start interviewing people. Witnesses are not equal in importance. You may not be ready to talk to a particular witness because you need to talk to another witness first or because you aren't yet sufficiently prepared to question that particular person. You may want to pay a visit to the scene before talking to a certain witness or to first gather and read documents or examine physical evidence. The point is that there are different types of witnesses and you will want to interview them with a view toward eliciting different types of information or setting the stage for a hearing.

Percipient Witnesses

A percipient witness is someone directly involved in the incident being investigated, an eyewitness to it or who otherwise has direct, firsthand knowledge of the matter.

Percipient witnesses should generally be interviewed first. Often you will need to reinterview them after developing facts or other information from other witnesses and sources.

The most important percipient witnesses in any investigation are: (1) the employees who allege they have been victimized because of race, religion, sex, etc., and the alleged harasser, or those who were injured in an accident; (2) other employees closely associated with the work activity at the time of the incident or accident; and (3) those employees responsible for supervising the work activity at the time of the event(s).

Fact Witnesses

A fact witness is any person who possesses information relating to, or explaining, the circumstances leading up to, and including, the issue in question.

An example of a fact witness might be someone who works in the same department as the parties directly involved in a dispute. The fact witness can testify about the normal working conditions and interactions of the parties in the past, working conditions in that department, and so forth.

Predicate Witnesses

A predicate witness is a person who may have no personal knowledge of the facts of the case but is necessary as a conduit to establish the legal predicate (foundation) for the admissibility of evidence—for example, your organization's payroll administrator or records clerk.

Character Witnesses

Character witnesses are individuals who have direct knowledge of the past actions of one or more of the parties in given situations or circumstances.

A character witness may be called to testify to an admissible character trait of the accused, another witness, or the complainant.

Expert Witnesses

An expert witness is a person whose education, training, skill, or experience is believed to give them more knowledge than the average person in a particular subject matter, industry, and so forth. That level of knowledge is deemed sufficient that others can legally rely on his or her opinion about evidence or a fact issue within the scope of his or her expertise.

A qualified expert witness, who may have no firsthand knowledge of the alleged crime, is permitted to venture admissible opinion testimony about disputed issues.

Investigatory Procedures

Steps in Questioning Any Witness

Basic steps in interviewing any witness are:

- Take detailed notes, as close to verbatim as possible, during each interview.
- Sign and date the notes.
- Identify the individual being interviewed at the top of a new page for each witness and place the names of those present at the interview and the date, time, and place of the interview.
- Pin each witness down to facts: specifically what the witness saw, heard, did, smelled, or felt. Distinguish matters that the witness has personal knowledge of from hearsay.
- Interview the witness—don't let the witness interview you. At the commencement of the interview, state what is being investigated without giving the witness specifics; for example, "We are investigating an employee complaint of improper conduct," not "We are investigating whether or not Simon tried to kiss Maya."
- Explain:
  - Information obtained during the interview will be reported to those within and possibly outside the company who have a "need to know" of it.
  - The seriousness of the investigation.

- The importance of accurate information and the individual's obligation to provide truthful, thorough information.

- Caution the witness against discussing your interview or any information the witness obtains during the interview with any other persons.

- Ask the witness to list all individuals who may have knowledge of any of the events and identify in as much detail as possible what information the witness believes the individuals possess.

- Follow up on answers with appropriate additional questions by developing questions to corroborate or refute information provided by other witnesses or evidence typically without disclosing the source. For example, if the complainant (Betsy) states that a coworker (Ian) tried to kiss her while she was clocking in and she says Eric saw the event, then when you interview Eric, rather than ask him if he saw Ian try to kiss Betsy, ask Eric if he saw anything unusual while he was near the time clock when he was clocking in. Let Eric tell you in his own words what he saw.

- Start with open-ended questions and move to more narrow, focused, and even leading questions after the witness has sketched the limits of the events as he or she recalls them, for example, "Marc, did you see Alana yesterday?" "Okay, when you saw her, was she with Lydia?" "So, you say you did see them directly approach Charlene?'"

- Avoid using compound questions, for example, "Do you remember when Shawn saw Rachel in the office and she became upset?" *Do you remember* is one question and *she became upset* is another. Ask one question at a time. Typically, ask questions that force the witness to relate events chronologically to ensure thorough coverage.

- Try to save unfriendly or embarrassing questions until the end of the interview. Hostile or tough questions usually cause the interviewee to become defensive. However, do not conclude the interview without asking the tough questions, even if the interviewee is uncomfortable.

- Never give the impression that you disbelieve any witness.

- Guard your emotions and do not express an opinion, either by outright statement or by verbal intonation, as to whether something inappropriate occurred during this fact-gathering process. In other words, saying, "I can understand why she might feel that way," is neutral. However, saying, "I can understand why *she* might feel that way," expresses a negative opinion of the person or what she said.

- Prior to concluding the interview, ask if the witness has any other information that may be relevant. Ask if there are any questions that were not asked that the witness feels should have been asked. Let the witness know that if he or she has forgotten or later recalls any information or documents, the witness should call you immediately when additional information comes to mind.

- At the conclusion of each interview, review with the witness the points contained in your notes to confirm their accuracy and determine whether the interviewee has anything to add. Review and finalize the notes immediately on completion of the interview or other communication.

- Remember that, in general, tape-recording interviews is not advisable. Tape recorders often frighten interviewees and make them hesitant to share the facts they have.

- If you will be sending the witness a statement, declaration, or memorandum for review and signature, explain what you will be doing and obtain a promise of cooperation.

- Stress the importance of not disclosing the questions asked, information given, or other information about the interview to others to facilitate a thorough, impartial investigation.

- Avoid discussing theories, strategy, assessment, or other evidence with the witness.

- Do not include in your interview notes your own interpretations, beliefs, assumptions, or conclusions about the information given to you by the interviewee.

The Complainant/Victim

1. When interviewing the complainant/victim, consider asking the individual to write down, either before or at the start of the interview, all incidents of improper conduct in chronological order, and all facts and witnesses that establish what occurred. A handwritten statement by (or at least one prepared by) the complainant/victim

is desirable at this early stage before he or she has counsel who may recast the events in a more negative light. It is helpful to have a checklist/questionnaire form to assist you in capturing basic facts during a witness interview. For example:

1. Information about complainant

Name (Last, First , Middle)			
Address		City	Zip
Home Phone	Work Phone	Cell Phone	
Job Title	Immediate Supervisor	Date of Hire	
Race/Ethnicity	Sex	Age/Date of Birth	
Religion		Other	

2. Information about alleged harasser

Name (Last, First , Middle)			
Address		City	Zip
Home Phone	Work Phone	Cell Phone	
Job Title	Immediate Supervisor	Date of Hire	
Race/Ethnicity	Sex	Age/Date of Birth	
Religion		Other	

3. Basis of charge of discrimination/harassment

☐ Race	☐ Sex/Gender (M/F, pregnant)	☐ Disability
☐ Color	☐ Sexual Orientation (heterosexual,	What is the disability?
☐ Ancestry	homosexual, bisexual)	_____
☐ National	☐ Gender Identity	
Origin	☐ Marital Status	☐ Other
☐ Age	☐ Genetic Predisposition	_____
☐ Religion	☐ Retaliation (opposed	☐ Other
	discrimination)	_____

4. Discriminated by being:

☐ Fired/Discharged	☐ Denied Promotion
☐ Not Hired	☐ Denied Transfer
☐ Forced to Quit	☐ Refused Pay Raise
☐ Laid Off	☐ Unequal Pay
☐ Sexually Harassed	☐ Unequal Hours
☐ Harassed	☐ Suspended
☐ Refused Accommodation	☐ Other (specify): _____

5. Date of last discriminatory action: _____

6. Summary of facts

Dates of Discrimination	Description of Discriminatory Adverse Actions

2. You should also ask the complainant/victim the following questions:

 • Did you ever indicate that you were offended or somehow displeased by the act or offensive statement? (Don't give the impression that unless the complainant said or did something to display displeasure he or she has "hurt" his or her credibility. The *Meritor* case indicates that circumstances may force the victim to submit to the harasser and such acquiescence is not neces-

sar-
ily interpreted to mean that the harasser's actions were welcome.)

- What did you say to show your displeasure? (Try to get exact words spoken.)

- What did you do to show your displeasure? (Try to get the exact words and/or actions.)

- What was the harasser's response to your act or statement? (Try to get exact words spoken.)

- When did you indicate your displeasure?

- Did you ever specifically tell the harasser to stop?

- Did you ever specifically say that you found the conduct to be offensive or to constitute illegal harassment?

- Did you speak to anyone else about the offensive behavior or statement?

- With whom did you speak?

- When did this conversation take place?

- What did you and he or she say [exact words used]? (Also ask about verbal intonation.)

- Did you ever make any notes or record of this incident?

- Did you tape-record it? When?

- What do your notes or recordings say?

- Where is a copy?

- Can we obtain one? (You may want to have a notary public certify that the copy given to you is a true and correct copy of the original it was made from. This can help get something into evidence later on.)

- What did you do after the offensive statement or incident? (Find out if the individual was able to return to normal activi-ties. It is very important to ascertain if the employee was able to return to normal activities because actions constitute hostile environment harassment only if they unreasonably interfere with the victim's ability to do his or her job.)

- Did you ever seek any medical treatment or counseling as a result of the incident or offensive statement?

- When did you first learn of the company's antiharassment policy and complaint procedure?

- To whom did you first report the offensive incident or statement?

- If the individual did not use the complaint procedure promptly: Why did you wait so long to use the complaint procedure to report the incident or statement?

- What action do you want the company to take? (Make no representations regarding what actions the organization may or may not ultimately take! Remember that just because a complainant/victim indicates that he or she wants or doesn't want the company to take certain action does not mean that the individual will not later file a lawsuit claiming that the action taken was inadequate. Also, the victim will always want the harasser severely punished. Job death may be disproportionate to the facts in question.)

3. Before concluding the interview with the complainant/victim you should:

- Thank the employee for raising the issue.

- Reaffirm that the company does not permit retaliation or reprisal for making an honestly believed complaint.

- Ask the employee to keep the investigation and information provided during the interview confidential.

- Express the company's commitment to conclude the matter in a timely manner.

- Confirm that all facts, evidence, and persons with potential information have been disclosed to the best of the individual's ability.

The Accused

The Cat's Paw or Dupe Theory of Liability Always interview the accused party and allow the person the opportunity to fully and fairly tell his or her side of the story. Do not rely solely on information about an employee that you receive from someone else.

In several jurisdictions, the EEOC has successfully argued that an employer should be liable for discrimination even if it did not know that the disciplined employee was a member of a protected class. An example can be drawn from *EEOC v. BCI Coca-Cola Bottling Co. of Los Angeles*, No. 04–2220 (10th Circuit, June 7, 2006). The EEOC successfully argued that Coca-Cola could be liable for race discrimination even though the human resources decision maker was unaware of the employee's race. She made her decision based solely on information she received from the employee's allegedly biased supervisor, who made her his "cat's paw" or dupe.

Steps and Questions for the Accused

1. Identify and give the individual an opportunity to respond to each alleged improper statement or action.

2. Disclose the incidents/statements in full detail so that the accused has a full opportunity to refute or disprove them.

3. Ascertain the extent and nature of the interactions the accused has had with the alleged victim. For example:

   • Have gifts, cards, or notes been exchanged?

   • Has there been a dating, sexual, social, or working relationship?

   • Has the alleged victim initiated or participated in any sexual or otherwise inappropriate discussions, jokes, or gestures? Remember, you are trying to ascertain whether a reasonable person in the same circumstances as the alleged harasser would have deduced that his or her words or actions would be welcome.

   • Has the alleged victim ever indicated any displeasure with anything the accused has said or done or ever asked the accused to stop?

4. Ask the accused for any facts that show anyone else may have a motive to fabricate the allegations against the accused. If the accused denies wrongdoing and claims that the person raising the issue is lying, explore possible reasons.

5. Ask why the accuser would make the claim.

6. Ask if anything has happened between the two individuals that would explain why one would make a meritless complaint.

7. Give the accused an opportunity to provide any alibis or mitigating circumstances.

8. Ask the accused to identify all persons he or she believes should be

interviewed as part of the investigation and what relevant information each is likely to have.

9. Request that the accused provide you with all relevant documents and other evidence.

10. Ask the accused what steps he or she believes should be taken to ensure a thorough investigation.

11. Explain to the accused that the company prohibits any retaliation or reprisal against anyone making a complaint of illegal harassment or anyone who provides information concerning the complaint.

Weingarten Rights

Union employees have a right to union representation at investigatory interviews if they request such representation and reasonably believe the interview will result in their being disciplined. See *NLRB v. Weingarten, Inc.,* 420 U.S. 251, 88 LRRM 2689 (1975 Supreme Court case).

Employees have *Weingarten* rights only during investigatory interviews. An investigatory interview occurs when a supervisor questions an employee to obtain information that could be used as a basis for discipline or asks an employee to defend his or her conduct.

• ***There is no duty to advise* (Weingarten *is not Miranda).*** Employers have no duty to advise employees of their *Weingarten* rights. Consequently, employers may conduct investigatory interviews without the participation of an employee representative if one is not requested.

If an employee makes the request to have union representation present and the employer does not want to grant that request, the employer can present the employee with the choice of (1) participating in the interview without a union representative or (2) having no interview and forgoing any attendant benefits (e.g., the chance to tell his or her side of the story).

• ***There is no right to counsel.*** The National Labor Relations Board (NLRB) has held that an employee's right to have a representative present at an investigatory interview does not include the right to be represented at the interview by a private attorney. See *McLean Hospital,* 264 N.L.R.B. 459, 474 (1982). This ruling has particular import for companies that cooperate in investigations by, for example, the Securities Exchange Commission and the Justice Department, since effectively interviewing employees who are sitting at the interview table with their attorneys may be unproductive or impossible.

- *A* **Weingarten** *representative cannot interfere in the investigation.* In *Weingarten*, the Supreme Court expressly stated that the representative's role is to assist the employee and "may do so by attempting to clarify the facts or suggest other employees who may have knowledge of them." The Court made clear, however, that the employer may "insist" on hearing only the employee's own account of the incident under investigation. Consistent with this principle, a *Weingarten* representative oversteps the bounds if he or she directs the subject of the interview not to answer questions or to answer questions only once. See *New Jersey Bell Telephone Co.*, 308 N.L.R.B. 277 (1992). An employer who ejects the representative who engages in such obstructionist tactics acts lawfully because "it is within an employer's legitimate prerogative to investigate employee misconduct in its facilities without interference from union officials."

- *The employer may proceed without delay.* Although an employee has a right to demand the presence of a representative, the employer is not required to unreasonably delay its investigation. If the requested representative is "unavailable either for personal or other reasons for which the employer is not responsible," and if another representative whose presence could be requested is available, the employer is not obligated to postpone the interview. See *Coca-Cola Bottling*, 227 N.L.R.B. 1276 (1977). Rather, because "the right to hold interviews without delay is a legitimate employer prerogative," the burden remains on the employee to request the presence of an alternative representative. Of course, if the requested representative is not then available, but would be shortly, the NLRB would likely find that no legitimate employer interest is impaired by delaying the interview until the chosen representative can attend.

Conclusion of Investigation

Results

If the results of the investigation are conclusive, take appropriate action. If the results of the investigation are inconclusive, document that outcome and take the most appropriate action reasonable under the circumstances at that time.

Advise the complainant and the accused of any disciplinary action or other corrective steps to be taken, and urge the complainant to come forward immediately if there is any recurrence of the activity or retaliation.

Communicate the outcome only to those members of management or the general staff with a "need to know."

Final Report

Investigative reports aren't book reports. They are detailed and logical documents that discuss the following:

- *Issue/Facts*—What were the allegations and facts?
- *Rule/Policy*—Was there a specific company rule, policy, or procedure, or a federal, state, or city law or ordinance covering the situation?
- *Analysis*—This part of the report compares the allegations and facts to the policy, rule, or law.
- *Conclusions*—These are the results of the analysis, including recommendations and determinations as to the validity of the allegation(s).

The final report provides a document that decision makers can use to determine appropriate action that should or should not be taken.

Workplace Violence

Employer's Duty to Provide a Safe Workplace

An employer's duty to provide a safe workplace can be directly derived from Section 5 of the Occupational Safety and Health Act of 1970 (OSHA), commonly known as the General Duty Clause.

The General Duty Clause says:

a. Each Employer:
   1. Shall furnish to each of his employees employment and a place of employment which are free from recognized hazards that are causing or likely to cause death or serious physical harm to his employees
   2. Shall comply with occupational safety and health standards promulgated under this act
b. Each employee shall comply with occupational safety and

> health standards and all rules, regulations, and orders issued pursuant to this act which are applicable to his own actions and conduct.

Anything can become a *recognized hazard,* including workplace violence, and OSHA applies to any private employer with one or more employees, federal employers, and public sector (state, county, or city) employers in twenty-six states and U.S. territories that have their own OSHA-approved programs.

OSHA invokes the General Duty Clause and levies penalties when the following criteria are met:

- There is not an applicable OSHA standard (regulation). There is no standard dealing with workplace violence.

- The employer failed to keep the workplace free of a hazard to which employees of that employer were exposed.

- The hazard is (or should have been) recognized by the employer.

- The hazard is causing or was likely to cause death or other serious physical harm.

- There is a feasible and useful method to correct the hazard.

Basically, because of the General Duty Clause, employers must provide a workplace that is safe from foreseeable workplace violence.

In addition, Section 5(b) puts a duty on each employee to comply with workplace rules, including those related to workplace violence. Therefore, it is important that you (the employer) have a written, published, and widely disseminated workplace violence policy. In this regard, many of the features of a sexual harassment policy should appear in your workplace violence policy. See "Employer's Discrimination/Harassment Policy" in this chapter.

Workplace Violence Definitions

- *Workplace violence* includes but is not limited to intimidation, threats, physical attack, domestic violence, or property damage and includes acts of violence committed by employees, clients, customers, relatives, acquaintances, or strangers against employees in the workplace.

- *Intimidation* is engaging in actions that include but are not limited to stalking or behavior intended to frighten, coerce, or induce duress.

- *Threat* is the expression of intent to cause physical or mental harm. An expression constitutes a threat without regard to whether the party communicating the threat has the present ability to carry it out and without regard to whether the expression is contingent, conditional, or future.

- *Physical attack* is unwanted or hostile physical contact such as hitting, fighting, pushing, shoving, or throwing objects.

- *Domestic violence* is the use of abusive or violent behavior, including threats and intimidation, between people who have an ongoing or prior intimate relationship. This could include people who are married, live together, or date or who have been married, lived together, or dated.

- *Property damage* is intentional damage to property and includes property owned by the organization, its employees, visitors, or vendors.

Types of Workplace Violence and Their Characteristics

Workplace violence occurs in a variety of forms, including violence by strangers, violence by customers or clients, violence by coworkers, and violence by personal relations.

Violence by Strangers

Violence by strangers involves verbal threats, threatening behavior, or physical assaults by an assailant who has no legitimate business relationship to the workplace. According to OSHA, violence by strangers is responsible for the majority of fatal injuries related to workplace violence nationally. Workplaces at risk of violence by strangers commonly include late-night retail establishments and taxicabs.

Violence by Customers or Clients

Violence by customers or clients involves verbal threats, threatening behavior, or physical assaults by an assailant who either receives services from or is under the custodial supervision of the affected workplace or the victim. Assailants can be current or former customers or clients. They can be

(1) individuals who have exhibited violent behavior in the past or (2) those who are situationally violent—for example, individuals provoked when they become frustrated by delays or by the denial of benefits or social services.

Violence by Coworkers

Violence by coworkers involves verbal threats, threatening behavior, or physical assaults by an assailant who has some employment-related involvement with the workplace, such as a current or former employee, supervisor, or manager. Any workplace can be at risk of violence by a coworker.

Violence by Personal Relations

Violence by personal relations involves verbal threats, threatening behavior, or physical assaults by an assailant who, in the workplace, confronts an individual with whom he or she has or had a personal relationship outside of work. Personal relations include a current or former spouse, lover, relative, friend, or acquaintance.

Identifying the Risk Factors and Symptoms of Workplace Violence

Employees as well as managers should be trained to recognize the stages of workplace violence. That recognition is essential for the employer to intervene in a timely and appropriate manner before a violent episode occurs. Management should have a plan in place for appropriate, early intervention.

The following indicators can signal the risk potential of violent episodes:

- Sudden and persistent complaining about being treated unfairly
- Blaming of others for personal problems
- Sudden change in behavior, deterioration in job performance
- Statement that he or she would like something bad to happen to a supervisor or coworker
- Paranoid behavior
- Sudden increased absenteeism

- Sexually harassing or obsessing about a coworker: sending unwanted gifts and/or notes, unwanted calling, stalking
- Increased demand of supervisor's time
- Alcohol or drug abuse
- Talking to oneself
- Instability in family relationships
- Financial problems combined with not receiving a raise or promotion
- Poor relationships with coworkers or management
- History of violent behavior
- Previous threats, direct or indirect
- Presenting and talking about reading material that is violent in nature
- Carrying a concealed weapon, or flashing one around
- Quiet seething, sullenness
- Refusal to accept criticism about job performance
- Sudden mood swings, depression
- Sudden refusal to comply with rules or refusal to perform duties
- Inability to control feelings: outbursts of rage, swearing, or slamming of doors

If an employee begins demonstrating any or a combination of the previous indicators, it is important that management refer him or her to the employee assistance program (EAP) or other counseling services as soon as possible. To assist the employee, to protect other workers, and to avoid liability, it is imperative that management respond in an empathic, caring, and non-shaming manner, remembering that time is of the essence.

Prevention Strategies

Environmental Designs

Some common environmental violence prevention strategies include, but are not limited to, the following:

- Cash-handling policies in using locked drop safes, carrying small amounts of cash, and posting signs and printing notices that limited cash is available.

- Providing physical separation of employees from customers, clients, and the general public through the use of bullet-resistant barriers or enclosures.

- Making high-risk areas visible to more people and installing good external lighting.

- Controlling access to and exits from the workplace, the ease with which nonworkers can gain access to work areas because doors are unlocked, and the number of areas where potential attackers can hide.

- Using numerous security devices such as closed-circuit cameras; alarms; two-way mirrors; electronic control access systems; panic-bar doors locked from the outside only; and trouble lights or geographic-locating devices in mobile workplaces, such as trucks, vans, and cars.

Administrative Controls

Administrative violence prevention and control strategies include, but are not limited to, the following:

- Publishing a workplace violence policy and distributing it to all employees.

- Establishing a system for documenting violent incidents in the workplace. Such statistics are essential for assessing the nature and magnitude of workplace violence in a given workplace and quantifying risk.

- Using security guards or receptionists to screen persons entering the workplace and to control access to actual work areas.

- Developing appropriate work practices and staffing patterns during the opening and closing of establishments and during money drops and pickups.

Behavioral Strategies

Behavioral violence prevention and control strategies include, but are not limited to, the following:

- Enforcing workplace violence policies.

- Training employees in nonviolent response and conflict resolution.

- Emphasizing the appropriate use and maintenance of protective equipment, adherence to administrative controls, and increased knowledge and awareness of the risk of workplace violence.

A proactive approach can greatly help in reducing workplace violence and in mitigating its impact if it does occur.

CHAPTER 8

Privacy Issues

Introduction

Defining Privacy

Privacy has become an important issue in the modern workplace; however, there is no one overriding and definitive body of law, either statutory or regulatory, that defines what *privacy in the workplace* actually means or what its boundaries are. What does exist is a complex and confusing set of federal and state laws, state constitutional doctrines, and a variety of (and sometimes conflicting) court cases based on tort (civil wrongs) and contract theories.

Making matters even more confusing is that different laws dealing with employment discrimination, defamation, intrusion upon seclusion, occupational safety and health, physical impairments, personal health information, and so forth have different objectives and mandates.

This chapter approaches the subject of privacy by discussing various aspects of the conflict between the employer's legitimate business interests in obtaining and maintaining information about a job applicant or employee, as well as in observing, evaluating, and regulating employee conduct related to the work relationship, and the employee's interest in individual autonomy and the right to be left alone.

The Employer's Dilemma—Liability for Wrongful Acts of Employees

When recruiting, selecting, hiring, and retaining employees, employers often run into the problem of having federal and state laws forbidding inquiry into many aspects of the applicant's personal life, such as: "Have you ever filed a workers compensation claim?" or "Have you ever been arrested?" Other laws and especially case law require employers to carefully screen applicants or run the risk of becoming liable for *negligent hiring*.

A number of these problems can be avoided by carefully making lawful, job-related inquiries and decisions. See Chapter 1, "Hiring," for a full discussion of lawful hiring practices.

The Doctrine of Respondeat Superior

It is well-settled American law that the employer is liable for the wrongful acts of its employees committed in the course of their employment. This is called the doctrine of *respondeat superior*.

Employees act within the scope of their employment when they perform services for which they are employed or when they do anything that is reasonably related to their employment. The issue is "were their action(s) foreseeable"—not were the actions authorized or forbidden by the employer.

Subject to the issues raised in the following section of this chapter, if the worker's wrongful conduct was motivated by purely personal reasons unrelated to the employer's business, then the employer is not liable.

An analysis of four questions can help you determine if the worker acted within the scope of his or her employment:

1. What was the purpose of the employee's act(s)?
2. Did the employee have authority, either express or implied, to perform the act(s) in question?
3. Was the act(s) reasonably foreseeable by the employer?
4. When was the act committed, such as during work hours? (This last consideration is a minor one. The others carry more weight.)

Negligent Hiring

An action for negligent hiring tries to hold an employer accountable for injuries caused by an employee acting outside the scope of his or her employment if the employer (a) knew or should have known that the worker had a propensity to act the way he or she did and (b) did nothing to prevent the employee from committing the wrong.

The elements of negligent hiring are that:

- The perpetrator and the victim would not have met had the employer not hired the wrongdoer.

- Had the employer performed a reasonable background check or engaged in other reasonable hiring practices it would have determined that the perpetrator was unfit for the position.

- The employer did not exercise reasonable care to select an employee competent and fit for the work assigned to him or her.

- The employer hired the wrongdoer.

- The victim was harmed by the employer's negligence.

The danger of negligent hiring is a primary reason for an employer to verify the information provided on an application and to undertake a preemployment background investigation suitable to the position in question. For example, jobs involving access to customers' homes or property or occupying a position of trust with regard to third parties will almost always impose a duty to carefully investigate the employee's background and suitability.

Background Checks

Depending on your company's industry, you may be required by law to conduct background checks on your employees and may be precluded from hiring employees convicted of particular offenses—for example, employees in child care and education or employees associated with the sale of securities.

Regardless of whether the law requires your company to do so, conducting background checks makes good sense in that it allows you to verify the accuracy of information in a prospective employee's job application form and potentially prevents future negligent-hiring lawsuits.

The "Okay" Four

When Answering Inquiries

Attorneys often advise their clients not to be forthcoming when organizations call them and attempt to get background information about former employees unless the other entity has provided them with a signed consent form from the ex-employee in question.

It is generally all right to respond to the following four questions even without having been provided with a consent and release:

1. Did the applicant work for you?
2. What were the applicant's dates of employment?
3. What was the applicant's job title or general job duties?
4. Did the applicant make [compensation]? *Do not* volunteer information regarding the ex-employee's compensation. It is all right to confirm or deny what the caller states that the former worker represented to him or her.

Do not answer medically related questions. See Chapter 1 regarding the Americans with Disabilities Act (ADA) and pre-offer stage inquiries.

When Making Inquiries

When asking questions yourself, some common background inquiries are:

- How long have you known the candidate? In what relationship or capacity?
- What was the candidate's position? To whom did he or she report?
- What were the candidate's responsibilities? Scope?
- How did the candidate get along with superiors, peers, and subordinates?
- Describe the candidate's attitudes and other personality factors.
- What were some of the candidate's outstanding accomplishments?
- How effective was the candidate in terms of quantity and quality of work?
- How creative was the candidate? How much initiative did he or she display? Motivation? Resourcefulness?

- Describe the candidate's leadership ability and responsibility levels.

- What were the candidate's strengths? Aptitudes? Weaknesses?

- How well does the candidate express himself or herself orally? In writing?

- Did the candidate meet deadlines?

- What was the candidate's salary? Did he or she receive any bonuses? (You can ask these questions, but just don't answer them if they are posed to you in this format.)

- Why did the candidate leave?

- Would you rehire the candidate? (This is probably one of the most important questions to ask, if it is answered honestly.)

- Do you feel that the candidate can work effectively as a [title of job]?

Consent Forms

Consumer Reports and Investigative Consumer Reports

When obtaining background history information on employees or prospective employees, keep in mind that the federal Fair Credit Reporting Act (FCRA), 15 USC Section 1681 et seq., regulates how you obtain and use background history information. The FCRA applies to consumer reports and investigative consumer reports prepared by consumer-reporting agencies (which include background check vendors, private investigators, and detective agencies) for the purpose of providing information to a third party, such as the employer.

Consumer reports may consist of background reports, credit history checks, and Department of Motor Vehicles (DMV) records. Investigative consumer reports contain information regarding an applicant or employee's character, general reputation, personal characteristics, or mode of living obtained through personal interviews with friends, neighbors, or business associates, as well as through employment verification with prior employers.

If you use a consumer-reporting agency to procure background history information, you are required to adhere to the FCRA's steps for compliance, including disclosure and authorization, certification, advance notice of adverse action, and notice of adverse action.

Employers who intend to obtain background checks on employees and applicants need to:

- Provide a written notice to the employee/applicant explaining that a consumer report will be obtained, and if an investigative consumer report is to be obtained, then the notice must specifically indicate that fact.
- Obtain the employee's signed consent for the background check *in a document separate from an employment application or an employee handbook.*

Example of Consent for a Consumer Report or an Investigative Consumer Report

I hereby authorize [the Company] and its designated agents and representatives to conduct a comprehensive review of my background causing a consumer report and/or an investigative consumer report to be generated for employment purposes.

I understand that the scope of the consumer report/investigative consumer report may include, but is not limited to, the following areas:

Verification of Social Security number; current and previous residences; employment history including all personnel files; education including transcripts; character references; credit history and reports; criminal history records from any criminal justice agency in any or all federal, state, county jurisdictions; birth records; motor vehicle records to include traffic citations and registration; and any other public records or to conduct interviews with third parties relative to my character, or general reputation.

I further authorize any individual, company, firm, corporation, or public agency (including the Social Security Administration and law enforcement agencies) to divulge any and all information, verbal or written, pertaining to me to [the Company] or its agents. I further authorize the complete release of any records or data pertaining to me that the individual, company, firm, corporation, or public agency may have, to include information or data received from other sources.

I hereby release [the Company], the Social Security Administration, and its agents, officials, representatives, or assigned agencies, including officers, employees, or related personnel both individually and collectively, from any and all liability for damages of whatever kind, which may, at any time, result to me, my heirs, family, or associates because of compliance with this authorization and request to release information.

I understand from time to time [the Company] may receive a request from a client for whom I am performing services, or in anticipation of my providing such services, to provide information obtained during the background investigation. I hereby authorize [the Company] to release and/or disclose information obtained in the background investigation to such clients, said information to include, but not be limited to, consumer investigation reports, criminal history, employment and education history.

Name: _____   Date: _____

- Certify to the consumer-reporting agency that the previous steps have been followed and that the employer will comply with the FCRA.

- Provide advance notice of any intended adverse action to the individual and provide a copy of the report to the individual, along with the "Summary of Your Rights Under the Fair Credit Reporting Act," written by the Federal Trade Commission prior to taking adverse action. (See www.ftc.gov.) The purpose of the notice is to give the individual an opportunity to dispute or explain any inaccurate or incomplete information in the background check report.

- Supply the applicant, upon taking adverse action, with a copy of the report, the "Summary of Your Rights" document and the contact information for the consumer-reporting agency that furnished the report, as well as a statement that the consumer-reporting agency did not make the adverse decision and cannot explain why it was made.

Failure to comply with the FCRA provisions can subject employers to damages, including actual damages, punitive damages, costs, and attorneys' fees. Employers may also be liable for fines and/or imprisonment if they knowingly and willfully obtain a consumer report under false pretenses.

Medical Information During the Hiring Process

The Americans with Disabilities Act

Pre-Offer Inquiries and Medical Exams

The ADA prohibits medical examinations or inquiries into an applicant's disability status prior to the employer's making a job offer conditioned on the individual passing a preemployment physical that tests the person's ability to perform the essential functions of the job.

The statute does allow post-offer medical exams and inquiries; however, it imposes strict limitations on the use and disclosure of medical information.

Medical Information—Confidentiality

Medical information must be kept in files separate from the employee's personnel file.

In addition, both the ADA (29 CFR 1630.14) and the Family and Medical Leave Act (FMLA) (29 CFR 825.500) require that medically related information be kept confidential, with the following exceptions:

- Supervisors and managers may be informed regarding necessary restrictions on the work or duties of the employee and necessary accommodations.

- First aid and safety personnel may be informed, when appropriate, if the disability might require emergency treatment.

- Government officials investigating compliance with the ADA and other federal or state laws prohibiting discrimination must be provided relevant information on request.

- Pertinent information may be provided to state workers compensation offices and insurance companies providing health or life insurance to the employee.

In addition, improper disclosure of medical information may expose the employer to liability for invasion of privacy. See "Invasion of Privacy" in this chapter.

Consumer-Reporting Agencies—Section 411, FACTA

Section 411 of the Fair and Accurate Credit Transactions Act of 2003 (FACT Act, or FACTA) amended the FCRA to provide that a creditor may not obtain or use medical information in connection with any determination of a consumer's eligibility, or continued eligibility, for credit, except as permitted by regulations or the FACT Act. Section 411 prohibits a consumer-reporting agency from furnishing a report containing medical information about a consumer for employment purposes unless the employee has given specific, written consent.

Employers must obtain from the applicant or employee a *specific* written consent in clear and conspicuous language describing the use for which the information will be furnished. The medical-related information sought by the employer must be job related, just as under the ADA and FMLA. For example, this provision would prevent an agency conducting a background investigation from being able to disclose any medical-related information inadvertently disclosed while conducting a background investigation unless the employer had already obtained a specific consent from the applicant or employee. In this regard, the legislation adds a further layer of privacy by specifically reminding employers that medical information should not be disclosed except as necessary to carry out the purpose for which the information was initially disclosed, or otherwise permitted by law.

Medical Information Under the FACT Act Defined

The FACT Act defines medical information broadly to mean information or data, whether oral or recorded, in any form or medium, created by or derived from a health-care provider, or the consumer, that relates to the past, present, or future physical, mental, or behavioral health or condition of an individual, the providing of health care to an individual, or the payment for the providing of health care to an individual.

Preemployment Drug Tests or Screens

Drug tests or post-offer medical examinations received about applicants are not necessarily subject to the FCRA. Reports prepared by health-care providers and laboratories at the request of an employer are not generally considered a consumer report because such communications fall within a different exception of the FCRA. For example, a physician or drug counselor who reports the results of a drug test is not creating a consumer report. However, if an entity obtains copies of drug tests and sells this information to third parties for a fee, then it could be considered a consumer-reporting agency and consent would be needed.

Genetic and Biochemical Testing

Recent years have brought dramatic scientific advances in the study of human genetics, such as the Human Genome Project. These genetic advances create opportunities for discrimination against individuals based on their genetic information, even where individuals have no symptoms of disease.

Discrimination based on genetic information appeared as far back as the early 1970s, when employers used genetic screening to identify and exclude African Americans carrying a gene mutation for sickle cell anemia. Individuals were denied jobs even though they were healthy and never developed the disease. There was also discrimination by insurance companies against individuals who were carriers of sickle cell anemia even though they were asymptomatic.

Federal Law

Executive Order 13145 to Prohibit Discrimination in Federal Employment Based on Genetic Information was signed on February 8, 2000, by President Bill Clinton. Although the executive order states that genetic discrimination is added to the list of forms of discrimination barred by Title VII of the Civil Rights Act of 1964, the scope of the order does not reach beyond applicants, employees, and former employees of executive branch departments and agencies. It does not cover employees in the private sector. Private sector employers are covered by the Genetic Information Nondiscrimination Act (see Chapter 6, "Employment Laws").

State Laws

There is a hodgepodge of state laws dealing with genetic information and testing. Although a number of states have passed laws prohibiting certain forms of genetic discrimination, these laws vary widely with (1) some narrowly targeting particular genetic conditions, (2) some prohibiting only certain types of screening but not prohibiting adverse employment actions based on genetic information, and (3) some addressing only genetic counseling and confidentiality.

The ADA and Genetic Information Discrimination

Some plaintiffs have argued that the ADA prohibits discrimination based on genetic information. Their contention is based on the fact that the ADA protects individuals who (1) have an impairment that substantially limits them in a major life activity, (2) have a record of such an impairment, or (3) are regarded as having such an impairment.

The argument is that people who experience discrimination on the basis of predictive genetic information are being regarded as having a disability. In light of recent Supreme Court cases, this is a difficult argument to make. To be covered under *regarded as* having a disability, the plaintiff would have to prove that he or she was regarded as substantially limited in performing a broad class of jobs, not just his or her own job. That is one of the messages of *Sutton v. United Airlines, Inc.,* 527 U.S. 471, 473–74 (1999) and *Murphy v. United Parcel Service, Inc.,* 527 U.S. 516, 516–17 (1999) in which the Court stated that a job requirement excluding individuals based on their impairments does not necessarily establish that the employer regards individuals excluded by this requirement as substantially limited in working. In other words, it may be difficult for plaintiffs with genetic markers who are denied employment due to an employer's concern about health insurance premiums or productivity losses to show that the employer regarded them as substantially limited in performing not only the job in question but a broad class of other jobs as well.

The Health Insurance Portability and Accountability Act

The Health Insurance Portability and Accountability Act (HIPAA) prohibits genetic discrimination by insurers, not employers, in very limited circumstances.

HIPAA prohibits group health plans from using any health status–related factor, including genetic information, as a basis for denying or limiting coverage or for charging an individual more for coverage. A plan can still establish limitations on the amount, level, extent, or nature of benefits or coverage provided to similarly situated individuals.

In addition, HIPAA regulations require patient consent for most sharing of personal health information by health insurers, providers, and health-care clearinghouses. Companies that sponsor health plans are prohibited from accessing personal health information for employment purposes unless the patient consents.

Basically, HIPAA does little to prevent genetic discrimination in the workplace.

Title VII, Civil Rights Act of 1964

Race and gender discrimination laws (see Chapter 6, "Employment Laws") may apply to certain forms of genetic discrimination in that they forbid an employer from having policies that have a disparate (disproportionate) negative impact on members of protected classes. Therefore, employment policies that deny employment or employment opportunities based on genetic markers, such as sickle cell anemia linked to race or breast or ovarian cancer linked to gender, may have a prohibited disparate impact on African Americans or women.

Drug and Alcohol Testing

Public Sector Employers

The Fourth Amendment to the U.S. Constitution protects citizens from unlawful searches and seizures by the state (government). The Supreme Court has ruled that blood, urine, and breath tests are searches under the Fourth Amendment; however, whenever there is an overriding interest in public safety and health, especially in heavily regulated industries, such as transportation, where there is no reasonable expectation of privacy, public entities almost always are allowed to demand drug and alcohol testing of their employees.

As a general set of rules governing drug testing in the private sector, the following applies:

- Job applicants can be tested for drugs.
- Random or universal testing of employees without any probable cause to believe there is a problem is generally prohibited except in cases (jobs) involving health, safety, or the public trust.
- If the employer reasonably believes an employee has a drug problem at work, it can demand testing ("suspicion" testing).
- The employer should not act on positive results without confirmatory tests.

Private Sector Employers

Preemployment drug testing is generally allowed in most states.

Reasonable suspicion testing is allowed.

Except in high-risk or safety-sensitive positions, a number of states prohibit random or universal drug testing or require it to conform to scientific and procedural standards.

To avoid liability and reduce or eliminate an employee's expectation of privacy, employers should have a written and widely distributed drugs-in-the-workplace policy dealing with preemployment testing, reasonable suspicion testing, and so forth.

Unionized Workplaces

Drug testing in a union setting is a mandatory subject of collective bargaining. Almost without exception, discipline for infractions of drug rules will be subject to the just cause provisions of collective bargaining agreements.

Employee Polygraph Protection Act of 1988

The Employee Polygraph Protection Act of 1988 (EPPA) generally prevents employers from using lie detector tests either for preemployment screening or during the course of employment, with certain exemptions.

The secretary of labor, through the Wage and Hour Division of the Employment Standards Administration, enforces EPPA. The Act empowers the secretary of labor to bring injunctive actions in U.S. district courts to restrain violations, and to assess civil money penalties up to $10,000 against employers who violate *any* provision of the Act.

Employers are required to post notices summarizing the protections of the Act in their places of work.

Prohibitions

Under the EPPA the employer cannot:

- Require, request, suggest, or cause an employee or prospective employee to take or submit to any lie detector test.
- Use, accept, refer to, or inquire about the results of any lie detector test of an employee or prospective employee.
- Discharge, discipline, discriminate against, deny employment or promotion, or threaten to take any such action against an em-

ployee or prospective employee for refusal to take a test, on the basis of the results of a test, for filing a complaint, for testifying in any proceeding, or for exercising any rights afforded by the EPPA.

Exemptions

The EPPA excludes federal, state, and local governments. Lie detector tests administered by the federal government to employees of federal contractors engaged in national security intelligence or counterintelligence functions are also exempt.

The EPPA also includes limited exemptions where polygraph tests (but no other lie detector tests) may be administered in the private sector.

A *polygraph* means an instrument that records continuously, visually, permanently, and simultaneously changes in cardiovascular, respiratory, and electrodermal patterns as minimum instrumentation standards and is used to render a diagnostic opinion as to the honesty or dishonesty of an individual.

A *lie detector* has a broader meaning than a polygraph. A lie detector includes a polygraph, deceptograph, voice stress analyzer, psychological stress evaluator, or similar device (whether mechanical or electrical) used to render a diagnostic opinion as to the honesty or dishonesty of an individual.

The employer can administer polygraphs as follows:

- To employees who are reasonably suspected of involvement in a workplace incident that results in economic loss to the employer and who had access to the property that is the subject of an investigation

- To prospective employees of armored car, security alarm, and security guard firms who protect facilities, materials, or operations affecting health or safety, national security, or currency and other like instruments

- To prospective employees of pharmaceutical and other firms authorized to manufacture, distribute, or dispense controlled substances who will have direct access to such controlled substances, as well as current employees who had access to persons or property that are the subject of an ongoing investigation

An employee or prospective employee must be given a written notice explaining the employee's or prospective employee's rights and the limitations imposed, such as prohibited areas of questioning and restriction on the use of test results. Among other rights, an employee or prospective employee may refuse to take a test, may terminate a test at any time, or may decline to take a test if he or she suffers from a medical condition.

The results of a test alone cannot be disclosed to anyone other than the employer or employee/prospective employee without the latter's consent or, pursuant to court order, to a court, a government agency, an arbitrator, or a mediator.

Under the exemption for ongoing investigations of workplace incidents involving economic loss, a written or verbal statement must be provided to the employee prior to the polygraph test that explains the specific incident or activity being investigated and the basis for the employer's reasonable suspicion that the employee was involved in such incident or activity.

Where polygraph examinations are permitted they are subject to strict standards concerning the conduct of the test, including the pre-test, testing, and post-test phases of the examination.

Civil actions for legal or equitable relief, such as employment reinstatement, promotion, and payment of lost wages and benefits, may be brought by an employee or a prospective employee in federal or state court against employers who violate the Act. The action must be brought within three years of the date of the alleged violation.

Monitoring Employees in the Workplace

Because of federal and state law restrictions on the interception of any wire, oral, or electronic communications, it is essential that you, the employer, have written and clear policies dealing with monitoring employees' communications and activities in the workplace and that these policies are made well known to all workers.

These policies should specifically cover telephone, electronic, computer, Internet, and all other forms of communication as well as dealing with workplace searches and surveillance, both human and mechanical, of employees.

The Electronic Communications Privacy Act of 1986

The Electronic Communications Privacy Act (ECPA) prohibits the interception of e-mail transmissions by (1) unauthorized individuals or (2) individuals working for a government entity acting without a proper warrant.

An employer that illegally monitors or discloses the contents of an employee's call can be liable for fines and imprisonment, and the worker can sue for actual and punitive damages, as well as reasonable attorneys' fees and other costs of litigation.

The ECPA has several exceptions to the prohibition of interception of electronic communications, namely where:

- One party consents.
- The provider of the communication service can monitor communications.
- The monitoring is done in the ordinary course of business.

E-Mail and Internet Monitoring

The ECPA prohibits the intentional interception of "wire, oral, or electronic communications" in transmission. However, employers whose facilities are used to provide electronic communication service may do so "while engaged in any activity which is a necessary incident to the rendition of his service or to the protection of the [provider's] rights or property." This provision excludes "random monitoring except for mechanical or service quality control checks." Therefore, unless an employer "just happens" to intercept e-mails while servicing the facilities over which they are transmitted, interceptions of e-mails in transmission will not pass muster under the ECPA.

As a result of the potential and likely application of "wire communications" to e-mails, an employer should obtain consent, either expressly through a signed annual statement or implicitly through notification to employees, for example, with a daily banner reminder at sign-on that e-mails may be monitored.

Sample E-Mail and Internet Policy Employee Consent Statement

The Company's e-mail system and other forms of communication now existing or established in the future, of whatever nature and type (the "System"), is primarily intended for business use. The System is valuable Company property and may be used only for Company business. Incidental and occasional personal use of e-mail is permitted. The System is not to be used for employee personal gain or to support or advocate for non-Company-related business or purposes. All use of the System is subject to management access pursuant to this Policy.

Your failure to comply with this Policy could lead to disciplinary action up to and including termination of your employment. This Policy does not limit or amend other Company policies or agreements that may be in force now or in the future.

Do Not Expect Privacy. The Company may access, read, monitor, intercept, copy, and delete your communications if the Company deems it appropriate; however, the Company would do so only when it feels, in its sole discretion, there is a legitimate business reason. By way of example and not of limitation, the Company might do so if the Company suspects any violation of law, breach of security, or violation of Company policies. Furthermore, the Company may disclose your communications to third parties if the Company deems it appropriate. Therefore, **you should not expect privacy in your System account or any communications on the System or on any other communications media of any nature and type provided for your use by the Company now or in the future.**

Deleted messages and e-mails. Simply deleting an e-mail, text, or other message from your account does not destroy the message. E-mail messages and other forms of messaging may remain on the Company's e-mail server and other servers, and the Company often makes back-up copies of its e-mail and other servers that may be stored for months or years. Even after the Company erases the back-up copies, various software products may be able to restore the erased messages. Furthermore, in the case of e-mail sent over the Internet, copies of the e-mail could persist on the recipient's system (or any person who receives a forwarded copy from this person) indefinitely. Therefore, **you should not expect privacy related to any e-mail or other messages you have deleted.**

Control of e-mails and other forms of messaging. You effectively have no ability to control who sees an e-mail or other forms of messaging once they are sent. E-mails sent over the Internet cannot be "retrieved." Furthermore, e-mails are often forwarded to people you did not anticipate would receive it. Also, the Company may be required in future litigation to produce copies of your e-mails in a court proceeding, and the Company may do so without notifying you or asking your permission. Therefore, **you should not expect privacy related to any e-mail or other messages you have sent.**

Prohibited Uses. The Company's general policies regarding employee communications also apply to communications made using the System. Without limiting the foregoing, you may not use the System to send, receive, store, or display communications or files that:

- Infringe any third-party intellectual property or publicity/privacy right.
- Violate any law or regulation.
- Are defamatory, threatening, insulting, abusive, or violent.
- Might be construed as harassing, derogatory, disparaging, biased, or discriminatory based on a person's age, sex, race, sexual orientation, religion, disability, national origin, or any other protected classification.
- Are obscene, pornographic, harmful to minors, child pornographic, profane, or vulgar.
- Contain any viruses, Trojan horses, worms, time bombs, cancel bots, or other computer programming routines that are intended to damage, detrimentally interfere with, surreptitiously intercept, or expropriate any system, data, or personal information.
- Are solicitations or advertisements for commercial ventures, religious or political causes, outside organizations, or other non-job-related activities.

Under no circumstances may you use the System to gain unauthorized access to third-party resources.

Without any further notice to you, the Company may use software that restricts your access to certain websites or that keeps a log of the websites you visit.

System Security. The System is not perfectly secure and is susceptible to break-ins. You may not share your System passwords with anyone else (including other company employees) and you may not gain access to other System accounts without prior management authorization. **The Company reserves the right to override your password for legitimate business reasons.**

System Integrity. You should not use the System in a way that disrupts or degrades its performance.

Corporate Communications. Every time you send an e-mail that contains the Company domain name or transmit files using the System, third parties might interpret these communications as official corporate communications or legally binding statements of the corporation. Therefore, at minimum, **you should not use the System to make any statements or take any action that might be interpreted as a press release or publicity statement without management approval.**

Amendments to This Policy. This Policy supersedes all prior communications, oral or written, regarding the System. **You agree that the Company may amend this Policy by sending you an e-mail containing the new policy, and the amended policy shall be effective as soon as it is sent by the Company.**

Acknowledgment: **I understand and agree to comply with this Internet and E-mail Use Policy, and in particular I understand and agree that the company may access, read, monitor, intercept, copy, and delete my communications if it deems it appropriate. I understand that my failure to comply with any of the provisions in this policy may lead to disciplinary action, up to and including termination of my employment.**

Signed: _____ Date: _____

Rather than intercept e-mails in transmission, it is more common for an employer to access e-mails while in storage. In these situations, the Stored Communications Act (SCA) applies. It prohibits access to stored e-mails except for the person or entity providing a wire or electronic communications service. As a result, an employer who provides an e-mail system for its employees may monitor e-mails without violating the SCA. If e-mails are transmitted through a third-party service provider, an employer may access e-mails if it has the employees' consent.

Another computer issue that arises in employee investigations is the monitoring of Internet use. Such action may prompt claims of invasion of privacy. In these cases, courts have considered who owns the computer and whether the employer notified the employee that computer use may be monitored.

Listening to Telephone Calls and Voice Messages

An employer may not listen to employees' telephone conversations unless one of two exceptions applies. The first is *consent*. This requires that one-party consent and monitoring is not for the purpose of committing any criminal or tortuous act.

Consent may be implied where an employer notifies employees that calls will be monitored and employees continue to use the phone system anyway. However, the scope of the consent is limited to the extent of the employer's monitoring policy. For example, an employer who notifies employees that it will monitor all sales calls may not listen in on personal calls. If a personal call is intercepted in that situation, the employer may listen only long enough to determine the nature of the call.

The other exception allowing an employer to listen to employees' telephone conversations is the *business use exception*. The interception of wire communications is prohibited only when it is accomplished through the use of an "electronic, mechanical, or other device." According to the ECPA, an electronic, mechanical, or other device is defined as:

> [A]ny device or apparatus which can be used to intercept a wire, oral, or electronic communication *other than*—(a) any telephone or telegraph instrument, equipment or facility, or any component thereof, (i) furnished to the subscriber or user by a provider of wire or electronic communication service in the ordinary course of its business and being used by the subscriber or user in the ordinary course of its business or furnished by such subscriber or user for connection to the facilities of such service and used in the ordinary course of its business. . . .

Therefore, to establish the business use exception, the employer must prove two elements:

> (1) [T]he intercepting equipment must be furnished to the user by the phone company or connected to the phone line, and (2) it must be used in the ordinary course of business.

Use in the ordinary course of business requires that the employer have a legitimate business reason for monitoring telephone calls and industry practice may help establish a legitimate business reason. However, the phrase "in the ordinary course of business" cannot be expanded to mean anything that interests a company. It excludes personal calls except to the extent necessary to determine the nature of the call. This is true even if the subject of the personal call may affect the company or comments related to the employer's business are interspersed with personal conversation; however, the business use exception doesn't insulate employees from interception of telephone conversations discussing personal opinions about the workplace.

You should have employees sign an acknowledgment that the employer may access, read, monitor (listen to), intercept, copy, and delete the employee's communications if the employer deems it appropriate.

Surveillance, Searches, and Other Intrusions

Surveillance

Basically, an employer can engage in surveillance or undertake searches if the employee has no expectation of privacy and the action(s) are reasonably related to the workplace or the employer's business.

Surveillance of union activities is an unfair labor practice under the Fair Labor Standards Act. In a union setting, surveillance will almost certainly be an issue that must be bargained for by the company.

Some states have enacted laws placing restrictions on surveillance. Common are restrictions on the use of any electronic surveillance system in areas designed for the health or personal comfort of employees or for safeguarding their possessions, such as restrooms, locker rooms, or lounges.

Employers should inform employees that monitoring can occur, through written notice and perhaps with signage, and conduct such activity only for legitimate business purposes.

Searches and Other Intrusions

Basically, an employer can search an employee's property to prevent theft, detect the presence of alcohol or drugs, or recover stolen property if the employee has no expectation of privacy and the action(s) are reasonably related to the workplace or the employer's business.

In the case of *O'Connor v. Ortega*, 480 U.S. 709 (1987), the Supreme Court said that for a workplace search to be legitimate it must be (1) "justified at its inception" (something reasonable triggered the search), and (2) "reasonably related in scope to the circumstances" that prompted the search. For example, it would not be reasonable to search a pencil drawer for a missing desktop computer.

Employers should expressly in writing inform employees that their desks, lockers, and other areas the organization allows them to use are not their personal area or space. They should not expect privacy in such areas or spaces, and the employer must be provided a copy of any keys or combinations to any locking mechanisms of such areas or spaces.

The employee's property includes motor vehicles on the employer's premises. In this regard the employer should advise workers, in writing, that if they are asked to allow a search of their vehicle and they refuse, they could be subject to disciplinary action up to and including termination.

Regulating Employee Off-Duty, Off-Premise Lifestyle

Off-duty, off-premise behaviors or incidents can affect the work environment, employee performance, morale, and the organization's reputation in the community, as well as impact its health insurance costs.

In the absence of a law prohibiting the employer from disciplining an employee or refusing employment to an applicant for his or her off-duty, off-premise behaviors the employer can, in fact, take such action(s). For example, many companies will not hire smokers.

A number of states have passed so-called lifestyle laws that fall into the following three categories:

1. *Prohibition of Discrimination Based on Off-Duty Smoking.* This is the most limited form of protection and is the most common.

2. *Prohibition of Discrimination Based on Off-Duty Use of All Legal Substances.* This expands coverage to off-duty, off-premise drinking of alcoholic products and, possibly, to people with high cholesterol or other conditions related to diet.

3. *Prohibition of Discrimination Based on Any Legal Off-Duty Behavior.* This is the broadest type of coverage and exists only in

a few states including California, North Dakota, New York, and Colorado.

Courts have been sympathetic to employer policies regulating off-duty, off-premise behaviors when the employer can show that the regulated conduct:

- Is directly related to the job assigned to the employee
- Clearly threatens the employer's business with substantial adverse impact in the absence of the employer's regulation

Invasion of Privacy

When conducting an internal investigation for any purpose, an employer must be careful to recognize its employees' reasonable expectation of privacy. What expectation of privacy is reasonable will differ depending on the facts of each situation.

Employers can reduce employees' reasonable expectation of privacy by putting employees on notice of restrictions on workplace privacy, possibly through statements in an employee handbook or personnel manual, written notification, or signs posted in the workplace. (See "Monitoring Employees in the Workplace" in this chapter.) However, regardless of an employer's representations, employees often have heightened expectations of privacy as to personal or confidential information.

Tort Claims for Invasion of Privacy

A treatise on civil wrongs (torts), *Restatement (Second) of Torts*, identifies four separate tort causes of action for invasion of privacy, several of which may have application in the workplace:

1. Intrusion upon the plaintiff's seclusion or solitude
2. Appropriation of the plaintiff's name or likeness to the defendant's advantage
3. Publicity that places the plaintiff in a false light in the public's eye

4. Public disclosure of embarrassing and private facts about the plaintiff

Public Disclosure of Private Facts

Certain intimate details about people, even though true, may be off limits to the press and public, such as publishing detailed information about a person's sexual conduct, medical condition, or educational records. In order to succeed in this kind of lawsuit, the person suing must show that the information was:

- Sufficiently private or not already in the public domain
- Sufficiently intimate
- Highly offensive to a reasonable person

Employers should develop and follow internal procedures that ensure that only persons with a true business-related reason have access to employees' private information, as well as internal controls regarding the disclosure of such information to anyone.

Placing a Person in a False Light

Placing a person in a false light is where false allegations about a person are published as fact either with malice or with reckless disregard for the truth, thereby creating a deliberately false and misleading impression.

Employers should disclose or publish only that information relating to employees that it knows to be factual and do so in a manner not calculated to mislead the reader or listener.

Intrusion upon Seclusion

To prevail on an intrusion upon seclusion claim, a plaintiff must establish that (1) another person has intentionally intruded, physically or otherwise, on the plaintiff's seclusion or solitude, and (2) such intrusion would be offensive or objectionable to a reasonable person.

This tort requires the plaintiff to show that the defendant actually committed an intrusion. To prove actionable intrusion, the plaintiff must show that the defendant penetrated some zone of physical or sensory privacy surrounding, or obtained unwanted access to data about the plaintiff—for example, peeped through his or her window or broke into his or her home, car, or purse. An intrusion occurs when the person intruding believes, or is substantially certain, that he or she lacks the necessary legal or personal permission to commit the intrusive act.

The tort does not require that anything be done with the gained information. Therefore, the tort is complete at the moment of intrusion.

The actionable means of intrusion vary, and courts have found them to include eavesdropping by wiretapping or microphones, peering through windows, persistent telephoning, unauthorized prying into a bank account, and opening personal mail.

As stated previously in "Invasion of Privacy," have employees sign a release or acknowledgment that they have no expectation of privacy in the workplace and require all employees to affirmatively consent to monitoring of electronic communication and workplace searches and surveillance.

Misappropriation

Appropriation of an employee's name or likeness, such as in advertising, without the employee's prior consent may form the basis for a misappropriation claim.

Individuals have the right to privacy that extends to their likeness, such as photos, videotapes, and audiotapes of themselves. Someone who uses another person's likeness—or even personal information about him or her—for commercial purposes without that person's consent could be liable for damages or other relief. This includes the use of the likeness in e-mails for commercial purposes.

Employers should obtain written consent from an employee before using his or her name or likeness (even in company newsletters).

Defamation, Libel, and Slander

In addition to invasion of privacy, an employer must also be wary of liability for defamation. In investigating workplace misconduct, employers must be careful not to draw unwarranted conclusions or make unfounded accusatory statements regarding employees under investigation. Such communications to a third party could constitute publication of that information for defamation purposes.

Defamation is a communication that tends to hold the plaintiff up to hatred, contempt, ridicule, or scorn or that causes him or her to be shunned or avoided; one that tends to injure his or her reputation as to diminish the esteem, respect, goodwill, or confidence in which he or she is held.

Elements of Defamation

Proving Defamation

As stated previously, defamation is the issuance of a false statement about another person that causes that person to suffer harm. To prove defamation, the plaintiff would have to prove:

- A false and defamatory statement has been made about him or her.
- Unprivileged publication of the statement to a third party (i.e., somebody other than the person defamed by the statement).
- If defamatory matter is of public concern, fault amounting at least to negligence on the part of the publisher.
- Damage to the plaintiff.

Defamation may arise in the context of intracompany communications that result in harm to an employee's reputation, including statements and discharge letters to the employee, office petitions, warning letters, performance evaluations, statements in management or employee meetings, and internal security reports.

Written vs. Oral Defamation

Written defamation is called libel and oral defamation is called slander.

- *Slander* involves the making of defamatory statements by a transitory (nonfixed) representation, usually an oral (spoken) representation.
- *Libel* involves the making of defamatory statements in a printed or fixed medium (e.g., a magazine, newspaper, or company newsletter).

Defamation Defenses

The principal defenses to a defamation action in the employment context are truth and privilege.

Truth

Truth (told in a manner not calculated to deceive) is an absolute defense to a defamation action.

> **EXAMPLE:** If an accounting clerk was terminated for misapplying funds through negligence, saying so is the truth. Although unflattering, this version of the truth is a defense to a defamation charge. However, saying that the person produced some "funny numbers" makes the person sound like a thief and is truth told in a manner calculated to deceive and would not protect the speaker from a defamation charge.

An absolute or a qualified privilege may also arise in the employment context. An absolute privilege is recognized for statements made in the course of judicial or legislative proceedings.

Privilege

A qualified privilege may exist where the statement was believed by the employer in good faith to be true when uttered, served a legitimate business purpose, and was disclosed to an appropriate individual who also had a legitimate business interest in receiving the communication.

The qualified privilege operates to protect an employer who questions employees in a reasonable manner or whose representatives discuss or evaluate the results of an internal investigation.

Opinion

Another defense to a charge of defamation is where the accused party can show he or she was merely expressing an opinion.

Intentional Infliction of Emotional Distress or Outrage

The tort of intentional infliction of emotional distress has the following elements:

- Defendant must act intentionally or recklessly.
- Defendant's conduct must be extreme and outrageous.
- Conduct must be the cause of severe emotional distress.

The defendant's conduct must be more than malicious and intentional. Liability does not extend to mere insults, indignities, threats, annoyances, or petty oppressions. The conduct must be "so outrageous in character, and so extreme in degree, as to go beyond all possible bounds of decency, and to be regarded as atrocious, and utterly intolerable in a civilized community." See *Restatement (Second) of Torts* Section 46 cmt. d (1965).

Employers should not engage in a purposeful effort to inflict emotional harm on an employee irrespective of what he or she has done.

False Imprisonment

False imprisonment occurs when someone intentionally and totally restrains another person without having the legal right to do so. It's not necessary that physical force be used—threats or a show of apparent authority are sufficient. False imprisonment in the workplace usually occurs when an overzealous employer investigates allegations of employee wrongdoing and tries to question the employee or coerce a confession.

Generally, an employer has the right to detain an employee for a reasonable time and in a reasonable manner to investigate employee theft. Employee interrogation is a normal part of the employment relationship. Reasonable interrogation or *voluntary* confinement cannot be regarded as false imprisonment and is not actionable.

False imprisonment will usually be actionable only if the employer confines an employee physically or by threat of force, although other forms of unreasonable duress may be sufficient. An at-will employee who submits to interrogation in return for continued employment is not considered confined because the employee has a clear option to leave.

Employers should not:

- Physically restrain an employee in order to question him or her.
- Lock the door of the room where an investigatory interview is being held.
- Place someone at the door to restrain the employee from leaving.

To be considered false imprisonment, a person must lack a reasonable means to safely escape the confinement.

In matters related to privacy in the workplace, the employer can avoid liability by only acting for legitimate business purposes in a reasonable manner.

CHAPTER 9

Firing and Separation

Introduction

Employment at will is the fundamental law in all states except Montana, where an employee may only be terminated *for cause*. Under at-will employment, the employer can discharge an employee for any reason or no reason at all, with or without notice, and the employee can leave the employer's employ at any time, for any or no reason at all, with or without notice.

Carefully note that virtually every collective bargaining agreement (union contract) will have provisions preventing the employer from firing a union member except for cause.

An employer's right to fire at will is a powerful privilege that allows termination of unproductive, marginal employees without having to laboriously build a file to support a for-cause separation. Employers should work hard to preserve the at-will nature of the relationship.

Although employment at will is still a rebuttable presumption, most states now recognize one or more exceptions to the doctrine.

Policy Statements May Alter At-Will Employment

The most common way that an employee can gain some protection against being fired without cause is through policy statements made by an employer in an employee handbook or other published policy statements. The language of these statements must be such that they would lead a reasonable person to conclude that employment for some fixed period has been established or that if the employee fulfills some set of conditions—for example, makes it through a probationary period—then the employer can fire only for cause. In other words, these statements may be read as an implied contract between the employer and the employee.

The bottom line is that provisions in employee handbooks are often interpreted as enforceable contractual provisions if a reasonable employee would believe that they were promises.

Removal of promissory language coupled with clear and prominent disclaimers can defeat the implied contract argument and preserve the at-will employment relationship.

Probationary Periods

Probationary periods destroy the at-will nature of the employment relationship. The view of the courts is that since the (nonunion) employer has unilaterally and voluntarily restricted its unfettered right to fire an employee for any reason or no reason at all, with or without notice, the employee is entitled to rely on the implied promise that if the worker makes it past the specified time period—for example, thirty, sixty, or ninety days—then he or she will be fired only for cause.

It doesn't matter what the probationary period is called—for example, *introductory period* or *learning period*—if the employer reserves the right to discharge at will during the time frame stated, then it is a probationary period.

Do not confuse a probationary period that goes into the formation of an employment relationship with an eligibility waiting period for company benefits. The fact that a new hire must wait some period of time before being eligible for vacation or other benefits does not relate to the formation of the employment relationship itself and, therefore, such eligibility waiting periods do not impact an employer's right to fire at will.

Give Notice Clauses

Another clause in an employee handbook that will destroy the at-will nature of the relationship is one that states that unless the employee provides no less than two weeks' written notice to the employer prior to a voluntary separation (quit), the employee will suffer some detriment—for example, won't be eligible for rehire.

At will is a two-edged sword—the employer can fire without consequence and the employee can walk out without consequence.

An employer that makes prior notice of a voluntary separation a mandatory obligation coupled with a punishment loses the benefit of the at-will privilege. There is nothing legally wrong with requesting a prior notice as long as the request is not coercive.

Job Security Statements

Statements to the effect that employees will be fired only for "good cause" or that it is company policy "to retain employees who perform their duties efficiently and effectively" are a kiss of death for the at-will nature of the relationship and should be removed from company materials.

How to Reestablish the At-Will Privilege

A (nonunion) employer can reestablish its right to fire at will.

Clause Removal

The first step in reestablishing the right to fire at will is to remove from the employee handbook and other policy memoranda of any nature and type probationary periods, give notice clauses, and other statements that can reasonably be interpreted as promising employment for some defined period of time.

Insertion of Disclaimer

The employer should place prominently displayed disclaimers in the employee handbook and other policy statements, receipts for employee handbooks, job application forms, and offer letters, as well as preceding or being part of progressive disciplinary policies. A disclaimer basically states that employment with the employer is on an at-will basis, is for no defined period of time, and can be terminated at any time with or without cause and with or without notice.

Disclaimer Language

A typical disclaimer might read:

> Employment at the [name of organization] is on an "at-will" basis and is for no definite period and may, regardless of the date or

> method of payment of wages or salary, be terminated at any time
> with or without cause and with or without notice. Other than
> [designee of the organization], no supervisor, manager, or other
> person, irrespective of title or position, has authority to alter the
> at-will status of your employment or to enter into any employ-
> ment contract for a definite period of time with you. Any agree-
> ment with you altering your at-will employment status must be in
> writing and signed by [designee].

Note: The language "regardless of the date or method of payment of
wages or salary" is to defeat any claims that an offer letter or other correspondence that puts forward a wage on a per-year basis promises employment for a defined period of time and, therefore, defeats the at-will nature
of the relationship.

It is a good practice to have new hires sign an acknowledgment that
they have received a copy of the employee handbook and understand and
acknowledge that their employment is on an at-will basis.

Disclaimers and Progressive Disciplinary Policies

Many employee handbooks provide for formal levels of progressive discipline leading up to discharge. To the extent that such provisions are written in mandatory language—for example, "the employer shall" or "the
employer will"—courts tend to find that they create contractual rights
obligating the employer to follow the progressive disciplinary procedures.
However, if the handbook provisions allow the employer discretion to
skip one or more levels of discipline, then the employee generally has no
enforceable right.

You should include disclaimer language in the handbook stating that
the employer may, but is not obligated to, follow the progressive disciplinary procedures set out in the handbook and is not obligated to follow the
procedures in any particular order.

In addition, when giving an employee a warning letter, you should
not create a miniprogressive disciplinary step preventing you from firing
someone during a stated period of time. For example, saying something
like, "You are hereby warned that you are on probation for the next thirty
days. If you are late during this time period you will be terminated," prevents you from terminating the employee if the employee makes it
through this time frame and then is late immediately afterward. It is a

much better practice to simply demand "immediate and sustained adherence" to the company's rules and expectations.

Giving Notice—Prospective vs. Retroactive At-Will Employment

In order to reestablish the right to fire at will (in a nonunion environment), an employer should give written notice to its workforce that as of a certain date employment at the organization will be on an at-will basis and will not be for any certain length of time.

A major issue to consider is whether the employer should try to make the new status retroactive or merely prospective.

Retroactivity

The argument in favor of making the at-will status retroactive—that is, attempting to impose the status on your existing workforce—is that the notice is an offer of continued employment with a new set of work rules and that by continuing to work for the employer, the employee(s) has accepted the offer.

This is a weak position and could result in expensive litigation with an employee arguing that he or she already has a contract with you, having fulfilled whatever conditions you had previously offered the employment under, for example, a probationary period.

Prospectively Establishing At-Will Employment

A stronger legal position would be to establish at-will employment for new hires employed after a future date.

Existing employees have no emotional ownership in new hires and a new hire joining an organization with the understanding that his or her employment is on an at-will basis accepts the job offer with full knowledge of the condition.

In summary, you should:

- Retain the right to unilaterally modify the handbook.
- State that the handbook provides only "guidance" as to the employer's policies.
- Expressly disclaim any length/term of employment.
- Expressly disclaim any inference that the handbook is intended to constitute a contract.

- Expressly reaffirm the employment at-will relationship.
- Do not include language that allows the employee to negotiate any part of the handbook.

Progressive Discipline

To ensure fair, equitable, and nondiscriminatory management of employees, many organizations follow progressive disciplinary policies.

Coaching and Counseling

Coaching and counseling efforts are aimed toward ensuring that employees know what is expected of them.

These efforts should be used when infractions are minor or infrequent and the supervisor believes that counseling or verbal warnings will likely preclude a recurrence of the misconduct.

A best practice is to have the employee's manager document that the counseling was provided.

Retraining, if Necessary

Sometimes poor performance is more a matter of "can't do" or "don't know how to do" than "won't do." Therefore, an employer should determine if training or retraining can correct the problem.

Training documentation should include the name of the person trained, date of the training, subject matter trained on, and identity of the trainer.

In the absence of a law defining a longer time period—for example, retention of blood-borne pathogen training records for three years—training records should be retained for a minimum of one year.

Verbal Warning

A verbal warning serves as a notice of the specific acts for which the employee is being reprimanded, gives guidance of the corrective steps the employee is expected to take, and warns that disciplinary action may result if the unacceptable conduct continues.

A best practice is to have the employee's manager document that the verbal warning was given together with the essence of what was said.

Written Warning

A written warning is a recapitulation of the problem together with a history of the interaction between the employer and employee, and a statement about the employee's future status if the problems aren't corrected.

The objectives of good documentation and especially warning letters are to show that:

- The employer clearly communicated its expectations.
- Those expectations were enforced uniformly and evenhandedly.
- The employer gave clear notice that the employee's performance or behavior was unacceptable.
- The consequences of continued unacceptable performance or behavior were clearly stated.
- The employee was given meaningful opportunities to improve.
- The employer offered to assist the employee in every reasonable manner.

Therefore, a warning letter should:

- Identify the rule or standard that was violated.
- State the legitimate reason for that rule or standard or why the rule or standard is fair (e.g., in situations involving a performance standard, note that all employees are expected to and do comply).
- Demonstrate how the rule or standard was communicated (e.g., "You received the employee handbook on. . . .").
- Describe any previous counseling or discipline given for related events or previous steps in the progressive discipline process.
- Recount the effect on the organization of the employee's failure to satisfy the rule or to meet the standard in the then most recent incident.
- Clearly state future expectations, even if that means restating the rule.
- Invite the employee to ask if he or she has any questions regarding what is expected, thereby leaving no room for any claimed misunderstanding.
- Plainly state the consequences of an additional violation.

- Expressly state the organization's willingness to assist in any reasonable manner possible.

- Be dated.

- Identify the author.

- Be signed and dated by the employee indicating he or she has read and received a copy of the letter. If the employee refuses to sign the acknowledgment block, note the date and time that the employee was presented with the document and the fact that he or she refused to sign it; then sign the document yourself under the notations.

- Be handled in a confidential manner by distributing it only to those with a real need to know.

- Be legible.

- Use plain, nontechnical language that a jury can understand.

- Avoid hyperbole or conclusory, inflammatory language.

Some good rules to follow when writing warning letters are:

- Use the who, what, where, when, why, or how paradigm.

  EXAMPLE: "On May 27, 20XX, at 3:00 P.M. [when] you stood very close to your supervisor, Charlene Barash, while raising your voice well above a normal conversational level, [what] which Ms. Barash understood to be an attempt to intimidate her." [why]

- Use your senses in describing events.

  EXAMPLE: "I saw you . . ." "I heard you . . ." "I sensed . . ." "I felt . . ." "I smelled . . ." "I perceived . . ."

- Make the subjective into the objective.

  EXAMPLE: No: "You were hostile toward a customer, Maya Baellow." [subjective]

  Yes: "You were rude and abrupt with a customer, Maya Baellow, when you told her you didn't care if the order got there before 11:00 A.M." [objective]

- State negative organizational impact of the employee's actions.

EXAMPLE: "Consequently, you violated company Policy AB123." "You interfered with the work flow, resulting in a 5 percent decrease in normal productivity."

- Whenever possible, capture the employee's responses.
  EXAMPLE: "When I asked you . . . , you replied . . ."

Suspension

Under most circumstances, you should suspend before you terminate. It clearly evidences that the employee knew his or her job was in jeopardy.

Sometimes a company will enter into a last-chance agreement (LCA) with an employee. If you decide to follow that step before firing someone, be sure to make it clear in the agreement that the employer has grounds to terminate now but is agreeing to forgo that right in exchange for the employee's commitment to abide by the terms of the LCA. Also make it clear that compliance with all workplace rules is mandatory.

Even where the reason for the LCA stems from substance abuse, the terms of the LCA should be focused on the performance deficiency and correcting that behavior. Therefore, the LCA should identify the specific performance deficiencies and include dates of prior communications with the employee concerning the recurring performance deficiencies.

In the LCA, provide a clear description of the employer's expectations for improved performance and state that the improved performance must be continued and sustained and that any violation of the terms of the LCA will result in immediate termination.

Expressly state in the LCA that the employee remains an employee at will and can be terminated at any time with or without notice, with or without cause.

Termination

The employee should have "fired himself" (or herself) by not complying with all of the formerly made statements, guidances, and so forth.

The Termination Session

You should carefully prepare for the termination session. It is advisable to have a checklist so that you don't forget any important points or matters during what is usually an uncomfortable event. It is also advisable to have a witness present.

Before the meeting, disable any security access codes the employee has to computers, security doors, and so on.

The actual termination meeting should be relatively short, such as ten to fifteen minutes, and have as its sole purpose providing a simple and concise statement of the decision to terminate the employment relationship. If you have followed a progressive disciplinary procedure, simply allude to the various steps you have taken in the past and the employee's failure to correct his or her behavior or bring his or her work up to the expected standards of performance.

Surprise terminations, especially those where the employee is not given some reasonable, if brief, explanation for the dismissal and where there is little or no documentation in the file, are those that lead to litigation. If it is a surprise dismissal, it is advisable to let the employee give his or her side of the story and to vent his or her emotions.

Make it clear that the decision is final. Take the position that the decision has already been made and that all alternatives were considered.

If your state requires that a terminated employee's final check be paid on termination rather than no later than the next regularly scheduled pay period, provide this last check to the person.

If the employee is a participant in the organization's health plan, provide COBRA information. See Chapter 4, "Benefits." Also cover any benefits you may be offering, such as severance pay or outplacement services.

Explain your job reference policy. If it is your policy to provide only job title, dates of employment, and salary history, say so. If you normally give more information when it is requested in writing by a prospective employer with the terminated employee's written consent to release the information and to hold the employer (you) harmless from any and all liability for providing the information, tell the employee. In some states, you may be required to provide a service letter stating dates of employment, job title, compensation information, and the true reason for the discharge. (The reason for firing the person doesn't have to be kind—just truthful.)

Collect any keys, communications devices, company car, company credit cards, or any other property belonging to the organization from the employee. Make it clear that the payment of any severance pay or other benefits after discharge depends on the employee's cooperation with you in this area.

Advise other employees that the fired employee no longer works at your organization. This will help ensure that an unknowing employee does not allow the terminated employee access to the building or files.

Wrongful Discharge

Exceptions to the doctrine of employment at will are:

1. Firing someone because he or she is a member of a protected class (e.g., termination based on the employee's race, religion, sex, national origin, or age or other protected characteristic). The federal and state laws relating to civil rights are discussed in Chapter 6, "Employment Laws."
2. A tort (civil wrong) concept generally known as *wrongful discharge*. The concept is that the employer owed some sort of duty to the employee and breached that duty by firing the worker.

Whether or not an employee can claim and enforce some sort of wrongful discharge theory is very much dependent on the law of the state in which the harm is alleged to have occurred.

Wrongful discharge suits are generally based on claims that there has been (1) a violation of a public policy or (2) some sort of breach of a contract or contract right.

Violation of Public Policy

Public policy exceptions to the employment at will doctrine come into play when an employee is fired for performing an act that public policy would encourage or allow, or for refusing to do something public policy does not allow.

Two basic views exist as to what a public policy is: (1) a principle by which a society lives and (2) a specific statutory scheme or judicial precedent that forbids or requires some sort of action.

Under the first notion, a public policy principle doesn't have to be actually enshrined in a law or case for an employee to have a cause of action. This is a *fairness view*. Under the second approach, unless the worker can point to some right grounded in statute, such as the right to file a workers compensation claim, he or she will not have a cause of action.

Which view is taken is a matter of state law or state case law.

As a general rule, employees should not be disciplined or discharged:

- For taking military leave
- For exercising legal rights (e.g., filing a workers compensation claim)
- For meeting legal obligations (e.g., responding to a subpoena)
- For refusing to take part in illegal activities
- As retaliation for reporting safety hazards or violations of law

Covenant of Good Faith and Fair Dealing

As a general principle of contract law in most jurisdictions, all contracts, whether oral or written, contain an implied promise of good-faith dealing by the parties. On the basis of this principle, employees have argued that their employment contracts, even though at will, contain an implied term obligating each party to carry out the contract in good faith and to deal fairly with the other party or, at a minimum, to refrain from acting in bad faith.

Most courts have rejected the implied covenant theory, reasoning that this implied obligation does not alter the general rule of at-will employment.

Even in states in which the theory has been accepted, the courts generally apply a strict standard for the plaintiff to establish a cause of action. There must generally be some sort of special relationship between the parties that has been breached. For example, if a salesperson had earned a commission and the employer fired him or her in order to avoid paying the amount due, then in states accepting this implied covenant theory, the salesperson could sue for wrongful discharge.

The Worker Adjustment and Retraining Notification Act

The Worker Adjustment and Retraining Notification Act (WARN) requires covered employers to provide written notice at least sixty calendar days in advance of covered *plant closings* and *mass layoffs*.

Covered Employers

A WARN notice is required when a business with a hundred or more full-time workers (not counting workers who have less than six months on the job and workers who work fewer than twenty hours per week) is laying off at least fifty people at a single site of employment, or employs a hundred or more workers who work at least a combined four thousand hours per week, and is a private for-profit business, private nonprofit organization, or quasi-public entity separately organized from regular government.

Plant Closing

A plant closing is the permanent or temporary shutdown of a single site of employment, or one or more facilities or operating units within a single site of employment, if the shutdown results in an employment loss at the single site of employment during any thirty-day period for fifty or more employees excluding part-time employees. All of the employment losses do not have to occur within the unit that is shut down. For example, if a forty-five-person department is eliminated and, as a result, five positions in a clerical support staff are eliminated, a covered plant closing has occurred.

Mass Layoff

The term *mass layoff* means a reduction in force that:

- Does not result from a plant closing.
- Results in an employment loss at the single site of employment during any thirty-day period for:
  - At least 50 to 499 employees if they represent at least 33 percent of the total active workforce excluding any part-time employees.
  - At least 500 or more employees excluding any part-time employees. In this case, the 33 percent rule does not apply.

Covered Employees

Affected employees are those who may be expected to experience an employment loss. They may be hourly and salaried workers, including managerial and supervisory employees and nonstrikers.

Affected employees include:

- Employees who are terminated or laid off for more than six months or who have their hours reduced by 50 percent or more in any six-month period as a result of the plant closing or mass layoff.
- Employees who may reasonably be expected to experience an employment loss as a result of a proposed plant closing or mass layoff. If the employer has a seniority system that involves bumping rights, the employer should use its best efforts to give notice to the workers who will actually lose their jobs as a result of the system. If that is not possible, then an employer must give notice to the incumbent in the position being eliminated.
- Workers who are on temporary layoff but have a reasonable expectation of recall. (This includes workers on workers compensation, medical, maternity, or other leave.)
- Part-time workers do not count when determining whether there has been a plant closing or mass layoff but they are entitled to receive WARN notice if there is one.

Employees Not Protected by WARN

The following employees are not protected under WARN:

- Strikers or workers who have been locked out in a labor dispute.
- Workers working on temporary projects or facilities of the business who clearly understand the temporary nature of the work when hired.
- Business partners, consultants, or contract employees assigned to the business but who have a separate employment relationship with another employer and are paid by that other employer, or who are self-employed.
- Regular federal, state, and local government employees.

Exceptions to the Sixty-Day Notice Requirement

There are three exceptions to the full sixty-day notice requirement. However, notice must be provided as soon as is practicable even when these exceptions apply, and the employer must provide a statement of the reason for reducing the notice requirement in addition to fulfilling other notice information requirements. The exceptions are as follows:

- *Faltering Company.* Prior to a plant closing, when a company is actively seeking capital or business and reasonably in good faith believes that advance notice would preclude its ability to obtain such capital or business, and this new capital or business would allow the employer to avoid or postpone a shutdown for a reasonable period.

- *Unforeseeable Business Circumstances.* When the closing or mass layoff is caused by business circumstances that were not reasonably foreseeable at the time that sixty-day notice would have been required (e.g., a business circumstance that is caused by some sudden, dramatic, and unexpected action or conditions outside the employer's control, like the unexpected cancellation of a major order).

- *Natural Disaster.* When a plant closing or mass layoff is the direct result of a natural disaster such as a flood, earthquake, drought, storm, tidal wave, or similar effects of nature. In this case, notice may be given after the event.

Contents of the Notice to Nonunion Workers

Notice to individual employees must be written in clear and specific language that employees can easily understand and must contain at a minimum the following requirements:

- A statement as to whether the planned action is expected to be permanent or temporary, and if the entire plant is to be closed, a statement to that effect
- The expected date when the plant closing or mass layoff will commence and the expected date when the individual employee will be separated
- An indication as to whether or not bumping rights exist
- The name and telephone number of a company official to contact for further information

The notice may include additional information useful to the employees such as available dislocated worker assistance, and if the planned action is expected to be temporary, the estimated duration, if known.

Notice to a Union Representative

A notice to the bargaining agent or chief elected officer of each affected union or local union official must contain at a minimum the following information:

- The name and address where the mass layoff or plant closing is to occur, along with the name and telephone number of a company contact person who can provide additional information
- A statement as to whether the planned action is expected to be permanent or temporary, and if the entire plant is to be closed, a statement to that effect
- The expected date of the first separation and the anticipated schedule for making separations
- The job titles of positions to be affected and the number of affected employees in each job classification

Notice to the Dislocated Worker Unit and the Local Chief Elected Official

Advance notice should also be given to the State Rapid Response Dislocated Worker Unit as well as to the chief elected official of the local government where the closing or mass layoff is to occur. If there is more than one such unit, the tiebreaker is the local government to which the employer paid the most taxes in the preceding year.

CHAPTER 10

Documentation and Records Retention

Introduction

Any employer must maintain records regarding its employees because (1) it makes good business sense to have personnel files and records that are well organized; (2) some federal and state laws mandate that employers keep detailed information about their employees and prescribe the length of time it should be kept, such as wage and hour laws and safety and health laws; and (3) the day will probably come when these files and records will be needed for a hearing or litigation. If there is a charge of discrimination that the employer knows or has reason to believe will be filed with a federal or state fair employment practice agency and the employer allows its workers to destroy documents and records related to the charge, then there is a real danger that the employer will be charged with *spoliation*. If proven, a charge of spoliation can bring significant liability with it. See "Spoliation" in this chapter.

Federal rules are summarized in the book *Guide to Record Retention Requirements in the Code of Federal Regulations*. This publication is written in a digest form and tells the reader what records must be kept, who must maintain them, and for how long they must be kept. This volume, while extensive, is not all-inclusive and does not have the effect of any law, regulation, or ruling. However, it is useful.

Personnel Records in General

There is no absolute definitive list of items that should or should not be contained in an employee's personnel file. (See Exhibit 10-1.) Employers should develop and enforce internal procedures ensuring that only those with a legitimate business reason are allowed access to any type of personnel file.

Employee Access to Their Own Personnel File

Laws Permitting Access

An employee's right to view his or her personnel file depends on the law of the state where the employee is working or where the company is located and the file is kept. Generally, whatever law is most favorable to the worker will prevail.

There is no federal law requiring that employees in the private sector have access to their personnel files.

Restrictions on Access

In states that allow employees access to their files, employers have a reasonable amount of time to allow the viewing. Time frames, depending on the state's law, can range from forty-eight hours to fourteen business days. Also, some states restrict access to only once or twice per year.

A few states allow former employees to see their files for up to one year from the date of employment separation.

Generally, access can be restricted to regular business hours and at the employer's premises, with employees not being allowed to remove any of the contents of the files or records. Ordinarily, employees are allowed to obtain copies of items in their personnel file at a reasonable cost per page.

Even in states where employees do have a right to view their personnel files, there are some documents that can be withheld. Generally, these are documents or records that contain information related to third parties other than the employer and employee, such as reference letters or documents related to an internal investigation.

Exhibit 10-1. Items typically found in a personnel file.

Employment
- Request for application
- Employee's original employment application
- Prescreening application notes
- College recruiting interview report form
- Employment interview report form
- Education verification
- Employment verification
- Other background verification
- Rejection letter
- Employment offer letter
- Employment agency agreement if hired through an agency
- Employee handbook acknowledgment form showing receipt of handbook
- Checklist from new employee orientation showing subjects covered
- Veterans/disabled self-identification form
- Transfer requests
- Relocation offer records
- Relocation report
- Security clearance status

Payroll
- W-4 Form
- Weekly time sheets
- Individual attendance record
- Pay advance request record
- Garnishment orders and records
- Authorization for release of private information
- Authorization for all other payroll actions

Performance Appraisals
- New employee progress reports
- Performance appraisal forms
- Performance improvement program records

Training and Development
- Training history records
- Training program applications or requests
- Skills inventory questionnaire
- Training evaluation forms
- In-house training notification letters
- Training expense reimbursement records

Employee Separations
- Exit interview form
- Final employee performance appraisal
- Exit interviewer's comment form
- Record of documents given with final paycheck

Benefits
- Medical/dental/vision coverage waiver or drop form
- Vacation accrual/taken form
- Request for nonmedical leave of absence
- Retirement application
- Payroll deduction authorizations
- COBRA notification/election
- Hazardous substance notification and/or reports
- Tuition reimbursement application and/or payment records
- Employer concession and/or discount authorization
- Annual benefits statement acknowledgment
- Safety training/meeting attendance/summary forms

Wage/Salary Administration
- Job description form
- Job analysis questionnaire
- Payroll authorization form
- Fair Labor Standards Act exemption test
- Compensation history record
- Compensation recommendations
- Notification of wage or salary increase/decrease

Employee Relations
- Report of coaching/counseling session
- Employee Assistance Program consent form
- Commendations
- Employee written warning notice
- Employee written suspension notice
- Employee last-chance agreements
- Completed employee suggestion forms
- Suggestion status reports

If an employee disagrees with any item in the file (and the employer refuses to voluntarily remove it), some states allow the employee to submit a document to the file indicating the reasons why he or she feels the item is inaccurate.

Even in states that do not allow employees to access their personnel records, employers that thoroughly document worker performance and disciplinary matters may want to have an open personnel file policy. The reason is that it would be difficult for an aggrieved employee to secure the services of an attorney on a contingency basis rather than a cash-as-you-go basis if the lawyer knew that he or she faced a well-documented adversary.

Medical Information

Primarily because of the Americans with Disabilities Act (ADA), all medical information regarding an employee should be kept in a confidential medical file separate from the worker's general personnel file.

Examples of the types of documents that should only be in the employee's medical file are:

- Health insurance application form
- Life insurance application form
- Request for medical leave of absence, regardless of reason
- Personal accident reports
- Workers compensation report of injury or illness (If the Workers Compensation First Report of Injury form is used in lieu of the Occupational Safety and Health Administration (OSHA) Form 301, then on request, the employee, a former employee, or his or her personal representative must be given a copy of the report by the end of the next business day.)
- OSHA injury and illness reports (See "Employee Access to OSHA Injury and Illness Records" in this chapter regarding who is entitled to receive a copy of the OSHA Form 300 or the OSHA Privacy Case log.)
- Physician records of examination
- Diagnostic records
- Laboratory test records
- Drug-screening records
- Fitness for duty medical releases
- Any other medical records with personally identifiable information about individual employees

- Any other form or document that contains private medical information for a specific employee

Other Documents That Should Not Be Kept in a Personnel File

Form I-9

See Form I-9 discussion in Chapter 1, "Hiring."

Investigation Records

The following should not be kept in the worker's general personnel file:

- Discrimination complaint investigation information
- Legal case data
- Accusations of policy or legal violations

Security Clearance Investigation Records

The following should not be kept in the worker's general personnel file:

- Background investigation information
- Personal credit history
- Personal criminal conviction history
- Arrest records

EEOC Minimum Document Retention Rules Under Title VII

The One-Year Rule—Preservation of Records Made or Kept

Although the various federal laws dealing with the employer-employee relationship have varying document retention time frames—for example, retention of Form I-9 for the longer of three years from the date of hire or one year from the date of employment separation—the most basic retention rule is Title 29, Code of Federal Regulations, Section 1602.14, which states:

> Any personnel or employment record made or kept by an employer (including but not necessarily limited to requests for reasonable accommodation, application forms submitted by applicants, and other records having to do with hiring, promotion, demotion, transfer, lay-off or termination, rates of pay, or other terms of compensation, and selection for training or apprenticeship) shall be preserved by the employer for a period of *one year from the date of the making of the record or the personnel action involved, whichever occurs later.* [Emphasis added.] In the case of involuntary termination of an employee, the personnel records of the individual terminated shall be kept for a period of one year from the date of termination. Where a charge of discrimination has been filed, or an action brought by the Commission or the Attorney General, against an employer under title VII or the ADA, the respondent employer shall preserve all personnel records relevant to the charge or action until final disposition of the charge or the action. The term "personnel records relevant to the charge," for example, would include personnel or employment records relating to the aggrieved person and to all other employees holding positions similar to that held or sought by the aggrieved person and application forms or test papers completed by an unsuccessful applicant and by all other candidates for the same position as that for which the aggrieved person applied and was rejected. The date of *final disposition of the charge or the action* means the date of expiration of the statutory period within which the aggrieved person may bring an action in a U.S. District Court or, where an action is brought against an employer either by the aggrieved person, the Commission, or by the Attorney General, the date on which such litigation is terminated.

Note: The requirement to retain application forms submitted by "applicants" includes applications or résumés received over the Internet if the submittal is from an "electronic applicant." The federal *Uniform Guidelines on Employee Selection Procedures* (UGESP) state that in order for an individual to be an applicant in the context of the Internet and related electronic data-processing technologies, the following must have occurred:

1. The employer has acted to fill a particular position.

2. The individual has followed the employer's standard procedures for submitting applications.

3. The individual has indicated an interest in the particular position.

The bottom line is that if your organization is covered by Title VII, retain any personnel document for a minimum of one year from the date it was created or received, or from the last date of any personnel action related to it.

Equal Employment Opportunity Employer Information Report EEO-1

Nature of the Form EEO-1

The EEO-1 provides the federal government with workforce profiles by ethnicity, race, and gender, all divided into job categories. (See Exhibit 10-2 and Exhibit 10-3.) Most private sector employers with a hundred or more workers and those with fifty to ninety-nine workers and a federal contract with a dollar value of $50,000 or more are required to submit the EEO-1 annually.

The EEOC is looking for evidence of race, gender, or national origin discrimination—for example, if every executive of an organization is a white male and every service worker is a woman, a person of color, or has a Hispanic surname, the appearance of discrimination becomes obvious.

In addition, the Department of Labor's Office of Federal Contract Compliance Programs (OFCCP) uses EEO-1 data to determine which employer facilities to select for compliance evaluations. The OFCCP's system uses statistical assessment of EEO-1 data to select facilities where the likelihood of systematic discrimination is the greatest.

Authority for and Coverage of the EEO-1

The survey is conducted annually under the authority of Title VII of the Civil Rights Act of 1964, 42 USC 2000e, and the sections following, as amended. Under those laws, all employers with fifteen or more employees are covered by Title VII and are required to keep employment records as specified by EEOC regulations. Based on the number of employees and federal contract activities, certain large employers are required to file the EEO-1 with the EEOC (www.eeoc.gov/eeo1survey) by September 30 of each calendar year.

Exhibit 10-2. Form EEO-1 page 1.

Joint Reporting
Committee
● **Equal Employment
Opportunity Com-
mission**
● **Office of Federal
Contract Compli-
ance Programs (Labor)**

EQUAL EMPLOYMENT OPPORTUNITY

EMPLOYER INFORMATION REPORT EEO—1

Standard Form 106
REV. 01/2006

O.M.B. No. 3646-0007
EXPIRES 01/2009
106-214

Section A—TYPE OF REPORT
Refer to instructions for number and types of reports to be filed.

1. Indicate by marking in the appropriate box the type of reporting unit for which this copy of the form is submitted (MARK ONLY ONE BOX).

    (1) ☐ Single-establishment Employer Report

Multi-establishment Employer:
(2) ☐ Consolidated Report (Required)
(3) ☐ Headquarters Unit Report (Required)
(4) ☐ Individual Establishment Report (submit one for each establishment with 50 or more employees)
(5) ☐ Special Report

2. Total number of reports being filed by this Company (Answer on Consolidated Report only)_____

Section B—COMPANY IDENTIFICATION *(To be answered by all employers)*

OFFICE USE ONLY

1. Parent Company

    a. Name of parent company (owns or controls establishment in item 2) omit if same as label

a.

Address (Number and street)

b.

City or town	State	ZIP code

c.

2. Establishment for which this report is filed. (Omit if same as label)

    a. Name of establishment

d.

Address (Number and street)	City or Town	County	State	ZIP code

e.

    b. Employer identification No. (IRS 9-DIGIT TAX NUMBER)

f.

    c. Was an EEO–1 report filed for this establishment last year? ☐ Yes ☐ No

Section C—EMPLOYERS WHO ARE REQUIRED TO FILE *(To be answered by all employers)*

☐ Yes ☐ No   1. Does the entire company have at least 100 employees in the payroll period for which you are reporting?

☐ Yes ☐ No   2. Is your company affiliated through common ownership and/or centralized management with other entities in an enterprise with a total employment of 100 or more?

☐ Yes ☐ No   3. Does the company or any of its establishments (a) have 50 or more employees <u>AND</u> (b) is not exempt as provided by 41 CFR 60–1.5, <u>AND</u> either (1) is a prime government contractor or first-tier subcontractor, and has a contract, subcontract, or purchase order amounting to $50,000 or more, or (2) serves as a depository of Government funds in any amount or is a financial institution which is an issuing and paying agent for U.S. Savings Bonds and Savings Notes?

    If the response to question C–3 is yes, please enter your Dun and Bradstreet identification number (if you have one):

NOTE: If the answer is yes to questions 1, 2, or 3, complete the entire form, otherwise skip to Section G.

Exhibit 10-3. Form EEO-1 page 2.

EE 100 - Page 2

Section D-EMPLOYMENT DATA

Employment at this establishment – Report all permanent full- and part-time employees including apprentices and on-the-job trainees unless specifically excluded as set forth in the instructions. Enter the appropriate figures on all lines and in all columns. Blank spaces will be considered as zeros.

Number of Employees
(Report employees in only one category)

Race/Ethnicity

Job Categories	Hispanic or Latino		Not-Hispanic or Latino													Total Col A - N
			Male						Female							
	Male	Female	White	Black or African American	Native Hawaiian or Other Pacific Islander	Asian	American Indian or Alaska Native	Two or more races	White	Black or African American	Native Hawaiian or Other Pacific Islander	Asian	American Indian or Alaska Native	Two or more races		
	A	B	C	D	E	F	G	H	I	J	K	L	M	N		O
Executive/Senior Level Officials and Managers 1.1																
First/Mid-Level Officials and Managers 1.2																
Professionals 2																
Technicians 3																
Sales Workers 4																
Administrative Support Workers 5																
Craft Workers 6																
Operatives 7																
Laborers and Helpers 8																
Service Workers 9																
TOTAL 10																
PREVIOUS YEAR TOTAL 11																

1. Date(s) of payroll period used: _____

Section E - ESTABLISHMENT INFORMATION (Omit on the Consolidated Report.)

1. What is the major activity of this establishment? (Be specific, i.e., manufacturing steel castings, retail grocer, wholesale plumbing supplies, title insurance, etc. Include the specific type of product or type of service provided, as well as the principal business or industrial activity.)

Section F - REMARKS

Use this item to give any identification data appearing on the last EEO-1 report which differs from that given above, explain major changes in composition of reporting units and other pertinent information.

Section G - CERTIFICATION

Check   1   ☐   All reports are accurate and were prepared in accordance with the instructions. (Check on Consolidated Report only.)
one   2   ☐   This report is accurate and was prepared in accordance with the instructions.

Name of Certifying Official	Title	Signature	Date
Name of person to contact regarding this report	Title	Address (Number and Street)	
City and State	Zip Code	Telephone No. (including Area Code and Extension)	Email Address

All reports and information obtained from individual reports will be kept confidential as required by Section 709(e) of Title VII.
WILLFULLY FALSE STATEMENTS ON THIS REPORT ARE PUNISHABLE BY LAW, U.S. CODE, TITLE 18, SECTION 1001

The EEO-1 must be filed by certain employers.

Employers Covered by Title VII with a Hundred or More Workers All private employers who are subject to Title VII of the Civil Rights Act of 1964, as amended, with a hundred or more employees *excluding* state and local governments, primary and secondary school systems, institutions of higher education, Indian tribes, and tax-exempt private membership clubs other than labor organizations must file an EEO-1.

State and local governments, school systems, and educational institutions are covered by other employment surveys and are excluded from the EEO-1. Labor-management committees must report using the EEO-2, while unions must report using the EEO-3. States, counties, and cities use the EEO-4. There once were an EEO-5 and an EEO-6 used in the world of education; however, that same information is now embedded in other Department of Education reports and surveys.

Employers Covered by Title VII with Fewer Than a Hundred Workers The EEO-1 must also be filed by private employers that are subject to Title VII who have fewer than a hundred employees if the company is owned or affiliated with another company or there is centralized ownership, control, or management (such as central control of personnel policies and labor relations) so that the group legally constitutes a single enterprise, and the entire enterprise employs a total of a hundred or more employees.

Religious Organizations with a Hundred or More Workers Religious organizations with a hundred or more workers must also file the EEO-1.

It is the opinion of the general counsel of the EEOC that Section 702, Title VII of the Civil Rights Act of 1964, as amended, does not authorize a complete exemption of religious organizations from the coverage of the act or of the reporting requirements of the commission. See Chapter 6, "Employment Laws."

The exemption under Title VII that allows religious organizations to discriminate in favor of their coreligionists when hiring clergy, administrators, and so forth does not allow them to further discriminate within that group. Basically, it's all right for a Catholic religious group to hire only Catholics; however, it's not all right to hire only white Catholics, or only women Catholics, and so on. Therefore, since the Standard Form 100 does not provide for information as to the religion of employees, religious organizations must report all information required by the form.

Federal Contractor Private Employers Exempt from Filing There are certain federal contractor private employers who are exempt from filing the survey while others are not. 41 CFR 60-1.5 exempts from Title VII coverage private sector federal contractors that have:

- Transactions with the government of $10,000 or under
- Contracts and subcontracts for indefinite quantities
- Work outside the United States
- Contracts with state or local governments
- Contracts with religious entities
- Contracts with certain educational institutions
- Work on or near Indian reservations

Federal Contractor Private Employers That Must File Federal contractors that *do* have to file the survey are all federal contractors (private employers) who:

- Are not exempt as provided for by 41 CFR 60-1.5.
- Have fifty or more employees, as well as:
  - Are prime contractors or first-tier subcontractors, and have a contract, subcontract, or purchase order amounting to $50,000 or more.
  - Serve as a depository of government funds in any amount.
  - Are a financial institution that is an issuing and paying agent for U.S. savings bonds and notes.

Simply stated, if you are a private sector employer and have fifty to ninety-nine workers and a federal contract worth $50,000 or more, you must file the EEO-1.

Establishments in Puerto Rico, the Virgin Islands, or other U.S. Protectorates Only those establishments located in the District of Columbia and the fifty states are required to submit the EEO-1. No reports should be filed for establishments in Puerto Rico, the Virgin Islands, or other American Protectorates.

Single and Multiple Establishment Employers

An *establishment* (for purposes of the EEO-1) is an economic unit that produces goods or services, such as a factory, office, store, or mine. In most instances, the establishment is at a single physical location and is engaged in one, or predominantly one, type of economic activity. The definition used for the EEO-1 was adapted from the North American Industry Classification System (NAICS) that superseded the Standard Industrial Classification System (SIC) in 1999.

Single Establishment Employers Single establishment employers—for example, employers doing business at only one establishment in one location—must complete a single EEO-1 online data record or submit a single EEO-1 paper report.

Multiple Establishment Employers For multiestablishment companies, employment data, including parent corporations and their subsidiary holdings, must report all employees working at each company establishment or subsidiary establishment on a Consolidated Report. For the purposes of this Consolidated Report, the term *parent corporation* refers to any corporation that owns all or the majority stock of another corporation so that the latter relates to it as a subsidiary.

A company is said to be a subsidiary company only if the parent has controlling interest by owning over 50 percent of the issued share capital.

Subsidiaries are separate, distinct legal entities for the purposes of taxation and regulation. For this reason, they differ from divisions, which are businesses fully integrated within the main company, and not legally or otherwise distinct from it.

U.S.-based subsidiaries of foreign corporations must also file the EEO-1. If there is no U.S.-based headquarters, use the location that has the greatest number of workers as the headquarters for reporting purposes.

Units at different physical locations, even though engaged in the same kind of business operation, must be reported as separate establishments. For locations involving construction, transportation, communications, electric, gas, and sanitary services; oil and gas fields; and similar types of physically dispersed industrial activities, however, *it is not necessary* to list separately each individual site, project, field, line, and so forth unless it is treated by you as a separate legal entity. For these types of activities, list as establishments only those relatively permanent main or branch offices, terminals, and stations that are either (1) directly responsible for supervising such dispersed activities or (2) the base from which personnel and equipment operate to carry out these activities. (Where these dispersed activities cross state lines, at least one such establishment should be listed for each state involved.)

Multiestablishment employers must complete online the following:

- Report covering the principal or headquarters office
- Separate report for each establishment employing fifty or more people
- Separate report for each establishment employing fewer than fifty employees

Otherwise, the employer must complete an establishment list showing the name, address, and total employment for each establishment employing fewer than fifty people, including an employment data grid that combines all employees working at establishments employing fewer than fifty employees by race, sex, and job category.

Job Categories

Job categories are primarily based on the average skill level, knowledge, and responsibility involved in each occupation within the job category. You should report each employee in only one job category.

Officials and Managers Category The *officials and managers category* as a whole is to be divided into the following two subcategories that are intended to mirror the employer's own internal management.

Executive/Senior-Level Officials and Managers *Executive/senior-level officials and managers* are individuals who on behalf of their organization(s) plan, direct and formulate policies, set strategy, and provide the overall direction for the development and delivery of products or services within the parameters approved by boards of directors or other governing bodies.

These executives plan, direct, or coordinate activities with the support of subordinate executives and staff managers, and in larger organizations include those individuals within two reporting levels of the CEO, whose responsibilities require frequent interaction with the CEO.

> **EXAMPLES:** This group includes chief executive officers, chief operating officers, chief financial officers, line of business heads, presidents or executive vice presidents of functional areas or operating groups, chief information officers, chief human resources officers, chief marketing officers, chief legal officers, management directors, and managing partners.

First/Mid-Level Officials and Managers *First/mid-level officials and managers* are individuals who serve as managers other than those who serve as executive/senior-level officials and managers. They include those who oversee and direct the delivery of products, services, or functions at group, regional, or divisional levels of organizations.

These managers receive directions from the executive/senior-level management and typically lead major business units. They implement policies, programs, and directives of executive/senior management through subordinate managers and within the parameters set by executive/senior-level management.

> **EXAMPLES:** This group includes vice presidents and directors; group, regional, or divisional controllers; treasurers; human resources, information systems, marketing, and operations managers.

The first/mid-level officials and managers subcategory also includes those who report directly to middle managers. These individuals serve at functional, line of business segment, or branch levels and are responsible for directing and executing the day-to-day operational objectives of enterprises or organizations; conveying the directions of higher-level officials and managers to subordinate personnel; and, in some instances, directly supervising the activities of exempt and nonexempt personnel.

> **EXAMPLES:** This group includes first-line managers, team managers, unit managers, operations and production managers, branch managers, administrative services managers, purchasing and transportation managers, storage and distribution managers, call center or customer service managers, technical support managers, and brand or product managers.

Professional Category Most jobs in the *professional category* require bachelor and graduate degrees or professional certification. In some instances, comparable experience may establish a person's qualifications.

> **EXAMPLES:** This group includes accountants and auditors, airplane pilots and flight engineers, architects, artists, chemists, computer programmers, designers, dieticians, editors, engineers, lawyers, librarians, mathematical scientists, natural scientists, registered nurses, physical scientists, physicians and surgeons, social scientists, teachers, and surveyors.

Technician Category Jobs in the *technician category* include activities that require applied scientific skills, usually obtained by postsecondary education of varying lengths, depending on the particular occupation, recognizing that in some instances additional training, certification, or comparable experience is required.

> **EXAMPLES:** This group includes drafters, emergency medical technicians, chemical technicians, and broadcast and sound engineering technicians.

Sales Workers Category *Sales worker* jobs include nonmanagerial activities that wholly and primarily involve direct sales.

> **EXAMPLES:** This group includes advertising sales agents; insurance sales agents; real estate brokers and sales agents; wholesale sales representatives; securities, commodities, and financial services sales agents; telemarketers; demonstrators; retail salespersons; counter and rental clerks; and cashiers.

Administrative Support Workers Category *Administrative support workers* jobs involve nonmanagerial tasks providing administrative and support assistance, primarily in office settings.

> **EXAMPLES:** This group includes office and administrative support workers; bookkeeping, accounting, and auditing clerks; cargo and freight agents; dispatchers; couriers; data entry keyers; computer operators; shipping, receiving, and traffic clerks; word processors and typists; proofreaders; desktop publishers; and general office clerks.

Craft Workers Category Most jobs in the *craft workers category* include higher-skilled occupations in construction (building trades craft workers and their formal apprentices) and natural resource extraction workers.

> **EXAMPLES:** This group includes boilermakers, brick and stone masons, carpenters, electricians, painters (both construction and maintenance), glaziers, pipe layers, plumbers, pipe fitters and steamfitters, plasterers, roofers, elevator installers, earth drillers, derrick operators, oil and gas rotary drill operators, and blasters and explosive workers.

This category also includes occupations related to the installation, maintenance, and part replacement of equipment, machines, and tools, such as automotive mechanics, aircraft mechanics, and electric and electronic equipment repairers.

In addition, the *craft workers category* includes some production occupations that are distinguished by the high degree of skill and precision required to perform them, based on clearly defined task specifications, such as millwrights, etchers and engravers, tool and die makers, and pattern makers.

Operatives Category Most jobs in the *operators category* include intermediate skilled occupations and include workers who operate machines or factory-related processing equipment. Most of these occupations do not usually require more than several months of training.

> **EXAMPLES:** This group includes textile machine workers; laundry and dry cleaning workers; photographic process workers; weaving machine operators; electrical and electronic equipment assemblers; semiconductor processors; testers, graders, and sorters; bakers; and butchers and other meat-, poultry-, and fish-processing workers.

This category also includes occupations of generally intermediate skill levels that are concerned with operating and controlling equipment to facilitate the movement of people or materials, such as bridge and lock tenders; truck, bus, or taxi drivers; industrial truck and tractor (forklift) operators; parking lot attendants; sailors; conveyor operators; and hand packers and packagers.

Laborers and Helpers Category Jobs in the *laborers and helpers category* include workers with more limited skills who require only brief training to perform tasks that require little or no independent judgment.

> **EXAMPLES:** This group includes production and construction worker helpers; vehicle and equipment cleaners; laborers; freight, stock, and material movers; service station attendants; construction laborers; refuse and recyclable materials collectors; septic tank servicers; and sewer pipe cleaners.

Service Workers Category The *service workers category* includes food service, cleaning service, personal service, and protective service activities. Skill may be acquired through formal training, job-related training, or direct experience.

> **EXAMPLES:** This group includes cooks, bartenders, and other food-service workers. Examples of personal service positions include medical assistants and other health-care support positions, hairdressers, ushers, and transportation attendants. Examples of cleaning service positions include cleaners, janitors, and porters. Examples of protective service positions include transit and railroad police and firefighters, guards, private detectives, and investigators.

Race and Ethnic Identification

Self-Identification The instruction booklet for the EEO-1 states:

> Self-identification is the preferred method of identifying the race and ethnic information necessary for the EEO-1 report. Employers are required to attempt to allow employees to use self-identification to complete the EEO-1 report. If an employee declines to self-identify, employment records or observer identification may be used.
>
> Where records are maintained, it is recommended that they be kept separately from the employee's basic personnel file or other records available to those responsible for personnel decisions.
>
> Race and ethnic designations as used by the Equal Employ-

ment Opportunity Commission do not denote scientific definitions of anthropological origins.

**Self-Identification Form and Race and Ethnicity Category Defi-
nitions** A suggested form of the self-identification form that contains the
EEOC's race and ethnicity category definitions is shown in Exhibit 10-4.

EEO-1 Document Retention

You should retain either a hard paper or electronic copy of your last filing
until you file your next one, or forever if your workforce drops below
one hundred and you no longer have to submit the survey. In other words,
always have your last filing available.

Document Retention Policies

A *document retention policy* (DRP) is a set of guidelines that a company
follows to determine how long it should keep certain records, including
e-mail and Web pages. A DRP promotes business efficiency in that it frees
up valuable storage space at your business by destroying useless documents,
enables you to quickly locate important documents, reduces the time spent
handling and retrieving documents, and aids in any litigation that might
arise.

Any organization that does not have a DRP delegates (by default)
decisions about which records to create, retain, or destroy to all the employees who have access to record-making or record-keeping functions.

Minimum Elements of a Document Retention Policy

Identification of Documents That Should Be Retained

Here is a list of documents you should take into consideration in developing your DRP; however, it is not a complete list.

Employment Documents

- Employee records (Because lawsuits from current and former employees are common, employee records should be retained for the
  length of the employee's tenure with your business plus some term
  of years. Many document retention policies retain employee doc-

Exhibit 10-4. Self-identification form and race and ethnicity category definitions.

Our company, [NAME OF ORGANIZATION], is subject to certain governmental record-keeping and reporting requirements for the administration of civil rights laws and regulations. In order to comply with these laws, [NAME OF ORGANIZATION] invites you to voluntarily self-identify your race or ethnicity by checking the appropriate box below.

Race and ethnic designations as used by the Equal Employment Opportunity Commission and on this self-identification form do not denote scientific definitions of anthropological origins.

Submission of this information is voluntary and refusal to provide it will not subject you to any adverse treatment. The information obtained will be kept confidential and may be used only in accordance with the provisions of applicable laws, executive orders, and regulations, including those that require the information to be summarized and reported to the federal government for civil rights enforcement. When reported, data will not identify any specific individual.

PLEASE CHECK THE APPROPRIATE BOX:

☐ **Hispanic or Latino**—A person of Cuban, Mexican, Puerto Rican, South or Central American, or other Spanish culture or origin regardless of race.

☐ **White (Not Hispanic or Latino)**—A person having origins in any of the original peoples of Europe, the Middle East, or North Africa.

☐ **Black or African American (Not Hispanic or Latino)**—A person having origins in any of the black racial groups of Africa.

☐ **Native Hawaiian or Other Pacific Islander (Not Hispanic or Latino)**—A person having origins in any of the peoples of Hawaii, Guam, Samoa, or other Pacific Islands.

☐ **Asian (Not Hispanic or Latino)**—A person having origins in any of the original peoples of the Far East, Southeast Asia, or the Indian Subcontinent, including, for example, Cambodia, China, India, Japan, Korea, Malaysia, Pakistan, the Philippine Islands, Thailand, and Vietnam.

☐ **American Indian or Alaska Native (Not Hispanic or Latino)**—A person having origins in any of the original peoples of North and South America (including Central America), and who maintains tribal affiliation or community attachment.

☐ **Two or More Races (Not Hispanic or Latino)**—All persons who identify with more than one of the above five races.

☐ Male ☐ Female

Name: _____ Date: _____

uments for at least five years after an employee leaves the company. That time frame will cover most statutes of limitation for the filing of an employee claim.)

- Employment taxes
- Training manuals

Workplace Records

Businesses often collect and generate a number of records that may not be directly termed employment documents but may have a bearing on litigation brought by current or former employees.

- Safety documents
- Maintenance records
- Product manuals
- Travel and delivery schedules

Accounting and Corporate Tax Records

- Tax returns
- Gross receipts
- Purchases
- Expense receipts
- Travel, transportation, entertainment, and gift expenses

Legal Records

- Real estate records
- Contracts
- Patents, trademarks, and copyrights
- Citations, tickets, and other administrative penalties
- Legal pleadings
- Insurance policies
- Licenses and permits
- Government paperwork
- Vehicle registrations

- Electronic records (Maintenance and destruction of electronic records may be the most difficult part of the DRP.)
- Computer disks
- E-mail
- Hard drives
- Web pages (If you sell products online, you may be making representations and warranties about the products on your website and may also have privacy policies and other terms of dealing.)

General Forms of Media

- Photographs
- Audio recordings
- Letters (and reading files)
- Facsimiles
- Advertisements and promotional items (Advertisements and promotional items can form the basis for contracts between your business and the customer. Copies of these items should be maintained at least for the length of the contract statute of limitations in your state, and potentially for the state of any customer who may have received the advertisement. You should treat online advertisements the same way you treat all other advertisements.)

Period-Specific Types of Documents Should Be Retained

Define for how long, how, and where to store both paper and electronic records making sure you specify specific retention periods for specific categories of records.

Make sure you have considered all forms of electronic data in all devices and media (don't forget digital printers, copiers, and voice mail).

Job Advertisements and Postings Pursuant to the Americans with Disabilities Act (ADA), Age Discrimination in Employment Act (ADEA), and Fair Labor Standards Act (FLSA), job advertisements and internal postings should be retained for a minimum of one year.

Résumés and Applications The ADA, the Rehabilitation Act, Title VII of the Civil Rights Act, and the ADEA require employers to keep all résumés and job applications on file for one year. Because the ADEA further stipulates a two-year retention period for paperwork for individuals over age 40 (something that may be difficult to determine and is, of course, illegal to ask), consider making it your policy to hold on to all résumés and applications for that long.

Employment Action Records Records relating to promotions, demotions, transfers, and terminations must be retained for one year according to the ADA, ADEA, and Title VII. While training records, in general, should also be kept on file for one year, those related to safety and health must be retained for three years in accordance with OSHA.

Wage and Hour Records The FLSA and Equal Pay Act oblige you to keep basic employment and earnings records for two years and payroll records for three years.

Tax Records Information relating to income tax withholdings must be retained for four years according to the Federal Insurance Contribution Act (FICA) and Federal Unemployment Tax Act (FUTA).

Retirement and Pension Records The Employee Retirement Income Security Act (ERISA) mandates that employee benefit plan information, including summary plan descriptions (SPDs) and annual reports, be kept on file for six years.

Leave Records Information relating to leaves of absence under the Family Medical Leave Act (FMLA), such as time off and medical certification, must be retained for three years.

I-9 Forms Under the Immigration Reform and Control Act of 1986 (IRCA), I-9 Forms must be retained for three years after employment begins or one year following termination (whichever is later).

Job-Related Illness and Injury Records OSHA requires that information pertaining to job-related illness and injury (Forms 300, 300A, and 301) be kept on file for five years. In cases of exposure to toxic substances or blood-borne pathogens, medical exam results must be retained for thirty years after the employee's termination.

Process for Destroying Documents

Specify how records are to be destroyed when their retention period has expired. Some good rules to follow are found in the Disposal Rule of The Fair and Accurate Credit Transaction Act of 2003 (FACT Act, or FACTA), which requires disposal practices that are reasonable and appropriate to prevent the unauthorized access to—or use of—information in a consumer report. For example, reasonable measures for disposing of consumer report information could include establishing and complying with policies to:

- Burn, pulverize, or shred papers containing consumer report information so that the information cannot be read or reconstructed.
- Destroy or erase electronic files or media containing consumer report information so that the information cannot be read or reconstructed.
- Conduct due diligence and hire a document destruction contractor to dispose of material specifically identified as consumer report information consistent with the rule. Due diligence could include:
  - Reviewing an independent audit of a disposal company's operations and/or its compliance with the rule
  - Obtaining information about the disposal company from several references
  - Requiring that the disposal company be certified by a recognized trade association
  - Reviewing and evaluating the disposal company's information security policies or procedures

Circumstances Under Which Document Destruction Should Be Suspended

Duty to Preserve Documents When a company reasonably anticipates litigation, it has a common-law duty to preserve relevant information. A company's duty to preserve relevant documents arises when the company knows, or should know, through *notice* that the documents will become material to litigation or an investigation at some point in the future. Notice might come in the form of an inquiry from the government, service of a complaint or petition commencing litigation, or a third-party request for documents.

Courts consider the *totality of the circumstances* when determining if a reasonable person or company would have anticipated the litigation based on the information available.

Evidence That Must Be Preserved A company doesn't have to preserve every document in the company's hard-copy or electronic files. What the company has the duty to preserve are documents that (1) it knows or reasonably should know are relevant to the litigation, (2) are reasonably calculated to lead to the discovery of admissible evidence, (3) are likely to be requested during discovery, or (4) are the subject of a discovery sanction.

At the time the duty to preserve attaches, the company must initiate a *litigation hold* to suspend any document retention or destruction policy, and thus retain all documents relevant to the anticipated litigation then in existence and all relevant documents created thereafter.

Spoliation Spoliation is the intentional destruction of evidence, including the significant alteration of or the failure to preserve evidence.

The theory of spoliation is that when a party destroys evidence, it may be reasonable to infer that the party had consciousness of guilt or other motivation to avoid the evidence. Therefore, the fact finder may conclude that the evidence would have been unfavorable to the spoliator.

Spoliation has two consequences: first the act is criminal by statute and may result in fines and incarceration for the parties who engaged in the spoliation; and second, case law has established that proceedings that might have been altered by the spoliation may be interpreted under a *spoliation inference*. In other words, the court can order that a jury should infer that the missing documents would all have favored the plaintiff and should find accordingly.

Documentation of Compliance with the Retention Policy

You should monitor compliance with your DRP policy by conducting periodic audits. In addition, it is a good idea to periodically review and update the policy to ensure that it accurately reflects your current document-management practices.

Further, train employees on proper policy compliance. A document-management policy is effective only if it is consistently applied. If an organization follows the policy's guidelines for periodic destruction only when it anticipates an investigation or a lawsuit, the policy will not be a valid defense to a charge of obstruction of justice or spoliation of evidence. Therefore, it is critical to ensure that employees understand the policy and consistently adhere to it.

Make the document retention policy part of the employee handbook, have employees sign the policy, and have the handbook updated when the policy is updated.

OSHA Record Keeping

The Occupational Safety and Health Act contains an extensive set of document creation and retention rules.

Overview

This section provides you with a *basic* understanding of the OSHA record-keeping regulation, Title 29 Code of Federal Regulations Part 1904 ("Part 1904"). The rule requires employers to keep records of occupational deaths, injuries, and illnesses on OSHA's Forms 300, 300A, and 301, or their equivalents. (See Exhibit 10-5, Exhibit 10-6, and Exhibit 10-7.)

For detailed explanations regarding the mechanics of completing Forms 300, 300A, and 301, see the regulation itself (much of which is written in a question-and-answer style) and *Recordkeeping Policies and Procedures Manual*, CPL 02-00-135, both at www.osha.gov.

The record-keeping rule requires that states adopt occupational injury and illness recording and reporting requirements that are substantially identical to the requirements in the federal revision of Part 1904. The requirements for determining which injuries and illnesses are recordable and how they are recorded must be identical to those in Part 1904, so that national statistics are uniform. All other injury and illness recording and reporting requirements must be at least as effective as the federal requirements.

If you are complying with the illness and injury record-keeping rules of a governmental agency other than OSHA, OSHA will consider those records as meeting Part 1904's record-keeping requirements if (1) OSHA accepts the other agency's records under a memorandum of understanding with that agency or (2) the other agency's records contain the same information as Part 1904 that requires you to record, for example, a workers

Exhibit 10-5. OSHA's Form 300.

OSHA's Form 300 (Rev. 01/2004)

Log of Work-Related Injuries and Illnesses

Year 20___

U.S. Department of Labor
Occupational Safety and Health Administration

Form approved OMB no. 1218-0176

Attention: This form contains information relating to employee health and must be used in a manner that protects the confidentiality of employees to the extent possible while the information is being used for occupational safety and health purposes.

You must record information about every work-related death and about every work-related injury or illness that involves loss of consciousness, restricted work activity or job transfer, days away from work, or medical treatment beyond first aid. You must also record significant work-related injuries and illnesses that are diagnosed by a physician or licensed health care professional. You must also record work-related injuries and illnesses that meet any of the specific recording criteria listed in 29 CFR Part 1904.8 through 1904.12. Feel free to use two lines for a single case if you need to. You must complete an injury and illness incident Report (OSHA Form 301) or equivalent form for each injury or illness recorded on this form. If you're not sure whether a case is recordable, call your local OSHA office for help.

Establishment name _____

City _____ State _____

Exhibit 10-6. OSHA's Form 300A.

OSHA's Form 300A (Rev. 01/2004)

Summary of Work-Related Injuries and Illnesses

Year 20____

U.S. Department of Labor
Occupational Safety and Health Administration

Form approved OMB no. 1218-0176

All establishments covered by Part 1904 must complete this Summary page, even if no work-related injuries or illnesses occurred during the year. Remember to review the Log to verify that the entries are complete and accurate before completing this summary.

Using the Log, count the individual entries you made for each category. Then write the totals below, making sure you've added the entries from every page of the Log. If you had no cases, write "0."

Employees, former employees, and their representatives have the right to review the OSHA Form 300 in its entirety. They also have limited access to the OSHA Form 301 or its equivalent. See 29 CFR Part 1904.35, in OSHA's recordkeeping rule, for further details on the access provisions for these forms.

Number of Cases

Total number of deaths

(G)

Total number of cases with days away from work

(H)

Total number of cases with job transfer or restriction

(I)

Total number of other recordable cases

(J)

Number of Days

Total number of days away from work

(K)

Total number of days of job transfer or restriction

(L)

Injury and Illness Types

Total number of . . .
(M)

(1) Injuries ____
(2) Skin disorders ____
(3) Respiratory conditions ____
(4) Poisonings ____
(5) Hearing loss ____
(6) All other illnesses ____

Post this Summary page from February 1 to April 30 of the year following the year covered by the form.

Public reporting burden for this collection of information is estimated to average 58 minutes per response, including time to review the instructions, search and gather the data needed, and complete and review the collection of information. Persons are not required to respond to the collection of information unless it displays a currently valid OMB control number. If you have any comments about these estimates or any other aspects of this data collection, contact: US Department of Labor, OSHA Office of Statistical Analysis, Room N-3644, 200 Constitution Avenue, NW, Washington, DC 20210. Do not send the completed forms to this office.

Establishment information

Your establishment name ____

Street ____

City ____ State ____ ZIP ____

Industry description (e.g., Manufacture of motor truck trailers) ____

Standard Industrial Classification (SIC), if known (e.g., 3715) ____

OR

North American Industrial Classification (NAICS), if known (e.g., 336212) ____

Employment information *(If you don't have these figures, see the Worksheet on the back of this page to estimate.)*

Annual average number of employees ____

Total hours worked by all employees last year ____

Sign here

Knowingly falsifying this document may result in a fine.

I certify that I have examined this document and that to the best of my knowledge the entries are true, accurate, and complete.

____
Company executive   Title ____

(____) ____
Phone   Date ____

Exhibit 10-7. OSHA's Form 301.

OSHA's Form 301
Injury and Illness Incident Report

U.S. Department of Labor
Occupational Safety and Health Administration

Form approved OMB no. 1218-0176

Attention: This form contains information relating to employee health and must be used in a manner that protects the confidentiality of employees to the extent possible while the information is being used for occupational safety and health purposes.

This *Injury and Illness Incident Report* is one of the first forms you must fill out when a recordable work-related injury or illness has occurred. Together with the *Log of Work-Related Injuries and Illnesses* and the accompanying *Summary*, these forms help the employer and OSHA develop a picture of the extent and severity of work-related incidents.

Within 7 calendar days after you receive information that a recordable work-related injury or illness has occurred, you must fill out this form or an equivalent. Some state workers' compensation, insurance, or other reports may be acceptable substitutes. To be considered an equivalent form, any substitute must contain all the information asked for on this form.

According to Public Law 91-596 and 29 CFR 1904, OSHA's recordkeeping rule, you must keep this form on file for 5 years following the year to which it pertains.

If you need additional copies of this form, you may photocopy and use as many as you need.

Completed by _____

Title _____

Phone (_____) _____ - _____   Date _____ / _____ / _____

Information about the employee

1) Full name _____

2) Street _____

   City _____ State _____ ZIP _____

3) Date of birth _____ / _____ / _____

4) Date hired _____ / _____ / _____

5) ☐ Male   ☐ Female

Information about the physician or other health care professional

6) Name of physician or other health care professional _____

7) If treatment was given away from the worksite, where was it given?

   Facility _____

   Street _____

   City _____ State _____ ZIP _____

8) Was employee treated in an emergency room?
  ☐ Yes   ☐ No

9) Was employee hospitalized overnight as an in-patient?
  ☐ Yes   ☐ No

Information about the case

10) Case number from the Log _____ *(Transfer the case number from the Log after you record the case.)*

11) Date of injury or illness _____ / _____ / _____

12) Time employee began work _____ AM / PM

13) Time of event _____ AM / PM   ☐ Check if time cannot be determined

14) **What was the employee doing just before the incident occurred?** Describe the activity, as well as the tools, equipment, or material the employee was using. Be specific. *Examples:* "climbing a ladder while carrying roofing materials"; "spraying chlorine from hand sprayer"; "daily computer key-entry."

15) **What happened?** Tell us how the injury occurred. *Examples:* "When ladder slipped on wet floor, worker fell 20 feet"; "Worker was sprayed with chlorine when gasket broke during replacement"; "Worker developed soreness in wrist over time."

16) **What was the injury or illness?** Tell us the part of the body that was affected and how it was affected; be more specific than "hurt," "pain," or sore." *Examples:* "strained back"; "chemical burn, hand"; "carpal tunnel syndrome."

17) **What object or substance directly harmed the employee?** *Examples:* "concrete floor"; "chlorine"; "radial arm saw." *If this question does not apply to the incident, leave it blank.*

18) **If the employee died, when did death occur?** Date of death _____ / _____ / _____

Public reporting burden for this collection of information is estimated to average 22 minutes per response, including time for reviewing instructions, searching existing data sources, gathering and maintaining the data needed, and completing and reviewing the collection of information. Persons are not required to respond to the collection of information unless it displays a current valid OMB control number. If you have any comments about this estimate or any other aspects of this data collection, including suggestions for reducing this burden, contact: US Department of Labor, OSHA Office of Statistical Analysis, Room N-3644, 200 Constitution Avenue, NW, Washington, DC 20210. Do not send the completed forms to this office.

compensation first report of injury form that generally contains the same information sought on Form 301.

Keeping OSHA Injury and Illness Records

Federal Agencies

Effective January 1, 2005, 29 CFR Part 1960, Subpart I made the federal sector's record-keeping and reporting requirements essentially identical to the private sector by adopting applicable OSHA record-keeping provisions in 29 CFR Part 1904.

Private Sector Employers

With two exemptions, all organizations covered by the Act must maintain these forms. The exemptions are based on an organization's size—for example, the number of workers—or its Standard Industrial Classification Code (SIC).

Note: The exemptions are called *partial exemptions* because no organization covered by the Act is exempt from the OSHA reporting requirements. See "Reporting Fatalities and Multiple Hospitalization Incidents" in this chapter.

Size Exemption

If your company had ten or fewer employees at all times during the last calendar year, you do not need to keep OSHA injury and illness records unless OSHA or the Bureau of Labor Statistics (BLS) informs you in writing that you must keep records under Section 1904.41 or Section 1904.42. See "Survey of Occupational Injuries and Illnesses Form" in this chapter.

The partial exemption for size is based on:

- Number of employees in the entire organization—not per site
- Organization's peak employment during the immediate past calendar year

If you had no more than ten employees at any time in the immediate past calendar year, your company qualifies for the partial exemption for size.

SIC Code Exemption Industry Definitions used in BLS programs come from the 1987 *Standard Industrial Classification (SIC) Manual*, which can be researched on the OSHA website at www.osha.gov.

In 1999, the SIC system was superseded by the North American Industry Classification System (NAICS). The NAICS system can be researched on the OSHA website. As of August 1, 2008, OSHA was still basing its industry exemptions on the SIC system. The chart of exempt SIC codes starting August 1, 2008, is found in Exhibit 10-8.

Survey of Occupational Injuries and Illnesses Form OSHA and BLS may send a covered or an otherwise exempt organization an annual survey form. If they do, it will arrive prior to the commencement of a calendar year, and during that upcoming year, the employer is required to complete and return the survey form to the sending agency.

Time Frames

The forms referred to in Part 1904 must be maintained on a calendar year basis and are retained for five years.

If the employer sells the business, the forms must be given to the new owner for retention; however, the new owner does not have to update the previous owner's forms even if new information about a case becomes available.

Reporting Fatalities and Multiple Hospitalization Incidents

Basic Requirement

Within eight hours after (1) the death of any employee from a work-related incident or (2) the in-patient hospitalization of three or more employees as a result of a work-related incident, all employers covered by OSHA orally report the fatality or multiple hospitalization by telephone or in person to the OSHA area office that is nearest to the site of the incident. You may also use the OSHA toll-free central telephone number, 1-800-321-OSHA (1-800-321-6742).

Information Requested

For each fatality or multiple hospitalization incident, provide OSHA with the following information:

Exhibit 10-8. Partially exempt industries.

Nonmandatory Appendix A to Subpart B—Partially Exempt Industries

Employers are not required to keep OSHA injury and illness records for any establishment classified in the following Standard Industrial Classification (SIC) codes, unless they are asked in writing to do so by OSHA, the Bureau of Labor Statistics (BLS), or a state agency operating under the authority of OSHA or the BLS. All employers, including those partially exempted by reason of company size or industry classification, must report to OSHA any workplace incident that results in a fatality or the hospitalization of three or more employees (see §1904.39).

SIC Code	Industry Description	SIC Code	Industry Description
525	Hardware Stores	725	Shoe Repair and Shoeshine Parlors
542	Meat and Fish Markets	726	Funeral Service and Crematories
544	Candy, Nut, and Confectionery Stores	729	Miscellaneous Personal Services
545	Dairy Products Stores	731	Advertising Services
546	Retail Bakeries	732	Credit Reporting and Collection Services
549	Miscellaneous Food Stores	733	Mailing, Reproduction, and Stenographic Services
551	New and Used Car Dealers	737	Computer and Data-Processing Services
552	Used Car Dealers	738	Miscellaneous Business Services
554	Gasoline Service Stations	764	Reupholstery and Furniture Repair
557	Motorcycle Dealers	78	Motion Picture
56	Apparel and Accessory Stores	791	Dance Studios, Schools, and Halls
573	Radio, Television, and Computer Stores	792	Producers, Orchestras, Entertainers
58	Eating and Drinking Places	793	Bowling Centers
591	Drug Stores and Proprietary Stores	801	Offices and Clinics of Medical Doctors
592	Liquor Stores	802	Offices and Clinics of Dentists
594	Miscellaneous Shopping Goods Stores	803	Offices of Osteopathic Physicians
599	Retail Stores, Not Elsewhere Classified	804	Offices of Other Health Practitioners
60	Depository Institutions (banks and savings institutions)	807	Medical and Dental Laboratories
61	Nondepository Institutions (credit institutions)	809	Health and Allied Services, Not Elsewhere Classified
62	Security and Commodity Brokers	81	Legal Services
63	Insurance Carriers	82	Educational Services (schools, colleges, universities, and libraries)
64	Insurance Agents, Brokers, and Services	832	Individual and Family Services

(continues)

Exhibit 10-8. (Continued)

Nonmandatory Appendix A to Subpart B—Partially Exempt Industries

Employers are not required to keep OSHA injury and illness records for any establishment classified in the following Standard Industrial Classification (SIC) codes, unless they are asked in writing to do so by OSHA, the Bureau of Labor Statistics (BLS), or a state agency operating under the authority of OSHA or the BLS. All employers, including those partially exempted by reason of company size or industry classification, must report to OSHA any workplace incident that results in a fatality or the hospitalization of three or more employees (see §1904.39).

SIC Code	Industry Description	SIC Code	Industry Description
653	Real Estate Agents and Managers	835	Child Day Care Services
654	Title Abstract Offices	839	Social Services, Not Elsewhere Classified
67	Holding and Other Investment Offices	841	Museums and Art Galleries
722	Photographic Studios, Portrait	86	Membership Organizations
723	Beauty Shops	87	Engineering, Accounting, Research, Management, and Related Services
724	Barber Shops	899	Services, Not Elsewhere Classified

- Establishment name
- Location of the incident
- Time of the incident
- Number of fatalities or hospitalized employees
- Names of any injured employees
- Your contact person and his or her phone number
- Brief description of the incident

Caution: Do not speculate! Provide OSHA with whatever facts are available to you at the time of the call. Speculation might cause you to "admit" a violation of the standards that did not, in fact, occur. Investigate the incident immediately.

Injury and Illness Recordable Incidents That Are Not Reportable

Recordable, but not reportable, are work-related incidents such as:

- Fatality or multiple hospitalization incident(s) that results from a motor vehicle accident occurring on a public street or highway, and that does not occur in a construction work zone

- Fatality or multiple hospitalization incident(s) that occur on a commercial or public transportation system (e.g., commercial airplane, train, subway, or bus accident)

Penalty for Not Reporting

An *other-than-serious citation* will normally be issued for failure to report a fatality or multiple hospitalization occurrence, with an unadjusted penalty of $5,000.

Establishments

Definition

You must maintain the forms for each establishment. An *establishment* is a single physical location where business is conducted or where services or industrial operations are performed. For activities where employees do not work at a single physical location—such as construction; transportation; communications, electric, gas, and sanitary services; and similar operations—the establishment is represented by main or branch offices, terminals, or stations that either supervise such activities or are the base from which personnel carry out these activities.

More Than One Location

An establishment can include more than one physical location under certain conditions. An employer may combine two or more physical locations into a single establishment only when:

- The employer operates the locations as a single business operation under common management.
- The locations are all located in close proximity to each other.
- The employer keeps one set of business records for the locations, such as records on the number of employees, their wages and salaries, sales or receipts, and other kinds of business information. For example, one manufacturing establishment might include the main plant, a warehouse a few blocks away, and an administrative services building across the street.

One Location with More Than One Profit Center

Normally, one business location has only one establishment. Under limited conditions, the employer may consider two or more separate businesses that share a single location to be separate establishments. An employer may divide one location into two or more establishments only when:

- Each of the establishments represents a distinctly separate business.
- Each business is engaged in a different economic activity.
- No one industry description in the *Standard Industrial Classification Manual* (1987) applies to the joint activities of the establishments.
- Separate reports are routinely prepared for each establishment on the number of employees, their wages and salaries, sales or receipts, and other business information.

> **EXAMPLE:** If an employer operates a construction company at the same location as a lumber yard, the employer may consider each business to be a separate establishment.

Telecommuters

For employees who telecommute from home, the employee's home is not a business establishment and a separate Form 300 is not required. Employees who telecommute must be linked to one of your establishments for record-keeping purposes.

Multiple Business Establishments

Worksites Scheduled to Continue for a Year or More A separate Form 300 must be maintained for each establishment. The log may be maintained either at the site or at an established central location provided the employer can:

- Transmit information about the injuries and illnesses from the establishment to the central location within seven calendar days of receiving information that a recordable injury or illness has occurred.
- Produce and send records from the central location to the establishment within four business hours when the employer is required

to provide records to a government representative or by the end of the next business day when providing records to an employee, a former employee, or an employee representative.

Worksites Scheduled to Continue for Less Than a Year A separate Form 300 need not be maintained for each establishment. One Form 300 may be maintained to cover (1) all such short-term establishments or (2) all such short-term establishments within company divisions or geographic regions.

Work Related

Only work-related injuries, illnesses, or deaths are recordable.

A case is presumed work related if and only if an event or exposure in the work environment is a discernable cause of the injury or illness or of a significant aggravation to a preexisting condition. The work event or exposure need only be one of the discernable causes—it need not be the sole or predominant cause. Basically, anything that happens to the employee in the *work environment* is considered to be work related.

Work Environment

OSHA defines the work environment as "the establishment and other locations where one or more employees are working or are present as a condition of their employment. The work environment includes not only physical locations, but also the equipment or materials used by the employee during the course of his or her work."

Exceptions to Work Relatedness

There are nine exceptions to work relatedness. An employer is not required to record injuries and illnesses if:

1. At the time of the injury or illness, the employee was present in the work environment as a member of the general public rather than as an employee.
2. The injury or illness involves signs or symptoms that surface at work but result solely from a non-work-related event or exposure that occurs outside the work environment.
3. The injury or illness results solely from voluntary participation in a

wellness program or in a medical, fitness, or recreational activity such as blood donation, physical examination, flu shot, exercise class, racquetball, or baseball.

4. The injury or illness is solely the result of an employee eating, drinking, or preparing food or drink for personal consumption (whether bought on the employer's premises or brought in).

    Note: If the employee is made ill by ingesting food contaminated by workplace contaminants (such as lead), or gets food poisoning from food supplied by the employer, the case would be considered work related.

5. The injury or illness is solely the result of an employee doing personal tasks (unrelated to his or her employment) at the establishment outside of the employee's assigned working hours.

    Note: For these types of incidents to not be recordable, the event must both involve personal tasks and take place outside of the employee's working hours.

    Also Note: Assigned working hours means those hours the employee is actually expected to work, including overtime.

6. The injury or illness is solely the result of personal grooming, self-medication for a non-work-related condition, or is intentionally self-inflicted.

    Note: Personal grooming activities are activities directly related to personal hygiene, such as combing and drying hair, brushing teeth, clipping fingernails, and the like. Bathing or showering at the workplace when necessary because of an exposure to a substance at work is not within the personal grooming exception.

7. The injury or illness is caused by a motor vehicle accident and occurs on a company parking lot or company access road while the employee is commuting to or from work.

8. The illness is the common cold or flu.

    Note: Contagious diseases such as tuberculosis, brucellosis, hepatitis A, or plague are considered work related if the employee is infected at work.

9. The illness is a mental illness. Mental illness will not be considered work related unless the employee voluntarily provides the employer with an opinion from a physician or other licensed health-care professional with appropriate training and experience (psychia-

trist, psychologist, or psychiatric nurse practitioner) stating that the employee has a mental illness that is work related.

Privacy Cases

The employer must not enter an employee's name on Form 300 when recording a privacy case. The following work-related injuries or illnesses are treated as privacy cases:

- An injury or illness to an intimate body part or the reproductive system.
- An injury or illness resulting from a sexual assault.
- A mental illness.
- HIV infection, hepatitis, or tuberculosis.
- Needlestick and sharps injuries that are contaminated with another person's blood or other potentially infectious material as defined by Section 1910.1030.
- Other illnesses if the employee independently and voluntarily requests that his or her name not be entered on the OSHA 300 log. (This does *not* apply to injuries.)

The employer must keep a separate, confidential list of the case numbers and employee names and provide it to the government on request. The only individuals or organizations that are allowed to see the log containing the privacy case employee names are OSHA, your workers compensation carrier, and a consultant you may hire to assist you with matters related to safety and health.

Form 300A

Form 300A is a summary of the injuries and illnesses recorded for the prior calendar year. It must be posted in a conspicuous place at the establishment for which it was kept from February 1 through April 30 of the year following the year for which the data was kept—for example, post Form 300A for 2008 from February 1 through April 30, 2009.

Form 300A must be certified. A company executive must certify that he or she has examined OSHA Form 300 and that he or she reasonably believes, based on his or her knowledge of the process by which the information was recorded, that the annual summary is correct and complete.

The company executive who certifies the log must be one of the following individuals:

- Owner of the company (only if the company is a sole proprietorship or partnership)
- Officer of the corporation
- Highest-ranking company official working at the establishment
- Immediate supervisor of the highest-ranking company official working at the establishment

Form 301

Within seven calendar days after you receive information that a recordable work-related injury or illness has occurred, you must fill out a Form 301 or an equivalent. Most state workers compensation, insurance, or other reports are acceptable substitutes if they contain all of the information asked for on Form 301.

Employee Access to OSHA Injury and Illness Records

OSHA has a long-standing policy of allowing employees and their representatives access to the occupational injury and illness information kept by their employers, with some limitations.

Employee and His or Her Representative

Section 1904.35 requires an employer covered by the Part 1904 regulation to provide limited access to the OSHA record-keeping forms to current and former employees, as well as to two types of employee representatives, as follows:

1. Personal representative of an employee or former employee who is a person whom the employee or former employee designates, in writing, as his or her personal representative, or is the legal representative of a deceased or legally incapacitated employee or former employee
2. Authorized employee representative, which is defined as an authorized collective bargaining agent of one or more employees working at the employer's establishment

Access Rights

Section 1904.35 accords employees and their representatives three separate access rights, as follows:

First, it gives any employee, former employee, personal representative, or authorized employee representative the right to a copy of the current OSHA 300 log, and to any stored OSHA 300 logs, for any establishment in which the employee or former employee has worked.

The employer must provide one free copy of the OSHA 300 log(s) by the end of the next business day.

Note: The employee, former employee, personal representative, or authorized employee representative is not entitled to see, or to obtain a copy of, the confidential list of names and case numbers for privacy cases.

Second, any employee, former employee, or personal representative is entitled to one free copy of the OSHA 301 Incident Report describing an injury or illness to that employee by the end of the next business day.

Finally, an authorized employee representative is entitled to copies of the right-hand portion of all OSHA 301 forms for the establishment(s) where the agent represents one or more employees under a collective bargaining agreement. The right-hand portion of Form 301 contains the heading "Information About the Case" and elicits information about how the injury occurred, including the employee's actions just prior to the incident, the materials and tools involved, and how the incident occurred, but it does not contain the employee's name. No information other than that on the right-hand portion of the form may be disclosed to an authorized employee representative.

The employer must provide the authorized employee representative with one free copy of all the 301 forms for the establishment within seven calendar days.

Index

Selected Titles from the
Society for Human Resource Management (SHRM)

Building Profit through Building People: Making Your Workforce the Strongest Link in the Value-Profit Chain
   By Ken Carrig and Patrick M. Wright
Diverse Teams at Work: Capitalizing on the Power of Diversity
   By Lee Gardenswartz and Anita Rowe
Employment Termination Source Book
   By Wendy Bliss and Gene R. Thornton
Essential Guide to Workplace Investigations: How to Handle Employee Complaints & Problems
   By Lisa Guerin
Expatriate Compensation: The Balance Sheet Approach
   By Roger Herod
Global Compensation and Benefits: Developing Policies for Local Nationals
   By Roger Herod
Hiring Source Book
   By Catherine D. Fyock
HR and the New Hispanic Workforce: A Comprehensive Guide to Cultivating and Leveraging Employee Success
   By Louis E.V. Nevaer and Vaso Perimenis Eckstein
Igniting Gen B & Gen V: The New Rules of Engagement for Boomers, Veterans, and Other Long-Termers on the Job
   By Nancy S. Ahlrichs
Investigating Workplace Harassment: How to Be Fair, Thorough, and Legal
   By Amy Oppenheimer and Craig Pratt
Investing in People: Financial Impact of Human Resource Initiatives
   By Wayne Cascio and John Boudreau
Managing to Stay Out of Court: How to Avoid the 8 Deadly Sins of Mismanagement
   By Jathan Janove
Outsourcing Human Resources Functions: How, Why, When, and When Not to Contract for HR Services, 2d edition
   By Mary F. Cook and Scott B. Gildner
Performance Appraisal Source Book
   By Mike Debleux

Proving the Value of HR: How and Why to Measure ROI
     By Jack J. Phillips and Patricia Pulliam Phillips
Solving the Compensation Puzzle: Putting Together a Complete Pay and Performance System
     By Sharon K. Koss
Strategic Staffing: A Comprehensive System of Effective Workforce Planning, 2d edition
     By Thomas P. Bechet
Supervisor's Guide to Labor Relations
     By T.O. Collier Jr.
Trainer's Diversity Source Book
     By Jonamay Lambert and Selma Myers
Weathering Storms: Human Resources in Difficult Times
     By SHRM